Campaigns of the American Revolution

AN ATLAS OF MANUSCRIPT MAPS

by

Douglas W. Marshall
and
Howard H. Peckham

The William L. Clements Library of the University of Michigan

THE UNIVERSITY OF MICHIGAN PRESS   ANN ARBOR
HAMMOND INCORPORATED   MAPLEWOOD, NEW JERSEY

Published with the gracious assistance of a grant from the
Michigan American Revolution Bicentennial Commission

Library of Congress Cataloging in Publication Data

Marshall, Douglas W
    Campaigns of the American Revolution.

    Includes index.
    1. United States—Revolution, 1775-1783—Campaigns
and battles—Maps.   2. Maps, Early—Facsimiles.
I. Peckham, Howard Henry, joint author.   I. Title.
G1201.S3P4   1976   911'.73   75-13657

ISBN 0-8437-3125-7 (Hammond Incorporated)
ISBN 0-472-23300-9 (The University of Michigan Press)

Published in the United States of America by The University of
Michigan Press and Hammond Incorporated and simultaneously
in Don Mills, Canada, by Fitzhenry & Whiteside, Limited.

Printed in the United States of America

Contents

Introduction

"There is no map of the inhabited provinces of any use, for there is none correct, even the roads are not marked." So wrote the commander in chief of the British army in North America to his principal surveyor in 1767. The situation had not improved appreciably by the time revolution broke out eight years later. Although a substantial body of colonial surveys had evolved by the mid-eighteenth century, few were of value within the theater of war or to military operations in America. To what extent the British were able to remedy the deficiency is the subject of this book.

The atlas is composed of 58 maps. All but eight are by British participants. British maps offer the most diversity, but we have also included four American maps, three German, and one French. We have attempted to identify the value of maps in proportion to other military considerations and in a format which, in our opinion, most effectively presents the evidence—a chronological and essentially narrative approach.

If the American Revolution is seen as a military conflict in which the outcome was decided by conventional armies at Saratoga and Yorktown, then maps have only a peripheral significance in relation to more important tactical elements. But maps have a fundamental role if the war is examined within a context of large-scale pacification efforts, vicious partisan raids, nonstationary fronts, and critical logistical requirements.

Breed's Hill, the New York campaign of 1776, Saratoga, the Philadelphia campaign of 1777, the South Carolina campaign of 1780, and Yorktown were the principal engagements between armies in America. They were fought using more or less conventional tactics and were commemorated by traditional battle maps made after the event. Thirty-two of the maps published in the atlas fall into this category. Their inclusion was predicated by our design to narrate the war and their general proportion to other forms of military cartography. Most were submitted by junior officers seeking to gain recognition and advancement. However, some distinction must be made within this classification. Twenty are elaborate small-area memorial maps, six show large-scale troop movements, and six are battlefield sketch maps.

Closely connected to battle maps in terms of survey method and drafting technique were fortification plans. These relate to the construction of forts and defensive positions or to siege operations—all of which were standard methods of European warfare in the eighteenth century. Most military maps of America made prior to the Revolution were of this type. They are represented here by six plans or sketches of the defenses at Penobscot Bay, Paulus Hook, Portsmouth, Savannah, and two of Yorktown.

Yet behind the ordered lines of colorfully uniformed fusiliers emerged another kind of war. It involved the ingredients of a colonial struggle—transoceanic supply lines, vast indefensible coastlines, and strategically inconsequential urban centers. In its more brutal application this other war utilized various forms of economic warfare, divisive partisan allegiances, Indian auxiliaries, and the tactical slyness of country folk. Some officers—both American and British—recognized and implemented these practices: Charles Lee, Daniel Morgan, and Francis Marion; and William Tryon, Patrick Ferguson, and John Graves Simcoe. In their operations, geographic considerations were of primary importance. Reconnaissance information had to be obtained, and maps were the optimal means of storing it and transmitting it up the chain of command. Reconnaissance maps did not supersede the other cartographic forms, but came to have a relative value, just as "irregular" methods of warfare did not supplant the conventional forms but came to coexist with them. In this atlas, a total of 20 can be classified as reconnaissance maps. They can be subdivided among ten maps showing general topography, three large-scale topographic surveys, three road surveys, a troop disposition chart, and three spy maps.

The ability of an army to obtain adequate reconnaissance depended in part on control of territory. British efforts to extend bases across New Jersey, South Carolina, and Virginia were unsuccessful. Consequently, military surveyors were unable to map accurately areas other than those which they occupied around New York City, and at various times Rhode Island, Boston, Philadelphia, Savannah, and Charleston. The careful surveys of Rhode Island (pp. 72–73) and New York harbor (pp. 128–29) should be compared with the large area map of New Jersey on the front endpaper. The last was probably constructed from verbal sources or printed maps. It has been overlaid with vectors to show the actual position of towns and the extent of geographic inaccuracy.

Maps also depended on the availability and training of cartographers. They were submitted from many sources within the British army. Of 38 maps with an identifiable cartographer included here, only 13 were drawn by members of the Corps of Engineers (some of whom held an additional appointment on the army staff). Other maps were submitted by assistant engineers, artillery officers, officers in loyalist units, and line officers attached to the staff or in the regular army. In comparison, the French army received most of its maps from a single source, a corps of topographic engineers with identical training. Uniformity of style or method did not exist among the thirty British cartographers whose work is represented here. Four were trained in the Drawing Room, three acquired skill in foreign territories, four attended the Royal Military Academy at Woolwich, six received instruction during their military service, and thirteen either had no formal training or its source cannot be identified.

The 50 British maps in the atlas represent roughly 5 percent of the surviving British manuscript maps of the Revolution. Thirty came directly from the British headquarters papers in the possession of Sir Henry Clinton. It is possible that a corpus of 20,000 once existed. This estimate is based on the proportion of 100 maps known to survive from the work of Capt. John Montresor, who drew, at a conservative estimate, perhaps 2,000 maps during his service in America. Six of his maps appear here.

Several questions remain to be considered in specialized studies. What is the value of maps in relation to other sources of military reconnaissance, such as guides or verbal instruction? Were maps comparatively less important to the American army which had better sources of local information? How many times did cartographic uncertainty influence desertion rates and logistical considerations? How frequently were maps consulted in the preparation of strategic decisions, and how important was their accuracy?

The British maps reproduced here invite comparison with maps of their opponents. French maps and views of America have been published in the recent study by Howard C. Rice and Anne S. K. Brown, *The American Campaigns of Rochambeau's Army 1780, 1781, 1782, 1783*. American maps have traditionally been regarded as inferior in quality and quantity to the British and French, and the product of "amateurs." Washington complained of their scarcity, but the employment of Robert Erskine as surveyor general in July, 1777, did produce capable road surveys. By early 1779, British officers held prisoner were commenting favorably on the American maps, and a year later Erskine indicated that he could compile "a pretty accurate map" of the middle colonies and Connecticut. The American army, with as many as six assistant surveyors, a draftsman and 18 chain bearers, had constructed maps with considerable reconnaissance value. Clearly their importance vis-à-vis the British maps must be reconsidered.

Printed maps, other than sea charts, were of negligible value in military operations. Their small scale or the limited areas which they depicted rendered them useless. Samuel Holland, the principal British prewar surveyor in America, disclaimed those printed maps which bore his name. British and American commanders often found them inaccurate and of little military significance. They can be analyzed in relation to the history of printing, the growth of literacy, and the diffusion of geographic knowledge, but these purposes are peripheral to the war and exceed the boundaries of this study. However, nine of the maps in this atlas were eventually printed in London and one, Hobkirk's Hill, is a printed map and was included because the manuscript from which it was engraved no longer exists.

Certain considerations limited the project. In order to concentrate on army operations in America, we excluded the war at sea, the war in the West Indies, and the global war. Our objective for general availability of the atlas, its size, and legibility of maps meant printing only sections of three maps and limiting margins on five others. Those who wish to obtain a photostat of any complete map may write to the authors. The maps herein were selected on their ability to reconstruct the war, in terms of their availability in the field, and to show how and when they were influential to the events themselves. In effect, the atlas is an interpretation of the evidence and a portfolio of source material. Over one-half of these maps have never been reproduced in any form.

This book was made possible through a generous grant from the Michigan Bicentennial Commission, then headed by Lt. Gov. James Brickley. Mr. Marshall was awarded a supplemental grant for study in England by the University of Michigan Division of Research Development and Administration.

We wish to acknowledge the many friends and archivists who aided our research, particularly Lt. Col. John Montresor RE, and Elizabeth Montresor; Maj. John T. Hancock RE; Lt. Col. J. T. South RE, and his assistant J. L. Longfield, Royal Engineer Corps Library, Chatham; Hugh M. T. Cobbe, Assistant Keeper, Department of Manuscripts, The British Library; Peter A. Penfold, Modern Records Section, Public Record Office; Sir Hugh Algernon Percy, Duke of Northumberland, and his librarian Mr. Graham, Alnwick; John C. Dann, Curator of Manuscripts, Clements Library, and Jean F. Preston, Curator of Manuscripts, the Huntington Library. In addition, we wish to thank the staffs of the Department of Rare Books, Cornell University Library; the Print and Photograph Division, Library of Congress; and the Manuscripts and Archives Division, New York Public Library, who permitted reproduction of their materials.

Scholars within the map community were supportive of this project and it could not have been produced in this form without the help of Walter W. Ristow and Richard Stephenson, who advised us on map content and arranged loan privileges for several maps under their supervision, Geography and Map Division, Library of Congress; Helen Wallis and Sarah Tyacke, Map Room, The British Library; John C. Long, Atlas of Early American History, Newberry Library; William P. Cumming, and Peter J. Guthorn. J. Brian Harley, Geography Department, University of Exeter, permitted us to review his manuscript on Revolutionary War cartography. Waldo Tobler, Geography Department, University of Michigan, added a dimension to our interpretation of cartographic accuracy.

Some historians were asked to comment on individual narratives in the text. We are grateful for the suggestions of J. Barton Starr, Troy State University at Fort Rucker; the Rt. Rev. Robert M. Hatch; and Arlene Phillips, Clements Library. R. Arthur Bowler graciously forwarded the page proofs of his book on logistics in the American Revolution.

The complex process of assembling a book of this type would not have been possible without the enthusiastic participation of The University of Michigan Press and Hammond Incorporated. The authors are indebted to two members of the Clements staff: Barbara Mitchell, who researched several narratives and coordinated editorial revisions, and James Bartlett, who researched and arranged the source section.

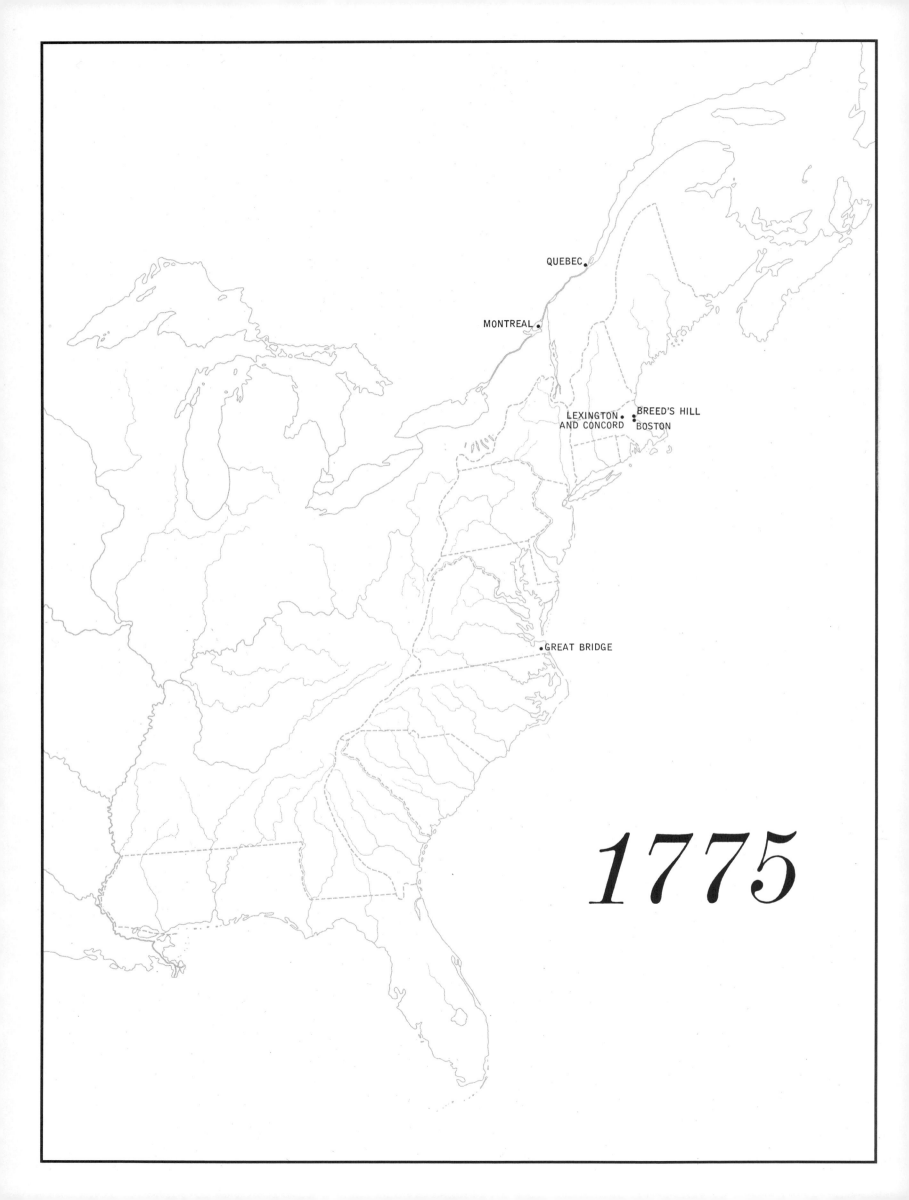

QUEBEC

MONTREAL

BREED'S HILL
LEXINGTON
AND CONCORD
BOSTON

GREAT BRIDGE

1775

In the spring of 1774 the H.M.S. *Lively* crossed the Atlantic from England in the remarkably fast time of four weeks. One passenger in particular may have compared the roll and pitch of the vessel with actions he was about to undertake in America. Lt. Gen. Thomas Gage was returning after a year's leave with the new title of Governor of Massachusetts. Moreover, he carried instructions to close the port of Boston and to quarter troops, if necessary, within the city. The citizenry would label these and later acts "intolerable." And, throughout the next year, Gage's officers were to watch him grow desperate and prematurely old. One of them recorded simply, "he feels no affection for the army."

Gage had spent 20 years as an officer of the British army in America, the last 11 years as its commander. He attained this high duty by prudent management of the Montreal district after the British conquest of Canada in 1760, and by political influence as a member of a noble family from Sussex. Although Gage earned no battlefield distinctions during six years of combat in the French and Indian War, he applied his abilities in the organization of a light infantry regiment. Traditional regiments were taught to line up in platoons and fire in unison. But they had difficulty using these techniques against Indians and French ranger units. In comparison, light infantry was adaptable to the requirements of war in America. One company from each regiment was trained to skirmish in irregular formations along broken terrain and through dense woods. These skills were not practiced systematically after 1763, to the belated regret of the British at Concord.

Aboard ship Gage had time to consider the problems of his command. The 1774 peacetime strength of the British army in America was about 6,000 men. This was 2,000 fewer than the force of 1763 and well below the wartime maximum of 16,000 soldiers assembled in 1760. As the earliest reductions occurred, the government decided to keep the original number of 15 regiments on service in America, but to lower the average size of each from 700 men to 350. Understrength regiments were common in years of peace.

The army also underwent geographical changes. In 1763 it was scattered along a thousand-mile arc of forts and garrisons between Newfoundland and Illinois, with a small corollary arc of outposts extending inland from the South Carolina coast. Most of the 8,000 troops occupied positions in the major cities of Canada and in the maritime provinces recently seized from the French. The remainder guarded the ports of New York and Halifax and entries to the 13 colonies in upper New York State and across Pennsylvania. The frontier areas of Illinois, West Florida, and South Carolina were protected by some isolated cantonments with a total of no more than 800 soldiers.

Over the next ten years British priorities shifted from the frontier to the seacoast. The army's preoccupation after 1770 was less with the maintenance of Indian boundaries than with the enforcement of the British ministry's statutes on the colonial populace. This revised function altered the army's distribution. More than 30 interior forts in North America were abandoned. Seven major garrisons remained: Montreal, Quebec City, Halifax, Boston, New York, Pensacola, and St. Augustine. Small posts were retained at Mackinaw, Detroit, Mobile, Kaskaskia, Ticonderoga, and Niagara. The abandonment of many forts was as much a result of physical decay as of political design. Those which remained were not necessarily sturdier. The 1774 estimate of fortification repair described once-mighty Ticonderoga as "most ruinous," and reported the same for the storehouses at Halifax. The barracks at Castle William in Boston Harbor were so far gone that repairs could be temporary at best. The fort at Mackinaw was scarcely defendable, and St. Augustine was forever falling into the sea. The engineer's estimate for the defense of Pensacola alone was £14,410, or over four times his projected expenditure for all forts in North America in 1773! The chronic disintegration of defenses could not be remedied by a commander whose peacetime administration was evaluated by his ability to cut costs.

When Gage disembarked at Boston on May 17, his orders to close the port soon paralyzed the local economy. Tension was increased in the fall of 1774 when regiments were sent to lodge among the unemployed longshoremen and mariners. At another level, the military commander's use of authority estranged the provincial leadership. Traditional prerogatives of assembly and colonial administration were suspended, and propagandists oiled their presses.

In September, 1774, 12 of 13 colonies sent delegates to a congress in Philadelphia that pledged support to Massachusetts in the event of British aggression. This congress also urged, among other measures, repeal of Gage's arrogated authority, and the removal of troops from Boston. That same fall, Massachusetts militia began to arm and drill in the open. The most readily available men in each town were organized into minutemen companies, and those less able to assemble quickly formed a reserve, called alarm men. Militia units in other colonies became active.

As one year ended and another began, armed camps smoldered throughout New England. On April 19, 1775, a night raid provoked an action that ricocheted down the Atlantic coastline. The year was to see British hegemony in North America reduced to the towns of Boston and Quebec, and the garrisons at Halifax, St. Augustine, Pensacola, Detroit, Niagara, and Mackinaw. In addition, a patriot regular army and government would take form, an invasion of Canada would be launched, and 142 recorded military engagements in 1775 would further diminish support for royal authority. The most important actions took place at Lexington and Concord, Breed's Hill, Montreal, Quebec City, and the Norfolk Great Bridge; each is described herein.

Lexington and Concord

Anxiously watching the growing hostility in Massachusetts, Gov. Thomas Gage, who also commanded the British Army in America, concluded that "nothing can be done but by forcible means." Throughout the winter Boston remained a tinderbox of resentment between the 3,000-odd soldiers and the populace of under 20,000. Actually Gage favored a naval blockade and suspension of the coercive acts that the colonials so warmly resisted. He felt whatever action the army took must be overwhelming.

On April 16, 1775, he received a delayed letter from the Secretary of State, advising him that "force should be repelled by force"; some reinforcements were coming, but Gage should act now with his present garrison and he ought to arrest the leaders of the Provincial Congress. Gage feared the letter meant war. He hesitated another two days until his spies brought word of the cannon, ammunition, tents, and equipment gathered by the rebels at Concord. There was the obvious target.

On April 18 he drafted sealed orders to Lt. Col. Francis Smith to march out that night with the grenadiers and light infantry, a corps of about 700 men. They were to be rowed across Back Bay to the Cambridge shore and then march by way of Lexington. In the city, loyalists and rebels alike witnessed the preparations and guessed the destination. Dr. Joseph Warren, a patriot leader, asked William Dawes and Paul Revere to leave Boston and ride with a warning to people along the route and particularly to John Hancock and Sam Adams, who were in Lexington.

Smith was slow in getting his expedition under way. As the redcoats marched northwestward they began to see lights in house windows and hear church bells and signal guns. Their secret was out. Smith hurried six companies (about 200 men) forward under Maj. John Pitcairn to secure the bridges over the Concord River. He also sent word back to Gage that resistance was likely and reinforcements were wanted.

Early in the morning of April 19, Pitcairn reached Lexington and found some 40 minutemen drawn up in two lines on the bright village green. Another 30 wandered around the nearby meeting house. These were the shock troops of the colonial militia. They did not block the road but stood back on the green in mute protest, making a show of arms. Pitcairn led his men on to the green and ordered the minutemen to drop their muskets and disperse. Their commander, Capt. John Parker, realized his disadvantage and told the men to withdraw and not fire. Then someone's musket flashed or was fired. Whose it was never has been known, and from which side issued the harmless pop has been hotly disputed. Several British soldiers then fired without orders and rushed on the retreating minutemen. As some of them fell, others swung around and returned the fire. Pitcairn shouted to his men to cease, but could not restrain them. Before he could get them back in line, one was wounded; and eight Americans lay dead and ten were wounded. Smith came up, and the column resumed its march to Concord, six miles beyond, with fifes and drums playing.

The Concord minutemen moved out of town as the redcoats entered. Smith used two-thirds of his men to search the town and sent seven companies to the North Bridge. He burned some gun carriages and flour, seized powder and musket balls, but learned that other stores had been removed. The militia again appeared and tried to force the North Bridge. Again it was disputed who fired first, but in this brief exchange three redcoats were killed and nine wounded. The British unit pulled back into town.

By noon Smith considered his mission accomplished and started his tired men back to Boston. Then his real troubles began. All morning the nearby towns had turned out their militia to converge on Lexington and Concord. The column of marching redcoats offered a wonderful target which they could fire on at will from behind trees or the stone walls that bordered much of the road. Used to orderly lines of skirmishers or platoons firing in unison on the open terrain of northern Europe, the British veterans considered this Indian-style sniping as unfair. On maps, legends such as "Provincials behind the Walls," "Hilly, broken ground," and "Each side lined with trees" indicate the disorientation of the British.

Within sight of Lexington they broke into a run and fled into the sheltering lines of a heavy reinforcement, about 1,400 men and two cannon under Brig. Hugh Percy. After a half-hour rest the march was resumed. The rebel potshotting revived, but Percy ordered flanking parties to keep the enemy at a distance and even used his field pieces to break up militia concentrations. Nevertheless, the road became a bloody chute all the way to Charlestown, where dusk ended the mauling.

The British lost 70 men killed, 182 wounded, and 22 missing in addition to their 13 earlier casualties — a total of 287. Perhaps 4,000 rebels had been involved at various times in the long day's engagement. Their casualties were 47 killed, 39 wounded, and 5 missing — a gratifyingly low total of 93. The Americans rebounded with dangerous enthusiasm over what they considered their first victory.

The colored map showing the area west from Boston has been attributed to the elusive Jonathan Carver. Doubtless it was drawn shortly after the rebels had ringed Boston but before the Charlestown peninsula was claimed by either side. Inaccuracies suggest that it was done by an officer or draftsman in the city garrison: Percy joined Smith at Lexington, not west of it, and the combined force retreated through "Monatomy" (Menotomy, or modern Arlington) on the lower road. A version was published in London that July, but this manuscript original remained in the possession of Percy.

The sketch map shows the area bounded by Medford, Menotomy, Cambridge, and Charlestown. Percy accurately foresaw the ambush the rebels were planning at Cambridge and steered his troops through the cutoff marked "Kent's Lane" to Charlestown, where they reembarked to Boston. The anonymous mapmaker depicts the route of the British not described in other contemporary accounts. This map was also drawn for Percy.

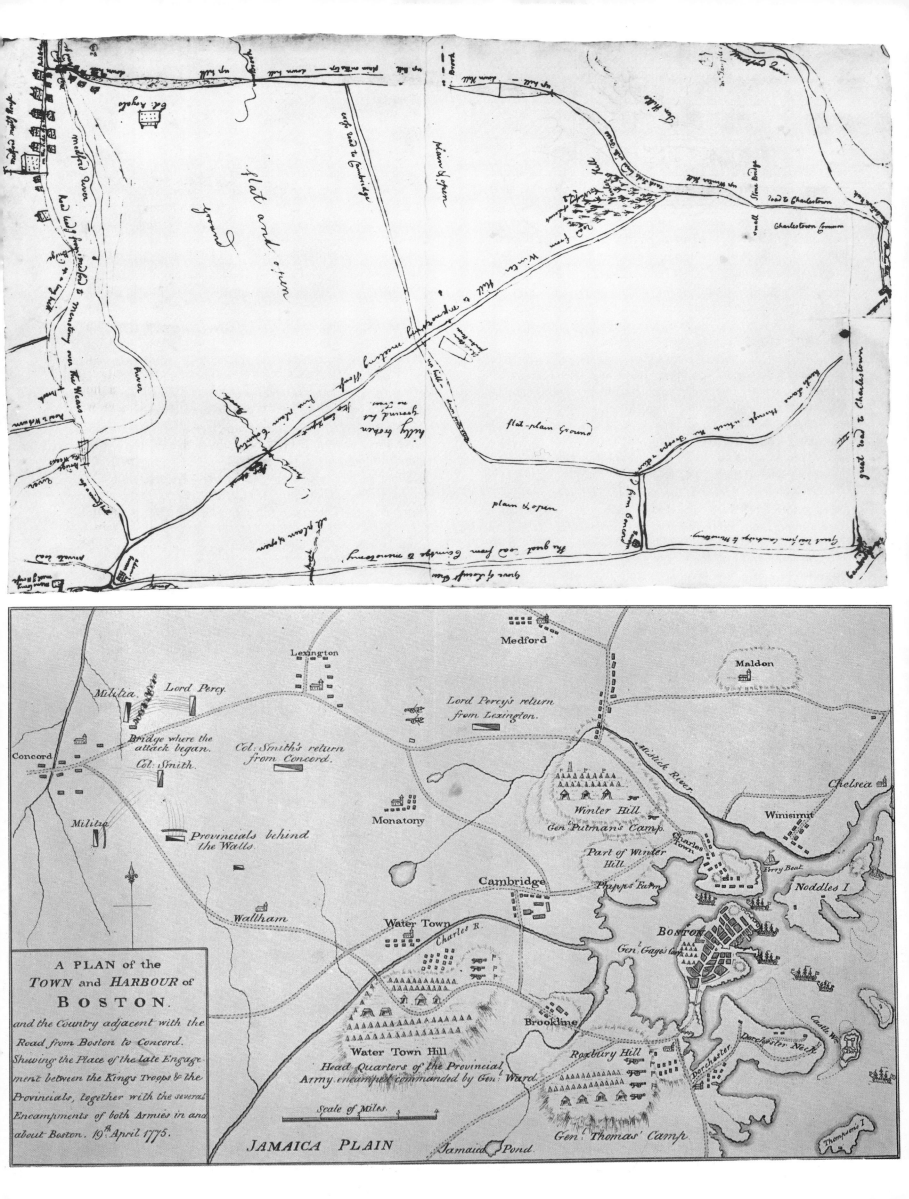

Siege of Boston

As the exhausted British regulars returned to Boston on the afternoon and evening of April 19, the retreating column was harassed by elements of the provincial militia. Maj. Gen. Hugh Percy, commander of the relief detachment to Lt. Col. Francis Smith at Concord, likened the rebel assault to a "moving circle." The circle closed about the British in Boston that night, and crude camps and sentry posts sprung up around a line from Roxbury to Cambridge. Overnight the ranks of the legendary embattled farmers and mechanics swelled to about 9,000. The British found themselves besieged.

Lt. Gen. Thomas Gage's army in Boston consisted of under 4,000 men in April, including fewer than 300 artillerymen and only one engineer, Capt. John Montresor. Adequate troop support was the most pressing need of the British. In 1774 Gage had assured the king that four regiments could control Boston. When reality intruded, he called for an army of 20,000 to subdue the rebels, but never received half that many.

The British entered the conflict well supplied with arms, munitions, and equipment. However, besides men, they lacked food, fuel, and forage—items difficult to ship from England. By July the army was consuming seven and one-half tons of food per day. This did not include the requirements for at least 6,500 civilians who stayed throughout the siege nor the minimum four and one-half tons of hay and oats per day needed to feed 500 army horses. Five hundred and fifty sheep, 290 hogs, and 200 tons of potatoes were sent to Boston in October and November, 1775, but not even 13 percent of each arrived in usable condition. The collection of provisions in America was to prove disappointing. Except for the seizure of 2,000 sheep and cattle on Long Island in July, raids on the mainland were generally unsuccessful. Some supplies were obtained from Canada, and, for a time, loyalist merchants in New York and elsewhere loaded food onto supply ships ostensibly bound for the West Indies. Local patriots, however, quickly caught on to the game that the Royal Navy was seizing a disproportionately high number of these ships and escorting them to Boston.

The British army in America was supplied by firms contracted to deliver food and equipment. Several family fortunes were bankrolled in this business—including that of John Hancock. A Boston contractor warned of potential disruptions in March, and by early fall another firm pleaded that fulfillment of orders was impossible. Overseas transport from England usually took from five to seven weeks for a one-way crossing. This system increased the danger of spoilage, piracy, and corruption. A modern quartermaster staff did not exist, and the attempt to improvise a supply network created interdepartmental friction, clumsy methods of business, and duplication of functions between branches.

Leadership was another problem. Unlike the Royal Navy, most officers in the army purchased their commissions from each other. The transactions required approval from the colonel of the regiment and the commander. The fee dissuaded many men of talent who could not draw together the necessary financing and influence. Still, whenever a commission became vacant, it brought forth a flood of petitions from all who wished to forward a particular candidate. More than one historian has mused that this business took up so much time, it was a wonder any other regimental duties got done. The purchase system worked to discourage experienced junior officers with only marginal influence from moving up in rank rapidly. Many turned gray and white waiting to obtain a higher commission. To young men with aspirations, especially those born in the colonies, it seemed better to choose another vocation. George Washington, among others, was a disappointed commission seeker.

Increasingly from 1763, the British army became a social and economic force in colonial society. Nearly 1,000 officers served here. Some were from aristocratic families, others were sons of other officers, and a few were soldiers of fortune. Many, like Gage himself, were younger sons. Denied family lands, they found a home in the army. Some made fine officers, and some were prone to chronic ignorance and incompetence. Drunkenness was pervasive. Perhaps their position within the family can explain, in part, this unusual combination of restlessness, ambition, and disillusion. The decision to keep a large peacetime army in America had been influenced by the British ministry's desire to maintain the size of the officer corps and thus assure a profession for the dispossessed.

For most officers, life in the army offered little more than security and, if they were lucky, the prospect of paying £3,500 to become a lieutenant colonel after as long as 25 years of service. Only the colonel of a regiment had a chance to earn any substantial income, while the pay of junior officers was not enough to afford comfort and was frequently two or three years in arrears. Frustrated in their attempt to obtain advancement or wealth within the army, several married into prominent colonial families and retired to provincial estates. Montresor and Gage are examples of officers who married well but stayed on.

For the common soldier, life in the army was almost hopeless. Redcoats enlisted for 20-year terms, pay was bad, and prospects for promotion were dismal. Enlistment quotas often were secured by less than honorable methods, such as recruits being forcefully inebriated and then pledged. Even so, these arrangements were less resented than the navy's resort to impressment gangs. Soldiers were obtained from the lower classes of society, and army service was sometimes offered in lieu of a prison term. County gaols occasionally gave up their charges to fill a regimental quota. Recent research has shown that some Scottish regiments were recruited from respectable men who had become insolvent, such as those displaced from the textile trade. Barracks were an attempt to prevent desertion. When the army had to be quartered within private houses, such as at Boston in 1768, desertion rates skyrocketed. Two regiments reported 70 men gone in the first two weeks. The situation was reexperienced when the army returned in 1774.

In addition, Gage suffered problems of command. British military tradition sanctioned a system of operation directed by a coterie of general officers, called the council of war. Although this arrangement distributed the burden of responsibility, it compromised a commander's direction of strategy and divided the allegiance of the field staff and the politicians in England. With the arrival of three major generals, William Howe, Henry Clinton, and John Burgoyne, on May 25, Gage felt prodded to begin an offensive. On June 17 the British drove the Americans from Breed's Hill in a costly attack that did not break the siege (see "Breed's Hill").

Vice Adm. Samuel Graves commanded the British fleet at Boston. His conduct proceeded from the assumption that the army and navy could maintain separate policies toward the colonists. This meant that while the army was at war, the navy was not. Warships continued to call at American ports down the coast to take on supplies and break the boredom of long voyages. Graves's neutrality soon cost the British their initiative at sea by permitting the birth of a fledgling American navy of whaleboats and privateers.

Comparatively, the patriot military problems were more serious. The citizen army that surrounded Boston on the night of April 19 was undisciplined and disorganized; in fact, it was less an army than an armed mob. The first duty of militia commanders Artemas Ward and John Thomas was to prevent the volunteers from simply melting away. As Thomas complained in a letter of April 24, "I shall be left all alone." Yet the Provincial Congress of Massachusetts had enacted orders to enlist 30,000 men. Regiments of 590 were to be recruited from the militia before Boston by officers whose commissions were recognized only if they filled their quotas. Initially, larger regiments had been requested, but local loyalties limited their size because soldiers would not serve with men from other towns. Troops were to be paid,

even though some voices suggested that liberty alone should compensate. The new army was chronically short of powder, shot, muskets, and cannon. Often, soldiers were enlisted unarmed and unequipped. A commissary, hospital, and supply services had to be improvised. The patriot camps around Boston were in wretched, overcrowded condition. Not until the first of May were latrines dug. Reports claimed that militiamen were "growing sickly and daily dying out of the barracks."

The Second Continental Congress convened in Philadelphia on May 10. It created a regular army by adopting the 24,500 New England troops, half of whom were home on leave from the Boston lines. George Washington of Virginia was elected commander in chief, in part to emphasize unified colonial participation. Washington arrived at Cambridge on July 2. His first reforms fell hardest on the officer corps. To the aristocratic commander, the customary election of officers among provincial militia had produced an unacceptable familiarity. Within a few weeks, ten officers were under arrest or had been discharged. A peaceful autumn gave Washington valuable time to drill troops, construct barracks, and obtain ordnance. The test came in December when the original enlistments expired. Washington faced the prospect of seeing one army fade away, then raising another. Soldiers felt they should not be asked to serve a second term since thousands of other sympathetic citizens were still at home. When veterans could not be persuaded to stay, New England militia was requested to fill the gap. These irregular units pulled the army through the crisis, as they were asked to do repeatedly in later years.

But for an occasional artillery duel, the British spent an inert summer and autumn in Boston refortifying their positions. The last major reinforcement arrived in July to bring troop strength to 6,000, with another 1,400 sick and wounded. Clinton suggested a preemptive strike on Dorchester Heights, but was overruled. Gage was recalled to England in October because of the carnage at Breed's Hill, and the British command in America was divided subsequently between Maj. Gen. Guy Carleton

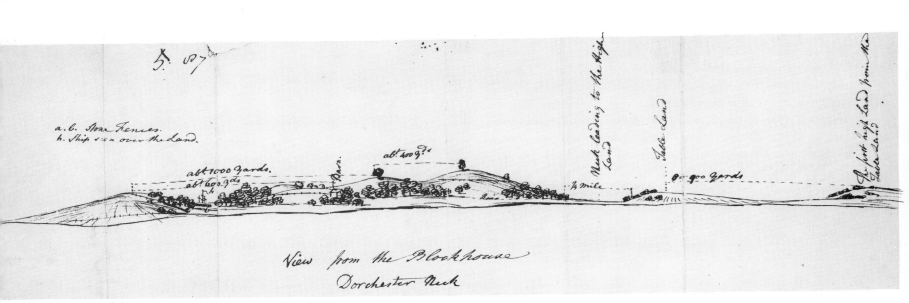

View from the Blockhouse
Dorchester Neck

in Canada and Howe in the 13 colonies. The siege would have continued longer had the provincials not seized old Fort Ticonderoga in upper New York in the spring of 1775. Surprised in its sleep, the weak British garrison surrendered to a mixed colonial force under Benedict Arnold and Ethan Allen. Sixty cannon were taken in this operation. They were then dismantled and sledded 300 miles to Cambridge that winter. Washington put the artillery on Dorchester Heights above Boston on the night of March 4, 1776, and aimed the guns down on the British. Howe evacuated the city on March 17. The British army temporarily withdrew to regroup in Halifax, Nova Scotia. Before they left, it was clear to the high command that the advantages of New York far outweighed Boston as a base of operations.

A reconnaissance of the Boston area had been attempted when the British army was first ordered there in 1768. At that time, Montresor was assigned to map the town and surrounding countryside. Gage felt that whatever he received would be of more use "than the bad maps that have been published." Knowledge of local topography was still scant in February, 1775, when Gage was forced to recruit and send out Ens. Henry De Berniere and Capt. William Brown disguised as country people. The two officers spent three days sketching the roads from Boston to Concord, Worcester, and Marlborough. Several times in danger of having their purpose discovered, they also narrowly missed being beaten by mobs.

Except for the brief tour of Lt. Thomas Hyde Page in June, Montresor alone represented the Corps of Engineers until Capt. Lt. Archibald Robertson and Ens. William Fyers arrived in November, 1775. Montresor designed most of the fortifications and drafted the large map. He constructed it from sketches such as the preceding view of Dorchester Heights. A small surveying instrument, probably a theodolite, was used to fix the distances. The Americans mounted cannon on the hill which appears at the far left of the sketch.

The elegant campaign map accurately depicts the siege. Here the patriot entrenchments are seen to encircle the British positions on the Boston and Charlestown peninsulas. Since the British fort on Bunker Hill is represented, the map was made after the battle of June 17, and perhaps in the leisure of fall or winter quarters. The map communicates a sense of isolation. Limited ship access to the ocean and the difficulty of maneuver in the harbor are displayed alongside the forbidding terrain. Military operations were impeded by the irregular landforms of New England. The British army was not to return here, and for the moment, the patriots were victorious.

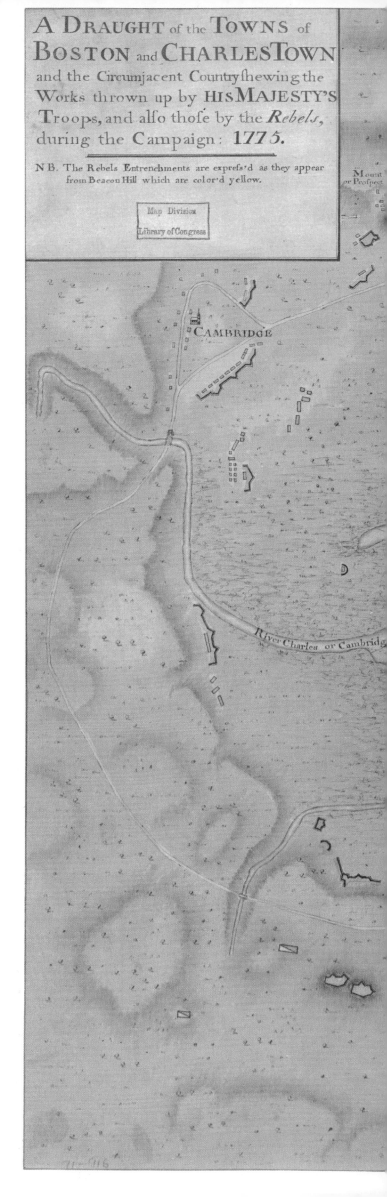

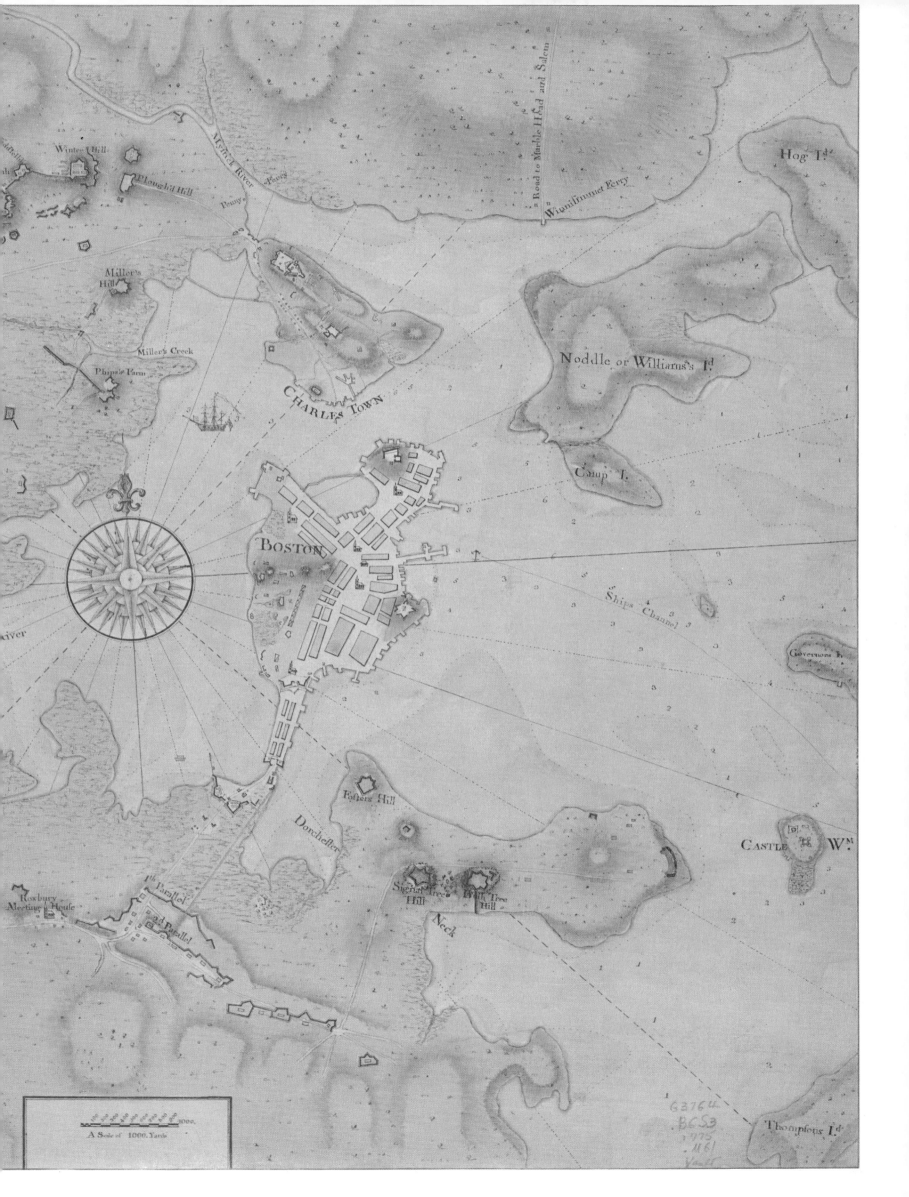

Breed's Hill

The Massachusetts Committee of Safety decided on June 15 to fortify Bunker Hill, an eminence of 110 feet rising a little more than half a mile northeast of Charlestown. The fort would tighten the ring which the Americans were forging around British-held Boston. Three Massachusetts regiments, an artillery company, and a working detachment from Brig. Gen. Israel Putnam's Connecticut regiment—all told, a force of 1,200 under the command of Col. William Prescott—marched out of Cambridge after dark on June 16 and crossed the narrow neck to the wider peninsula. On the way they were joined by Putnam with wagons of entrenching tools and by Col. Richard Gridley, chief engineer of Massachusetts troops.

They halted on the side of Bunker Hill, while the officers argued about the best site. Although not in command, Putnam insisted that the fortification be dug on Breed's Hill—a lesser hill of 62 feet, ahead of them and just east of Charlestown—and that a secondary work be constructed on Bunker Hill. Putnam's view prevailed, although the latter height could have been made almost impregnable. Breed's Hill had no advantage; but Gridley laid out a square redoubt about 45 yards on a side, and the men fell to digging at midnight. The subsequent battle has usually been named for Bunker Hill.

At daybreak on June 17 the British sloop *Lively* sighted the work party and opened fire. Her cannon awoke the troops in Boston. Lt. Gen. Thomas Gage called a council of war with his major generals, William Howe, Henry Clinton, and John Burgoyne. They knew what the threat of cannon placed on either hill meant. Their decision was to send Howe to disperse the rebels. Instead of landing at Charlestown or trying to seize the narrow neck and cut off the Americans, as Clinton advocated, Howe decided to have his force rowed around to Morton's Point at the southeast end of the peninsula and make a frontal assault. The boats would have to wait until high tide at 2:00 P.M.

Howe was given 1,550 of the best troops and 12 brass cannon, which were safely transported on 28 barges. Several warships moved into position to bombard both Charlestown and the redoubt. But once on the spot and having surveyed the enemy defenses, Howe sent back to Boston for 600 additional men. Meanwhile, he asked Vice Adm. Samuel Graves to fire "hot shot" into Charlestown and set it on fire.

What Howe observed was that Prescott had extended his line from the redoubt on Breed's Hill to the Mystic River by means of a trench and wooden fence ending in a stone wall on the beach. Another rail fence was rebuilt in front of it, neither one being bullet proof, but of great inconvenience to attackers. The Americans were now exhausted. Prescott welcomed reinforcements of two regiments of New Hampshire men under Cols. John Stark and James Reed. Stark led his men to augment the Connecticut force under Capt. Thomas Knowlton at the fence and wall. Prescott commanded in the crowded redoubt; Putnam moved about restlessly. Brig. Gen. Seth Pomeroy, aged 70, and Dr. Joseph Warren, president of the Massachusetts Provincial Congress, served as volunteers.

The British force now amounted to 2,200 men. Their attack began with an advance on Breed's Hill under Brig. Robert Pigot who was to hold the defenders in their redoubt. On his right the elite companies under Howe moved against the stone wall and wooden fence. It was 3:00 P.M. and hot; the troops not only wore their woolen uniforms, but also carried blankets and provisions on their backs. British artillery was out of action because the cannon balls were of incorrect diameter. Pigot's men, seeing smoke billowing across the field from burning Charlestown, moved uphill through the grass and over several stone walls. Howe's column marched four abreast along the Mystic River shore. Stark let them approach within 50 feet before he gave orders to fire. The first volley mowed down the first three companies of redcoats. Howe pulled back. His men were running. He quickly organized a second attack. It also was repulsed by the hail of bullets that seemed to aim at British officers. Pigot, too, had suffered so from the redoubt defenders that he had to withdraw and regroup his men for a second advance. That failed also. The field was strewn with the dead. The wounded were taken back to the boats. Prescott's men exulted, but they were running low on ammunition.

From Copp's Hill in Boston, Clinton watched anxiously the British failures. He sent over 400 fresh troops and then went to the battle himself—without orders. Howe shifted his men to the left to reinforce the frontal attack of Pigot, and at last let them drop their packs. The third assault by the determined British began. They pushed their way to the top edge of the redoubt. Suddenly the noise of American resistance ceased as gunpowder gave out. Shouting, the redcoats jumped down into the earthwork, only to be met by the powder-blackened faces of the enemy who were swinging their muskets as clubs. But the flight had begun; Warren fell dead in the retreat. The men at the fence had to fall back, too, and they swarmed up and around Bunker Hill. Clinton led the pursuit, but encountered a fighting rear guard. Slowly he pushed on to the higher hill.

Possibly 2,000 to 3,000 Americans saw action against the 2,600 British. The Americans lost 140 killed and 301 wounded, and 30 of the latter were captured. Two-thirds of them later died in prison. The British loss was staggering: 226 killed and 828 wounded. "A dear bought victory," Clinton wrote, "another such would have ruined us." The greatest casualty was the British myth that Americans could not stand against the regulars.

The crude sketch opposite is probably the first map to be made of the battle. The handwriting is that of Lt. Thomas Hyde Page, Pigot's aide. The "principal landing place" is Howe's landing on Morton's Point; the other landing is of reinforcements. The "rebels line of march" is their retreat across Bunker Hill. The two-pronged advance on the rebel fence and redoubt is clearly shown. The Mystic River flows on the right of the peninsula.

Sketch of different Passes into Canada
from our lower Provinces

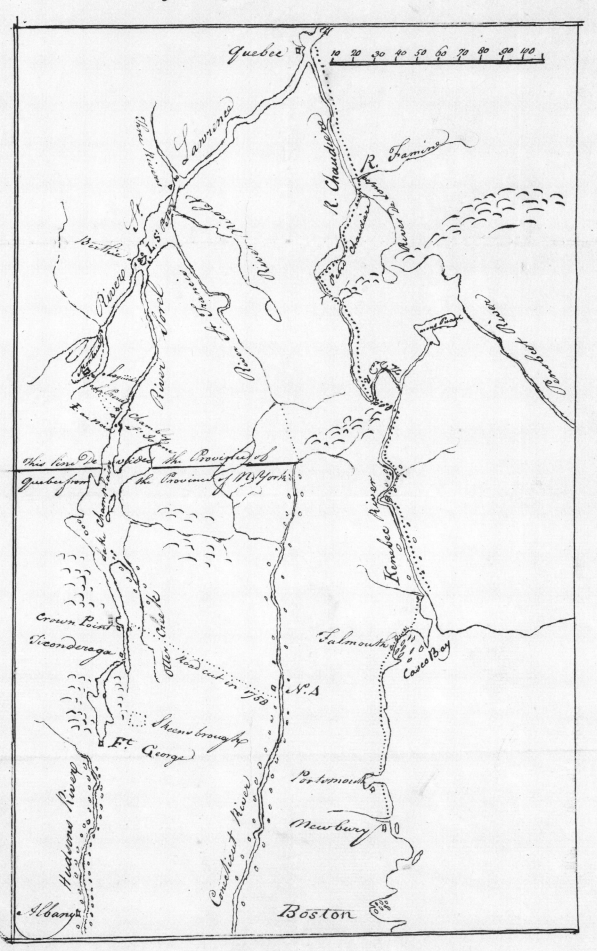

Quebec

10 20 30 40 50 60 70 80 90 100

Lawrence

St Lawrence River

R. Chaudiere

R. Famine

Berthie

River Sorel

River St Francis

River

Penobscot River

This line Devides the Province of Quebec from the Province of N: York

Lake Champlain

Kenebec River

Crown Point

Ticonderoga

Otter Creek R.

Road cut in 1759

N: A

Falmouth

Casco Bay

Skeensborough

Ft George

Portsmouth

Hudsons River

Newbury

Conecticut River

Albany

Boston

Arnold's Pass is marked . . . .

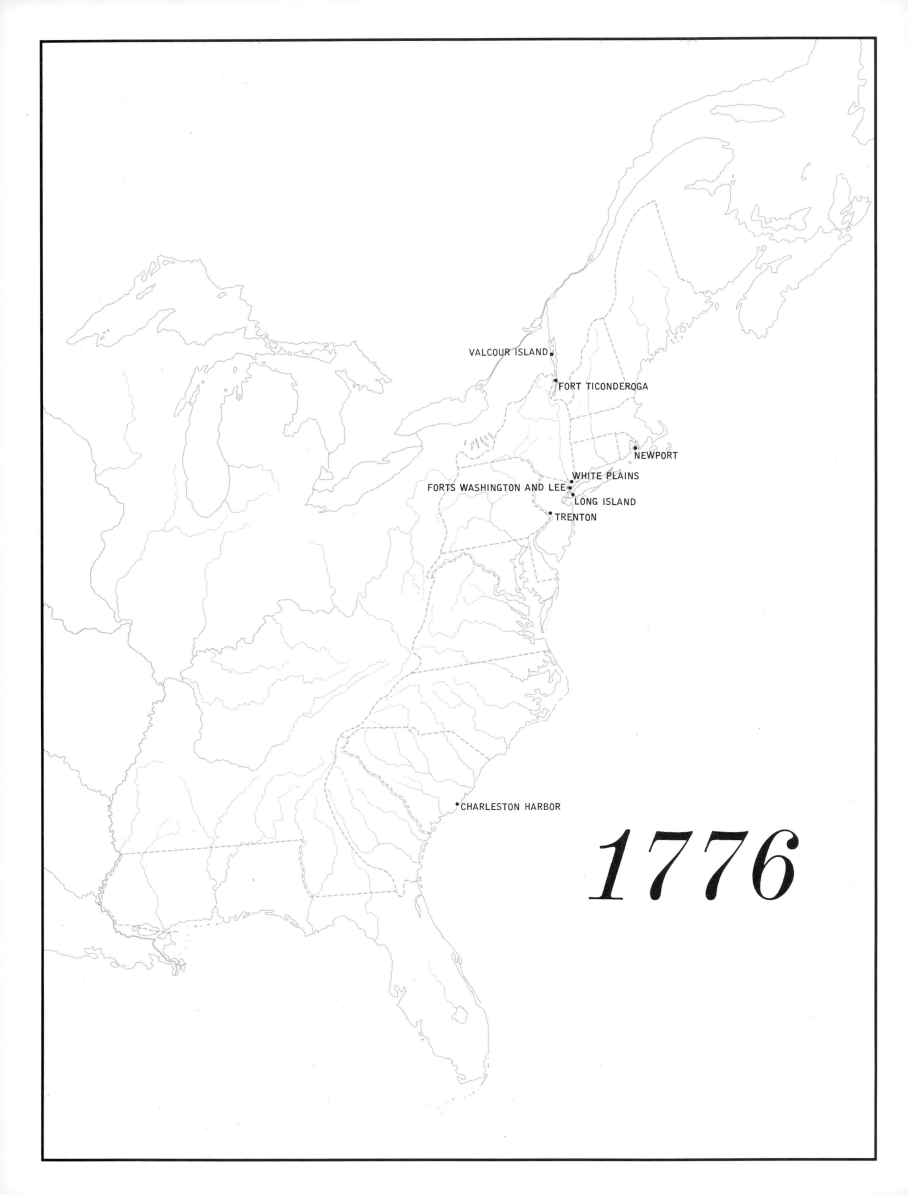

VALCOUR ISLAND

FORT TICONDEROGA

NEWPORT

WHITE PLAINS

FORTS WASHINGTON AND LEE

LONG ISLAND

TRENTON

CHARLESTON HARBOR

1776

The British began the year with small armies besieged in Boston and Quebec. By mid-March they had been forced from Boston. Almost everywhere in North America loyalist support was silent or subdued. Yet the American headquarters knew the British army would return—the question was when and where. The Quebec garrison was relieved in May by 10,000 troops from England and the Americans were driven from Canada. In July the British army that had left Boston was reinforced in Halifax, Nova Scotia. It sailed to Staten Island, and prepared to engage the Americans entrenched at Brooklyn.

Command of the British forces passed to the Howe brothers. Lord Richard Howe assumed control of the Royal Navy in American waters, and the 73 warships and 12,800 sailors represented 43 percent of all ships and men under the British flag. William Howe commanded an army of 23,800 by summer. The Howes were commissioned to pardon patriots who would submit to the crown, but they were not empowered to negotiate a peace without a surrender. The Americans had other ideas and these were not negotiable. On July 4, Congress dissolved the bond of empire and declared the colonies independent.

Successive British victories followed at Long Island, White Plains, and Forts Washington and Lee. By December, the main American army had been routed from positions in New York harbor and pushed westward across New Jersey. That same month, a British expedition seized Newport, Rhode Island. But other British ventures were less successful. A raid by Maj. Gen. Henry Clinton on Charleston harbor to establish a refuge for southern loyalists ended in disaster. Maj. Gen. Guy Carleton's expedition south from Montreal was delayed by a gunboat encounter on Lake Champlain; he withdrew back to Canada for the winter. Finally, the British outposts which stretched across New Jersey were rolled back 60 miles in a bold winter move by Washington on Christmas night at Trenton.

Tactically, both sides had learned painful lessons about war in America during the previous year. The rebels' practice of firing from behind the cover of trees along a line of retreat and especially the targeting of officers were considered unorthodox. Also, the steadiness of untested defenders on Breed's Hill disproved the widely held view of American cowardice and military inferiority. These unexpected realities caused confusion and rage. But the Americans were provoked in turn by the use of Hessian and other German regiments. Foreign mercenaries violated a colonial sense of paterfamilias, and their crude behavior did not improve support for the British cause. The employment of Indian auxiliaries as well was considered an unwarranted resort to terrorism, particularly by those Americans on the frontier.

The expansion of British military authority in North America and an increase in trained personnel better enabled the army to obtain reliable surveys in 1776. The limited base of operations at Quebec and Boston had been altered over the year to include all of Canada, Staten Island, Long Island, Manhattan, Rhode Island, and a portion of New Jersey. The area between Quebec and Montreal with river routes into the 13 colonies had been surveyed with care after the British took possession in 1760. Manhattan had also been fully surveyed before the Revolutionary War. Staten Island was quickly mapped in August, 1776, as was the route across New Jersey in December (see page 35). Triangulated surveys of Long Island and Rhode Island were not done immediately.

The best military cartography in America before the Revolution was the work of Capt. Samuel Holland. Holland had been employed by the Board of Trade since 1763 to survey the coasts and harbors in the Gulf of St. Lawrence, and by 1773 he had worked his way around to Boston. Next year the project involved a township survey of New Hampshire and a determination of New York State boundaries. Although the field work stopped in 1775, the project was still being financed four years later, probably to produce draft copies at Quebec of earlier surveys. When the war disrupted Holland's efforts, his staff of five deputy and assistant surveyors was disbanded. Holland fled his home in Amboy, New Jersey, and obtained an appointment as commissary of musters to the Germans and aide-de-camp to Brig. Philip von Heister. Moreover, four of his five staff members had obtained military commissions by 1777, none of whom joined in the Corps of Engineers. They provided a source of drawing talent to the army, and the maps of Newport and Long Island are examples of their work.

John Montresor was the only member of the Corps of Engineers on duty in America for the whole of 1775. But he was joined by 21 other members of this corps during 1776, over one-half of whom arrived in February. However, not all were able to construct a map. Only six of this group had been commissioned after service in the Drawing Room of the Tower of London. Besides the Royal Military Academy at Woolwich, the Drawing Room was the other major source of formal training for aspirants to the Corps of Engineers. It was administered under the Board of Ordnance, as were the Corps of Engineers and the Royal Artillery. In January, 1775, the master general of the Ordnance, George Townshend, became provoked by the lack of proficiency of Woolwich cadets and declared that admittance to the Corps of Engineers from the Drawing Room would be preferred. Over the next 6 years he commissioned 15 engineers with cartographic training from the Tower (as opposed to 8 from Woolwich), but none was destined to serve in America.

With the advent of a war of movement, the maps being produced in America changed. Earlier, at Boston and Charleston harbor, many of the maps drawn were actually watercolor views of the seacoast or countryside. Some were by artillery officers, who must have sought a quiet diversion from the sound of their guns. These views show evidence of skill at sketching and drawing rather than the more sophisticated techniques of making a survey. By 1776, the proportion of views gave way to a diversity of battle and reconnaissance maps represented here.

Charleston Harbor

What was launched in the secretary of state's office in London foundered in the waters of Charleston Bay in June, 1776.

In the fall of 1775 the governors of the four southernmost colonies assured the secretary, Lord Dartmouth, that allegiance to the king was strong in Virginia, the Carolinas, and Georgia, and that the loyalists would rise against the rebels if a force of redcoats landed on the coast. Loyal governments could then be restored. This equation seemed simple enough, except when considering its source. The governors had drawn these conclusions from opinions within their territorial jurisdictions—reduced now to the quarterdecks of men-of-war anchored off their respective capitals. It was all they had left. In the meantime, the British ministry realized that New England was not going to submit quickly, and it was looking elsewhere for an easier victory.

Command of the British army in America had passed from Lt. Gen. Thomas Gage to Maj. Gen. William Howe. Dartmouth wrote to Howe late in October that His Majesty had decided on a southern maneuver and had ordered five regiments to embark from Ireland by December 1 for Cape Fear River in North Carolina under the command of Maj. Gen. Charles Cornwallis. They were to carry 10,000 muskets for arming the loyalists and would be augmented by a naval squadron. Howe was asked to detach one of his generals to command the army and plan operations in the southern colonies.

Howe selected his second in command, Maj. Gen. Henry Clinton, to assume leadership of the land force and to share authority for the expedition with the naval leader, Commodore Sir Peter Parker. Clinton was allowed to take two light infantry companies and extra officers to organize those loyalists who would show themselves. Instructed to stop at New York, he took almost a month to reach the Chesapeake, arriving February 17. He was met by Virginia's Governor Dunmore, who told him Norfolk had been burned (see "Great Bridge").

Hoping to find more successful prospects for the royal cause in North Carolina, Clinton pressed on to Cape Fear. He was to rendezvous there with the fleet from England and join forces with the waiting loyalists. Neither happened. The North Carolina loyalists had been mauled and dispersed by a rebel force at Moore's Bridge while attempting to make their way to the coast. Upon learning that loyalists in neighboring South Carolina had fared no better, Clinton suffered "gloomy forebodings of my future success." He remained at Cape Fear for over a month, waiting for Parker's convoy.

Winter storms had prevented Parker from sailing. The 44 ships and 2,500 troops did not unite with Clinton until May. The commanders conferred with the two Carolina governors on exactly what action to take next. Plainly, the objective of restoring royal authority in the South and retaining it with local arms was no longer possible. Perhaps a southern port could be seized to serve as an asylum for loyalists before the summer sickness

set in. But where? Clinton favored a defendable island off Virginia. Howe's instructions, which arrived during the deliberations, suggested Charleston. A reconnaissance patrol to Charleston advised taking Sullivan's Island since it commanded the harbor mouth and was defended only by a crude fort. Parker supported this project and Clinton concurred. The town itself could be taken later.

Meanwhile, in the North, Howe had evacuated Boston and transported his troops to Halifax. George Washington assumed that the British would strike farther south, probably New York, and he marched most of his army there. The Chesapeake and Charleston were other possible points of attack; Washington dispatched Maj. Gen. Charles Lee, a former British officer and his second in command, to strengthen the defenses of the South. Lee reached Charleston on June 4. Three Continental regiments and the militia were ordered there. Fort Johnson on James Island had been captured by the rebels; it guarded the south side of the passage to Charleston. Sullivan's Island guarded the north side. Here Col. William Moultrie was building a fort. Its double walls were made of palmetto logs set 16 feet apart; the intervening space was filled with sand. The bastions were to hold 31 cannon. Lee thought little of the fort and wanted to withdraw the garrison, a suggestion the governor prudently ignored. Moultrie was confident he could hold his fort even though the western side was unfinished.

The British squadron sailed up and down Charleston harbor reconnoitering the American positions. Finally on June 9, Clinton asked to have the troops landed on undefended Long Island (now known as the Isle of Palms) which lay north of Sullivan's Island, separated from it by a channel called the Breach. At low tide this channel was reported to be only 18 inches deep. But after all the troops went ashore, Clinton discovered that the Breach was actually seven feet deep! The British were stranded. Clinton sent Brig. John Vaughan to confer with Parker, who replied that he thought the ships alone could reduce the fort to surrender, and that they would attack on June 23. Clinton and Cornwallis proposed to offer a diversion— to use rowboats on a rebel battery at Haddral's Point.

Contrary winds checked Parker's attempts to near Sullivan's Island until June 28; then the ships' pilots advised anchoring farther out than Parker wished. The three frigates that were to move to the west side of Long Island got stuck on a sand bar that day, and Clinton scuttled his landing at Haddral's Point. All he could do was watch the naval bombardment of Fort Moultrie.

The British fleet opened fire at 11:00 A.M. Moultrie's force was reduced to 485 men in the fort, as Lee had sent 800 men to the north end of the island to face Clinton across the Breach. The garrison aimed the fort's guns at the two biggest ships of the line, one of which was Parker's own flagship, and demonstrated what an Englishman called an "exceedingly well directed" fire. In return fire, the British cannon repeatedly struck the wall of the fort. But the spongy palmetto wood and sand fill simply swallowed up the balls. The projectiles from a bomb thrower came down inside the fort, buried themselves in the sand, and seldom exploded. The men within exhibited amazing courage. When the flagpole toppled, sending the flag over the wall, a Sgt. Jasper went out, retrieved it, and coolly nailed it up on another staff so that neither friend nor foe would think the fort had fallen. The British, spying Jasper atop the pole, incorrectly assumed that the Americans had hanged a man.

By nightfall the British were finished. They lifted anchor and pulled away. Casualties amounted to more than 200, of which 60 to 70 were killed. Commodore Parker suffered the ultimate indignity of having his breeches blown off. The Americans reported only 10 killed and 22 wounded. The next morning Clinton learned of the beating the navy had taken. Too many ships were damaged for them to try again, even though Moultrie was out of ammunition. The British army remained inactive on Long Island for another three weeks until Clinton decided it was time to rejoin Howe. The transports reembarked the troops and sailed northward reaching Sandy Hook on July 31. Howe, poised to open the campaign in New York, was encamped on Staten Island.

The British expedition had the character of an uncoordinated raid. The loyalists, who were to be its main strength, contributed to the failure by rising prematurely. Once this initial expectation was gone, Clinton became confused. His actions resembled those of the country squire who jumped on his horse and rode off in all directions. The options had been to find a refuge for southern loyalists, to blockade a major port with the prospect of taking over the town, or to make a show of force in the hope of discouraging the rebels. Clinton tried for all and accomplished none. Had he boldly attacked Charleston, and if he had not been diverted, he might have seized it. Instead, poor scouting of the Breach wasted the army; and Clinton exposed himself to ridicule. When the navy published Parker's report which blamed the defeat on the failure of the army to follow up the attack, Clinton was embittered. Problems in army-navy command were to prove a major difficulty for the British throughout the war.

After all their panicky preparations, the engagement for the Americans was a relief and a morale builder. The British navy's reputation was tarnished; the loyalists were subdued, and their lives now endangered. With the South temporarily safe, the Americans could concentrate full attention on New York.

This sketch shows the miscalculation of tidal depth between Sullivan's Island and Long Island which frustrated the British attack. With accurate reconnaissance, the oversight could have been avoided. The elaborate map on the next two pages depicts the plan of the entire operation in Charleston harbor.

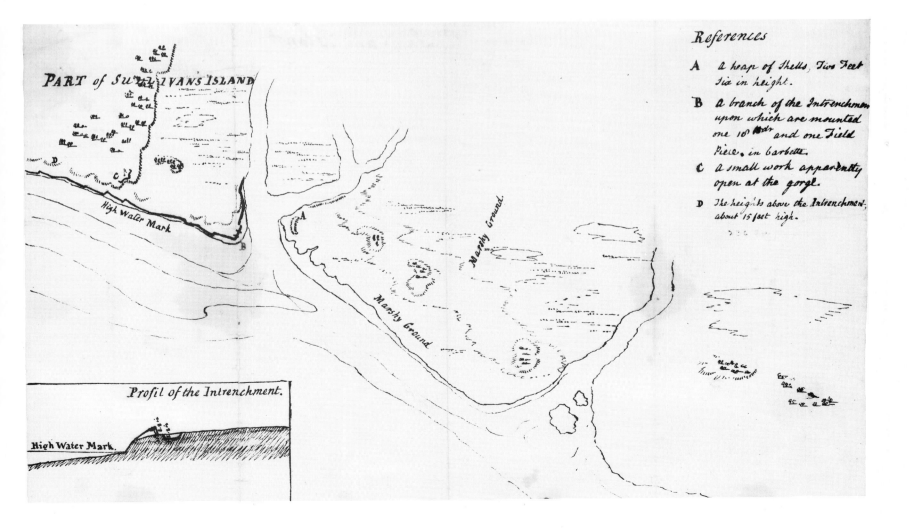

PART of SULLIVANS ISLAND

High Water Mark

Marshy Ground

Marshy Ground

Profil of the Intrenchment.

High Water Mark.

References

A   a heap of shells, Two Feet Six in height.

B   a branch of the Intrenchment upon which are mounted one 10 Pdr and one Field Piece, in barbette.

C   a small work apparently open at the gorge.

D   The heights above the Intrenchment, about 15 feet high.

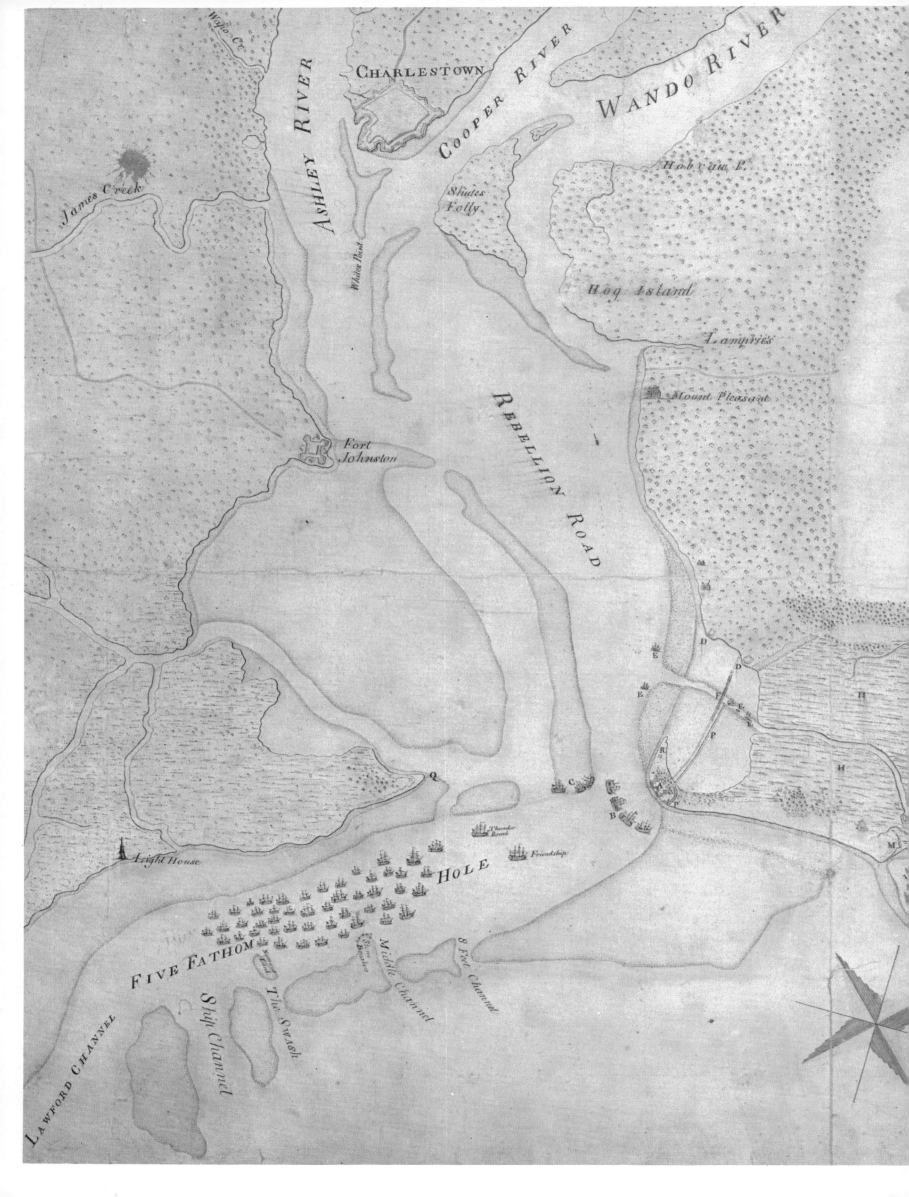

MILITARY REFERENCE'S.

A. *Fort Sulivan.*

B. *The Cannonade of Four Ships.*

C. *Three others which got aground early in the day of Action these were intented to be Stationed towards Heddrals Point.*

D. *Heddrals Point and Batteries.*

E. *Scooners and Floats to cover the Communication and Bridge of Boats.*

F. *Bridge of Boats.*

G. *Landing at Horse Island.*

H. *Impenetrable Bogs and Morasses.*

I. *Long Island.*

K. *Channels between it and Sulivans Island.*

L. *The Rebels First Intrenchment.*

M. *That which they removed to Afterwards.*

N. *A Battery of Small Ordnance Overflowed at high Water.*

O. *Disposition of Flatt Boats Pointing either to the Main or Sulivans Island.*

P. *Canal of five feet at high and two at low Water leading to Sulivans Fort and making it an Island.*

Q. *Cummins Point*

R. *Redoubt on Sulivan's Point*

S. *Strong Coppice in the Road from Horse Island in which they are Supposed to have had Works and a Camp.*

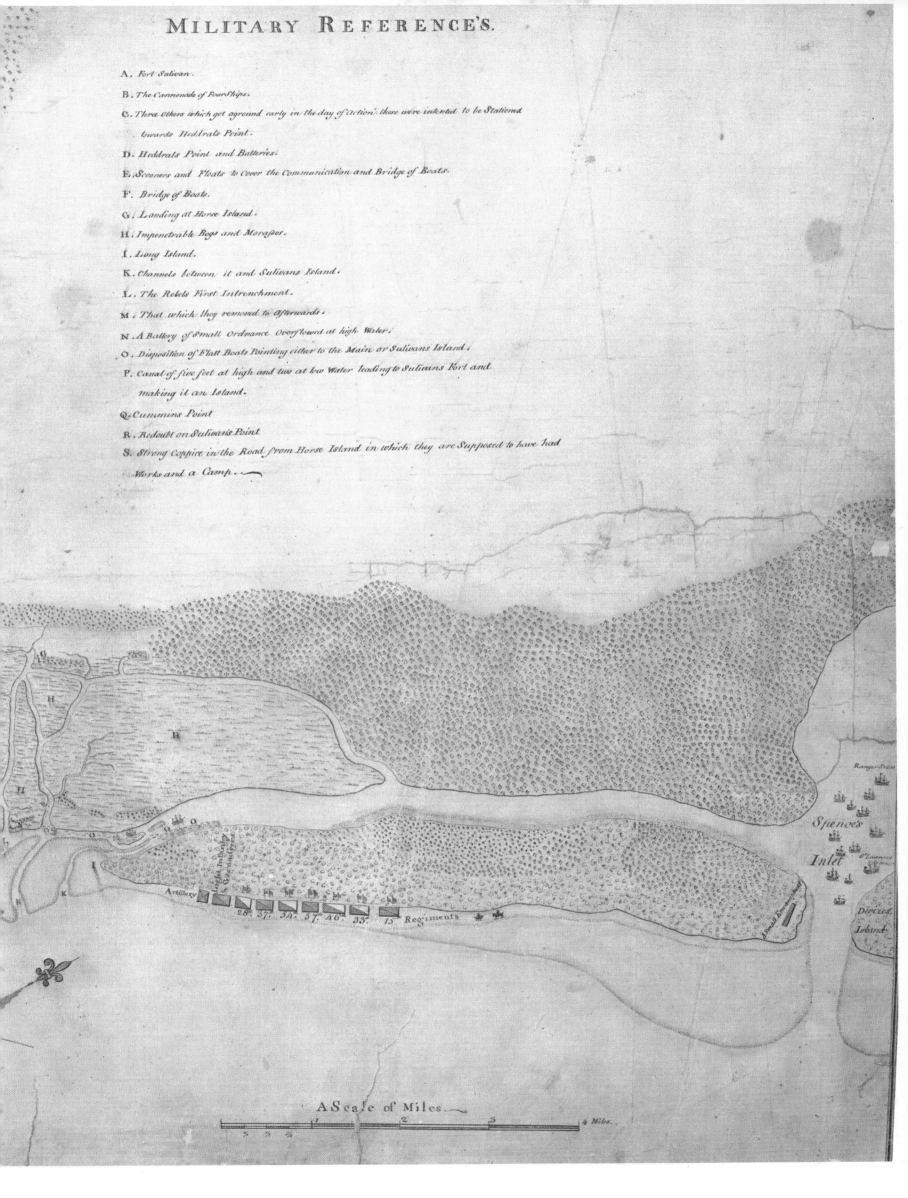

A Scale of Miles

Long Island

At the beginning of July, 1776, Maj. Gen. William Howe returned to the 13 colonies. New York was the logical base of operations. It was where Howe intended to achieve a decisive victory over the Continental army; the point from which Rhode Island could be secured and other raids launched to the north; and the juncture at which the Canadian army would meet Howe and thus isolate New England.

Just as crucial were the logistical advantages of New York. The area was believed to be a loyalist stronghold, and the inhabitants were expected to supply certain needs of the army. Most materials—munitions, tents, pots, stoves, candles, and blankets—could be obtained from England. But for food, forage, livestock, wagons, and additional horses Howe depended on local supply. Long Island especially, with its rolling farmlands, was viewed as an excellent source for these materials.

Procuring a sufficient number of ships to carry men and supplies contributed to Howe's delay in beginning his New York campaign earlier in the spring of 1776. When he left Boston that March, Howe packed 8,908 troops, 924 loyalists, and a great quantity of military stores into 78 ships—"never was an army so crowded in transports, owning to the want of shipping." Halifax was the optimal port in which to reorganize the troops until more ships arrived.

In England Lord George Germain was making preparations to send reinforcements of over 27,000 troops to Canada and New York. The problems of conducting large-scale transport operations were shared by several governmental agencies: the Navy Board, the Victualling Board, the Treasury, and the Board of Ordnance. Each had sometimes overlapping responsibilities to the army and navy. Delays and shortages occurred as the agencies competed with each other for ships, food, and other supplies.

Nonetheless, in 1776 the transport service did manage to assemble troops from widely distant ports in southern England, Ireland, Germany, and the Mediterranean along with vast military stores. Once the ships were at sea, other problems developed. Of the total number of men embarked to North America, about eight percent died en route. Sickness was common because the food procured by the Victualling Board was deficient in nutrition, dispensed to soldiers in two-thirds rations, and never better than one-half rotten. The over-crowded passage was described by one officer as "continued destruction in the foretops, the pox above-board, the plague between decks, hell in the forecastle, the devil at the helm." Horses fared worse than men. Of 950 embarked in June, 1776, only 538 reached America alive. Horses that survived the voyage often arrived unfit for service, and cavalry mounts were usually in scarce supply.

While casualties and sickness at sea reduced the number of horses and men, the weather made projected schedules improbable. Calms, storms, and contrary winds, added to a deficient system of navigation, imposed difficulties for a safe and short voyage in the eighteenth century. En route to New York in the summer of 1776 Vice Adm. Richard Howe's ship tossed about in head winds off Nantucket while his navigator assured him that they were near Long Island.

After landing his Halifax force at Staten Island with no resistance in July, Maj. Gen. William Howe waited for reinforcements. A portion of the troops from the abortive southern expedition arrived, and on August 4 a convoy of 22 ships from England joined them. With almost 14,000 men Howe felt he now had a large enough force to begin the offensive against the American works on Long Island. Yet he was concerned about the shortage of camp equipment, particularly kettles and canteens, to protect the health of his men in the field. Thus he remained inactive until August 12 when 10,000 men and a large quantity of equipment in 100 ships anchored off Staten Island.

For the next nine days Howe organized his troops and held back all action while his brother dispatched a plan of conciliation to Washington. This venture failed, and on August 21, Howe prepared to embark his troops to Long Island. The Hessians, however, who had arrived August 12, claimed they were still too weary from the voyage to take the field. Hoping the Germans would be inspired or shamed into action, Howe boarded his men in two contingents onto almost 90 boats and landed them at Gravesend on the southwest end of Long Island. By noon on August 22, 15,000 troops had disembarked. Three days later the Hessians arrived, and British strength rose to 22,000 men. The force moved inland about five miles through Flatbush until they came to a ridge of hills stretching eastward from Gowanus Bay, called the Heights of Guian. The elevation ranged from 40 to 80 feet, and the heights were covered by woods and dense thickets. There were, however, four roads or passes through the heights which made Brooklyn accessible.

Washington had about 19,000 effectives in the New York area. Lower Manhattan was fortified, and well-protected artillery was planted on the heights of Brooklyn. Maj. Gen. Nathanael Greene had commanded at Brooklyn with 10,000 men until he fell ill with fever and was relieved on August 20 by Maj. Gen. John Sullivan. Four days later Maj. Gen. Israel Putnam, who ranked above Sullivan, took general command. Neither Sullivan nor Putnam, unlike Greene, was familiar with the topography of the island; more unfortunate still was Putnam's incompetence as a field commander. Putnam distributed his advance forces in an extensive line along Guian Heights as follows: 550 at the Gowanus Road, farthest west; 1,000 near the pass out of Flatbush; 800 near the pass to Bedford; and 400 farther east on patrol. Jamaica Pass, at the eastern extreme, was guarded by a detail of five men.

On a scouting expedition August 24, Maj. Gen. Henry Clinton spotted Jamaica Pass as the key to the rebel position. His recommendation for a classic turning movement was adopted by Howe. Two diversionary forces would attack the left and center lines, while the main column marched east, then around and behind the Americans. At nightfall on August 26, Howe sent Maj. Gen. James Grant up the Gowanus Road with 5,000 men, stationed Brig. Philip von Heister on the Flatbush Road with another 5,000, and led 10,000 men under Clinton and Maj. General Charles Cornwallis toward Jamaica Pass.

Grant opened a moderate attack at 12:00 A.M. which through the night drew American reinforcements some under Brig. Gen. William Alexander (Lord Stirling) to the westernmost road. By morning Washington had crossed to Brooklyn with additional troops. At 9:00 A.M. Howe passed through the Jamaica gap and turned west on a road that led across the Americans' rear and directly to Brooklyn. Heister now began firing on Sullivan, whose force had been enlarged to 1,500 but was inadequate to hold up against Heister's 5,000. A regiment of Pennsylvania riflemen came upon Howe's rear baggage train, and nearly all were captured. A few fled back to report Howe's eastern approach to Putnam.

Sullivan and then Stirling discovered Howe's column behind them. As the Americans tried to move toward the entrenchments at Brooklyn, the heaviest fighting of the day developed. Trapped between the two British forces, Sullivan, Stirling, and scores of their men were taken prisoner. By noon Howe's efficient tactics had swept the Heights of Guian clear of the enemy. British losses were 63 killed, 282 wounded, and about 24 captured. American casualties were not carefully counted. About 200 were killed and 900 captured (some of them wounded), including 89 officers.

Howe reunited his army in a line less than two miles from the Brooklyn earthworks and decided to prepare formal siege operations. But on August 29 Washington chose to abandon Brooklyn. To the Americans' good fortune, a nor'wester kept British ships out of the East River. All available small craft were assembled. Col. John Glover's Massachusetts brigade of fishermen took charge of ferrying 10,000 men and all their equipment quietly through the rainy night to Manhattan. By the time a foggy dawn cleared, Washington himself stepped into one of the last boats.

An early morning British patrol found a forward American position abandoned. Cautiously, the redcoats pressed on and encountered no resistance. They found Brooklyn empty. By not pursuing the Americans after the battle, Howe had failed to achieve a decisive victory. He no longer seemed intent on destroying the Continental army. Possibly his change in strategy was influenced by his brother, Lord Richard, who believed that a steady advance by British troops, with minimum destruction, would not alienate the colonists and might improve the prospects for reunion.

Washington's masterful escape from Long Island only slightly redeemed his defeat. American troops had fought admirably, but Washington had been tactically outmaneuvered by Howe. Critics questioned Washington's failure to use cavalry to patrol the eastern pass and his approval of Putnam's thinly held line of advance. On Manhattan Washington considered whether it was possible to maintain a defense in the face of How's massed threat.

Ens. George Sproule was probably at Long Island with the 16th Regiment when he made a rough survey of the battlefield. The map developed from the sketch was given to Clinton, who never tired of reexamining his battles. Clinton added a note to the map and suggested a reason for Howe's excessive caution. "This map proves that there were no rebel works near the water side of Brooklyn 27 Augt. 76 & consequently S[ir] W[illiam] H[owe] was misinformed & that we might have taken possession at the close of the action and made the Island and all in it ours." The Guian Heights are not labeled, but they are the hills at the lower right, west of the two mill ponds. The road along which Grant advanced was defended below the mill pond by Stirling's forces. Jamaica Pass is off the map on the right, but the road from it to Brooklyn is shown.

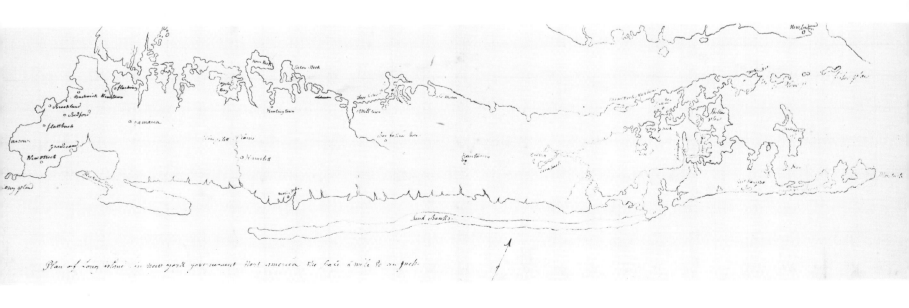

Plan of Long Island in new york government dont america the late dmile to an inch.

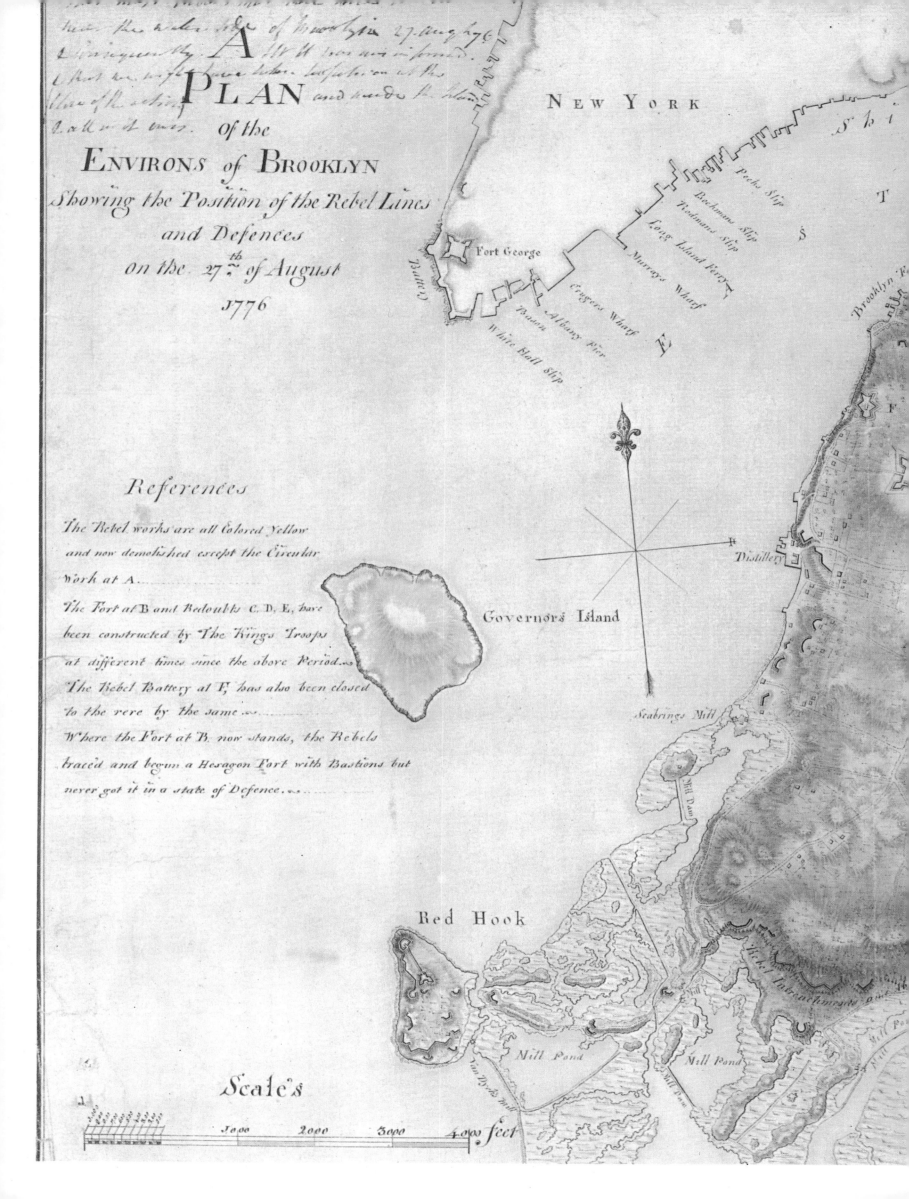

A PLAN

Of the

ENVIRONS of BROOKLYN

Showing the Position of the Rebel Lines
and Defences
on the 27.th of August
1776

References

The Rebel works are all Colored Yellow
and now demolished except the Circular
work at A.

The Fort at B and Redoubts C. D. E, have
been constructed by The Kings Troops
at different times since the above Period.

The Rebel Battery at F, has also been closed
to the rere by the same.

Where the Fort at B now stands, the Rebels
traced and begun a Hexagon Fort with Bastions but
never got it in a state of Defence.

NEW YORK

Fort George

Pecks Slip
Beekmans Slip
Roosmans Slip
Long Island Ferry
Murrays Wharf
Cruggers Wharf
Albany Pier
Paoun
White Hall Slip
Canel

Brooklyn

Distillery

Governors Island

Seabrings Mill

Mill Dam

Red Hook

Mill Pond

Mill Pond

Mill Pond

Rebel Intrenchments

Scales

1000   2000   3000   4000 feet

White Plains

After Washington's escape from Brooklyn to Manhattan, Vice Adm. Richard Howe initiated a conference with the rebels. On Staten Island, September 11, he offered surrender terms which representatives Benjamin Franklin, Edward Rutledge, and John Adams refused. The admiral's brother Maj. Gen. William Howe meanwhile made preparations to seize New York City.

British vacillation between peace and war disturbed prospects for success in either one. The Howes' hesitation can be viewed in part as sentiment for the colonials. Their earnest desire to negotiate peace in America limited their military objectives. They maneuvered for territory but did not seek to annihilate the enemy. Furthermore, military education had instilled in the Howes a duty to preserve their own carefully designed army at all costs and not to take unnecessary risks.

Washington spent his time haggling with Congress over the fate of Manhattan. He was troubled by the gloomy state of his troops, especially the militia. "Great numbers of them have gone off; in some instances, almost by whole regiments." Congress at last overcame its dread of a standing army and on September 16 authorized enlistments for the duration of the war. As for Manhattan, Maj. Gen. Nathanael Greene proposed to raze New York City thereby eliminating its utility as headquarters for the British. But Congress forbade the army to burn the city, whereupon Washington reorganized his forces and deployed them over several defensive positions on the island. When he felt Congress would not support him, Washington began an evacuation to the north.

Howe had earlier rejected Maj. Gen. Henry Clinton's plan to land forces at Westchester and trap the Continental Army on Manhattan. Instead, he took advantage of the awkward dispersal of patriot troops still remaining there. First he routed the panicky Connecticut militia at Kip's Bay and landed forces on September 15, but made no attempt to cut off the escape of those rebels left on the lower portion of the island. The following day an advance British guard was repulsed at Harlem Heights where Washington had quickly built up a strong position. This engagement lifted the Americans' spirits, and, along with a mysterious fire which burned a quarter of New York City, it served in some measure to stall Howe for nearly a month.

Waiting for reinforcements which he knew had sailed from England in July, Howe ordered fortifications built in lower Manhattan and at Harlem. Then on October 7 he embarked his troops for Throg's Neck, and delayed there for six days frustrated by bad weather and a lack of provisions. After reembarking his men to Pell's Point, farther north, his 4,000-man force was jolted by an attack from 750 Massachusetts soldiers under Col. John Glover. Glover prevented Howe from crossing the Bronx River where he would have directly confronted Washington's retreating army.

Finally, on October 25, Howe again advanced north in pursuit of Washington. His reinforcements, nearly 5,000 of them Hessians, had arrived. There were now over 11,000 German troops in America, almost one-third of the total number that would serve during the war. On October 28 Howe marched his 13,000 troops in two columns toward White Plains where Washington had halted seven days earlier. The Americans were deployed on a front three miles wide. On their right rose Chatterton's Hill, but it was not fortified. The narrow Bronx River circled part way around its base. Not until the British approached on the morning of the 28th did Washington order troops onto the hilltop. Sixteen hundred men and two cannon under Brig. Gen. Alexander McDougall occupied it and began digging in. Some militia were sent out to offer a delaying action but were driven back. The British and Germans, equal in number to the Americans, came in sight of Washington's lines and then stopped while Howe spread his men and prepared to assault Chatterton's Hill.

Three German regiments crossed the river and secured a height. Cannon opened fire from an easterly direction, and more troops followed across the Bronx. Brig. Alexander Leslie found a ford and led two regiments up the hill in a bayonet charge. McDougall drove him back with heavy losses. Howe began forming his men for a final advance. In this attack some American units resisted stubbornly, but the Massachusetts militia on the right gave way. A general withdrawal followed, and the British and Germans gained the top of the hill. It was now about 5:00 P.M. and fighting ended.

This field sketch by Capt. John Graves Simcoe shows the operation of October 28. Opposite the rebel position at Chatterton's Hill is the 35th Regiment in which Simcoe had formerly served. In his diary, this resourceful officer described making maps by "information of the country people, and by ocular observation." He once scaled a tree to draw the necessary reconnaissance. Here, Lt. Col. Robert Prescott with the main body of British troops is shown still on the east bank of the Bronx River. The American advance is poised to cross the river in support of their forward position below the hill. The Americans were driven back across the river through the unmarked town of White Plains and north along the eastern shore. Howe planned a further attack on October 31, but heavy rains postponed it. The next day he learned that Washington had retreated beyond the Croton River. The British commander decided not to press on farther north; he turned back on November 4.

American losses were 25 killed and 125 wounded—one-half of the British and German casualties of 313. British possession of the battlefield brought the victors no closer to either goal of dispersing the American army or of a negotiated peace.

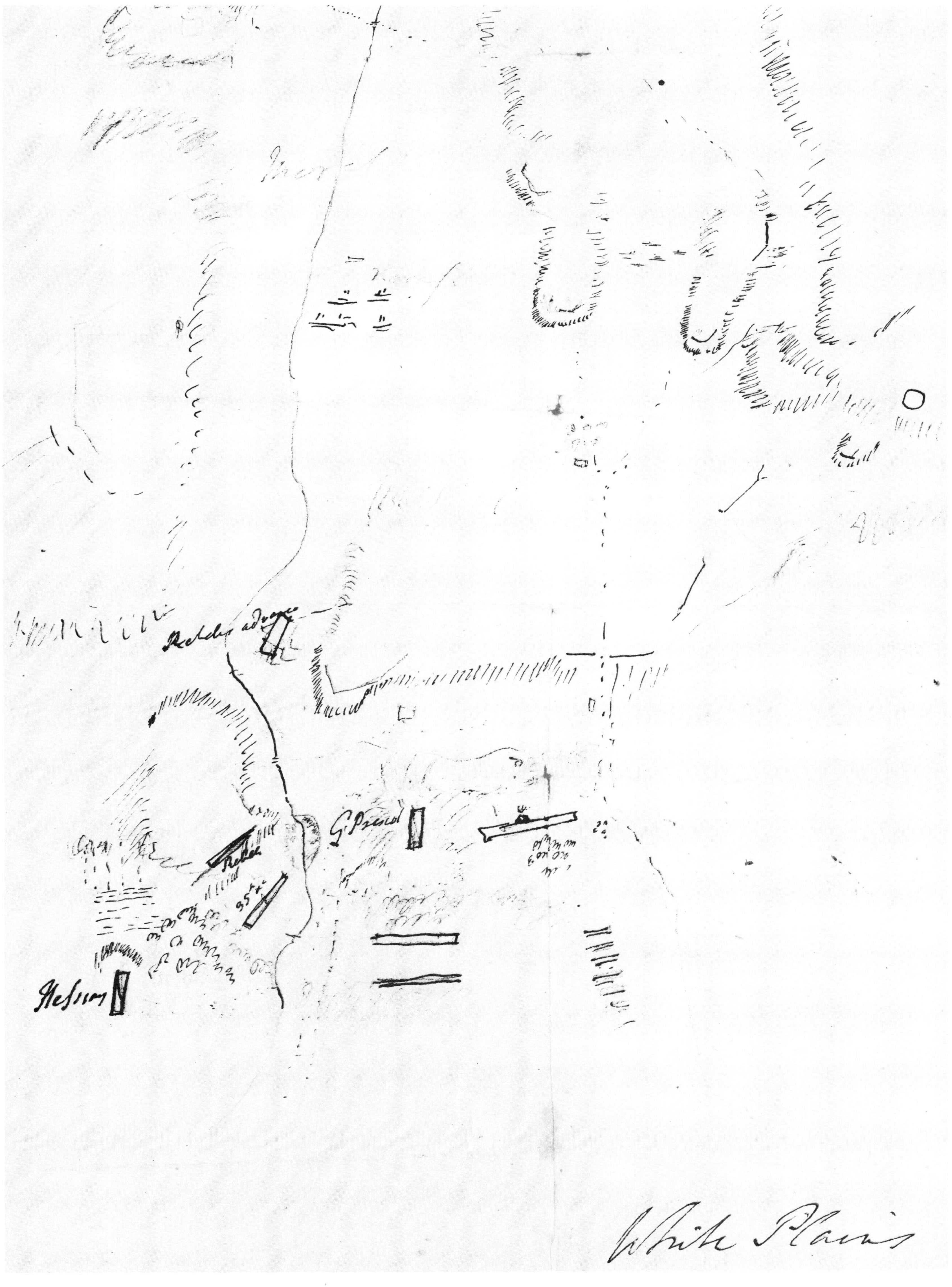

Rebels at house

G. French

Rebel

35th

Hessian

White Plains

Forts Washington and Lee

Heavy rains spoiled Maj. Gen. William Howe's planned second attack on the American army near White Plains on October 31. The next day the Americans were found to be apparently well entrenched at North Castle Heights. The rebel earthworks were composed largely of cornstalks pulled from nearby fields, whose roots, full of clinging soil, faced outward. Howe may have been discouraged by these illusory defenses, but his goal remained the complete removal of American troops from Manhattan, not the annihilation of Washington's army. His attention returned to Fort Washington which the American commander in chief had left garrisoned under Col. Robert Magaw after a general rebel evacuation of the island.

On the night of November 2 a defector, William Demont, entered the camp of Lord Hugh Percy at McGowan's Pass, south of Fort Washington. Demont had been Magaw's adjutant; the deserter placed the plans of the fort into Percy's hands. Although Howe had probably already begun to arrange operations against Fort Washington, exact knowledge of the fortification and its defenses would assist his attack.

Fort Washington's works, built the previous July, covered a hill 230 feet high (modern West 184th Street) and a mile long. Vertical cliffs rendered the fort unassailable from the Hudson River below. Additional protection was provided by Fort Tryon on the north, Laurel Hill on the east, and the old Harlem Heights defenses on the south. Fort Lee stood opposite Fort Washington in New Jersey. Between the two forts ran a line of sunken obstructions to prevent British ships from passing up the Hudson.

The natural defenses afforded by Fort Washington's position were superior, but the fort itself was less than ideal. A pentagonal earthwork without ditches or palisades, the structure lacked barracks, bombproofs, and an interior source of water. A captain stationed in the fort noted that it had none of "those exterior, multiplied obstacles and defenses, that . . . could entitle it to the name of fortress, in any degree capable of withstanding a siege." This weakness, recognized by some of the garrison, went unnoticed by Maj. Gen. Nathanael Greene, who was in charge of both forts.

Washington had been out of touch with Greene since October 22. Now, as Howe began moving south to direct the seizure of Fort Washington, the American commander had to consider the fort's defensibility. On November 5 three British vessels passed over the river barricades in the Hudson amidst rebel artillery fire and anchored, undamaged, at the northern tip of the island. Washington, in the process of deploying most of his troops in Westchester County, was much alarmed by this news and wrote to Greene on November 8, "I am inclined to think it will not be prudent to hazard the men and stores," but "as you are on the spot, I leave it to you to give such orders as to evacuating Mount Washington as you judge best."

Greene replied that the fort served some purpose beyond the prevention of ship passage up the Hudson. It hampered British communication between the island and the country to the north, compelled the maintenance of British troops at Kingsbridge (which connected Manhattan to Westchester County), and was clearly regarded as important by the British, or else they would not attempt its capture. These arguments were offset by Greene's assurance that if the situation grew dangerous, the stores and men could be shifted to Fort Lee at any time. Magaw said the garrison could hold out through December. But Washington's second in command, Maj. Gen. Charles Lee, expressed ominous concern. In a letter to Joseph Reed, the adjutant general, Lee wrote, "I cannot conceive what circumstances give to Fort Washington so great a degree of value and importance as to counterbalance the probability or almost certainty of losing 1,400 of our best troops."

With some 2,000 of his troops, Washington moved down the west side of the Hudson and reached Fort Lee on November 13. Meanwhile, Greene had reinforced Magaw's original garrison of about 2,000 men (Lee's figure was low) with an additional 900. Greene continued to favor a defense of the fort, and Washington finally relied upon his subordinate's judgment. The commander in chief would later write that Congress's desire to retain the area's defense and his own wish to keep an impediment in the enemy's way "caused that warfare in my mind and hesitation which ended in the loss of the garrison."

On November 4 Howe dispatched several brigades to march quickly south and reinforce Brig. Wilhelm von Knyphausen. His division had crossed the river at Kingsbridge on November 2 and began harassment of the rebels in the northern outpost of Fort Tryon. During the night of November 14, 30 British flatboats sailed up the river past Fort Washingon undetected by the Americans. The following day the enemy approached the fort in force.

Lord Cornwallis and Brig. Edward Mathew were to approach from across the Harlem River on the east, and Percy was to strike from the south. A British officer was sent to summon Magaw to surrender with the threat of no quarter if the fort was stormed. Magaw flatly refused. He had dispersed his forces at the various outposts on the three sides of the fort, posting minor detachments in between. The Americans covered a large perimeter of four to five miles. Early on the morning of November 16, Knyphausen opened the attack against Col. Moses Rawlings's Virginia and Maryland riflemen who managed to stall the Germans temporarily. Percy advanced on Lt. Col. Lambert Cadwalader's Pennsylvanians but then halted (to the Americans' surprise) to wait for a signal gun from Cornwallis or Mathew. Washington, Greene, Maj. Gen. Israel Putnam, and Brig. Gen. Hugh Mercer crossed to Fort Washington as the firing commenced, but they could do nothing to help Magaw and so returned to Fort Lee to watch the developing action.

Mathew, who had been somewhat delayed by the tide, pushed across the river and established a foothold on Laurel Hill. Cornwallis followed with more troops. Once the signal had gone out to Percy, pressure on the Americans began to mount. Rawlings was forced back, and Cadwalader withdrew. Confusion was rampant within the reduced perimeter; the retreating Americans poured into the fort. By 3:00 P.M. the Germans had reached Fort Washington from the north, and the British were in view on the east and south. Despite the original surrender terms, another flag was sent into Magaw to ask for capitulation. Realizing that to stand now would create a bloodbath within the crowded fort, Magaw surrendered.

The attack cost the British and Germans 67 killed, 335 wounded, and 6 missing. The Americans suffered 54 killed and 2,858 captured, including probably more than 100 wounded. The loss of all their arms and equipment was especially damaging.

Fort Lee was now untenable and Washington began transporting the ammunition out of the fort. On the night of November 19 the British brought boats through the Harlem River and carried a force under Cornwallis across the Hudson in the rain. They landed about six miles north of Fort Lee and began marching southward. Washington and Greene roused the garrison to a hurried flight and led them to Hackensack, then toward Newark and New Brunswick. Cornwallis marched into the empty fort on November 20 and found tents, military baggage, 50 cannon, and 1,000 barrels of flour. More than 100 skulkers were rounded up in the neighborhood; a few were killed.

Cornwallis pursued the Americans with some reinforcements sent from Howe and routed them at each New Jersey town where they stopped. Many of Howe's officers believed he would maintain this drive. As Lt. Frederick Mackenzie noted in his diary for November 21, "This is now the time to push these rascals, and if we do, and not give them time to recover themselves, we may depend upon it they will never make head again. A body of troops landed at this time at Amboy might, in conjunction with those already in Jersey, push on to Philadelphia, with very little difficulty." But Howe had begun preparations for an offensive in Rhode Island. He knew there was not time enough before winter's arrival to employ the same troop force in both New Jersey and Rhode Island.

In addition, Howe was criticized by some for sparing the garrison at Fort Washington. Capt. Lt. Archibald Robertson considered the rebels' losses "triffling." Thomas Jones, a former justice of the New York Supreme Court being held prisoner in Connecticut, believed that a general slaughter would have struck panic through the rebel countryside and forced congressional submission. "The most rigid severity at the first would have been the greatest mercy and lenity in the end." Of the nearly 2,900 Americans captured in the fall of the fort, over 100 were officers. Many of these were paroled and walked the New York streets in their uniforms to the chagrin and even fear of the loyalists and British. The soldiers were eventually put aboard prison ships in the harbor to languish; large numbers of them died under the atrocious conditions.

But Howe's victory had been decisive, and for the Americans, the aftereffects were serious. The loss of the garrison troubled Washington because the enlistments of many of his remaining troops were to expire in less than two months. An alarming percentage of his men were unfit for duty from sickness or want of clothes and shoes. Perhaps even more significant was the tremendous loss of precious materiel. The British had seized 146 cannon, 12,000 shot and shell, 2,800 muskets, and 400,000 cartridges. American resources had been dispersed and inadequate before this capture; now they were stretched very thin indeed. Washington would soon make his winter headquarters in New Jersey for a number of reasons, one of which was to protect the invaluable forges and furnaces in the northwestern part of the state.

The blame for squandering the men and supplies in the two forts rested naturally with Magaw, Greene, and Washington. Greene recognized that the lines around Fort Washington had been too extensive for 2,900 men to defend—especially in a disordered state. Since Washington had some early doubts about the fort's impregnability, his vacillation, finally favoring Greene's discretion, was inexcusable. Washington's trusted friend Reed termed this a "fatal indecision of mind." Many British were light-headed after their successful New York campaign and felt that the end of the war must be near. But Washington's error was not fatal. Nor was his disappointment so deep that he rejected thoughts of raising a new army.

The map, commissioned by Percy to depict his own action against Fort Washington from the south, is the work of cartographer Claude Joseph Sauthier. He was attached to the British army as a surveyor and draftsman. The geography of the map is faulty. One inaccuracy may explain the escape of the Americans after they abandoned Fort Lee in New Jersey. The map shows Cornwallis's crossing of the Hudson and his subsequent swoop southward on the fort. However, New Bridge over the Hackensack River is placed incorrectly farther south. In reality the bridge is north of Fort Lee, nearly opposite Cornwallis's landing. A British detachment could have easily seized New Bridge while the main column descended on the fort, thus blocking the escape route of the Americans. Perhaps the map reflects the cartographic confusion of Cornwallis. Or possibly he prevailed on the mapmaker to cover his oversight. In any case, the Americans slipped past the enemy lines over a road running northwest out of Fort Lee, crossed the Hackensack at New Bridge, and retreated into central New Jersey.

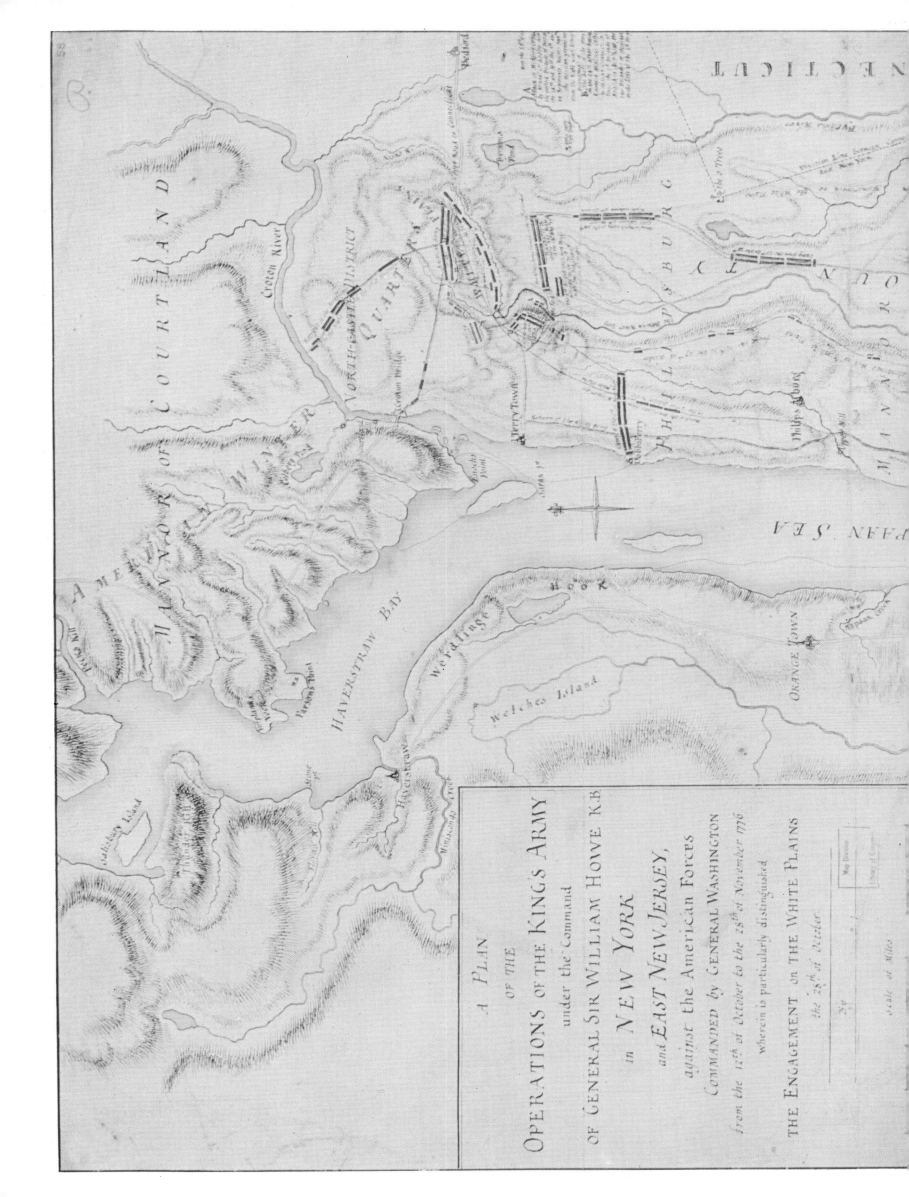

CONNECTICUT

COURTLAND

MANNOR of

Croton River

NORTH CASTLE DISTRICT

WINTER QUARTERS

Croton Bridge

PHILLIPSBURG

MANNOR

Welched Island

HOOK

HAVERSTRAW BAY

Weradinge

PPAN SEA

ORANGE TOWN

Haverstraw

A PLAN
OF THE
OPERATIONS OF THE KING'S ARMY
under the Command
OF GENERAL SIR WILLIAM HOWE K.B.
in
NEW YORK
and EAST NEW JERSEY,
against the American Forces
COMMANDED by GENERAL WASHINGTON
from the 12th of October to the 28th of November 1776
wherein is particularly distinguished
THE ENGAGEMENT on THE WHITE PLAINS
the 28th of October

Scale of Miles

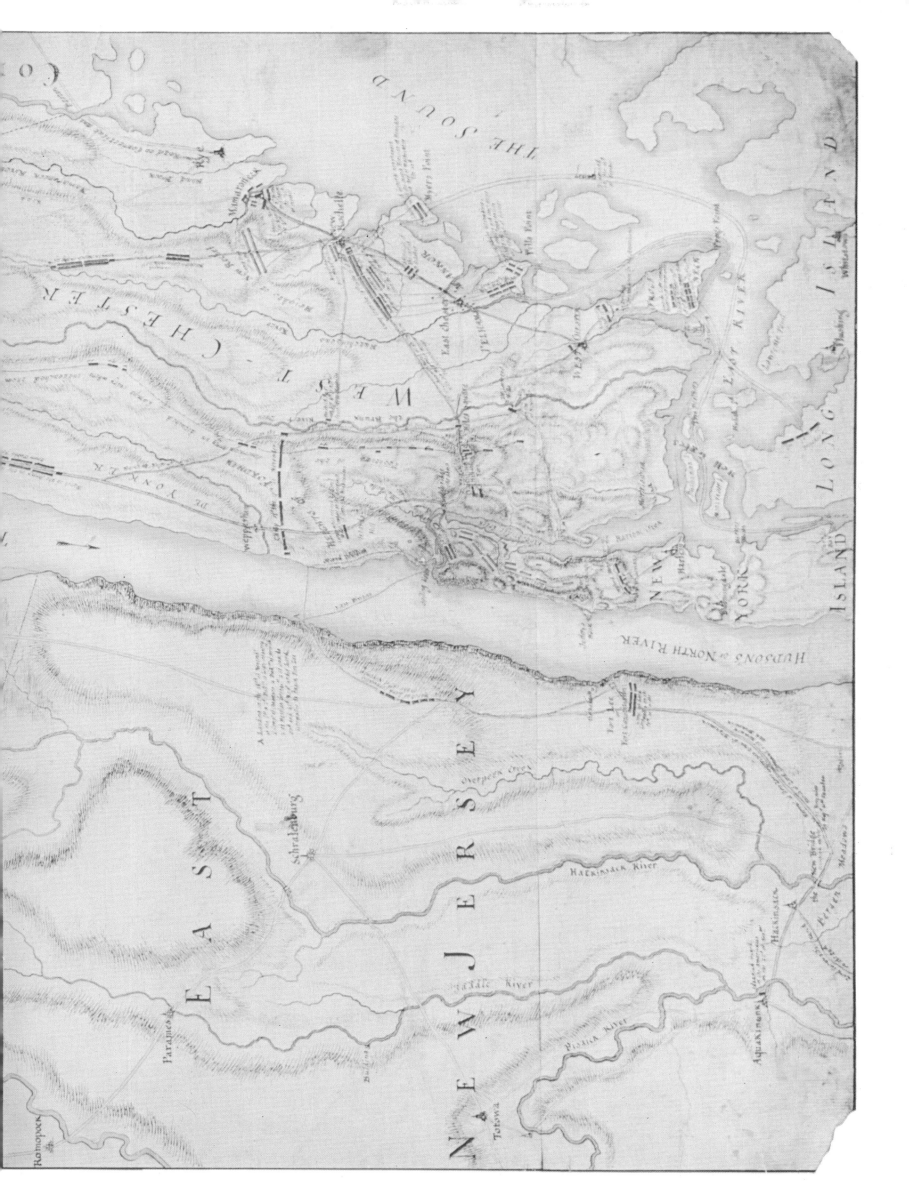

Newport

During October, while Maj. Gen. William Howe continued his drive to expel the Americans from Manhattan, a large fleet was being assembled in the harbor. Howe was looking beyond his New York campaign to the occupation of Rhode Island, as a supply base for the army and an ice-free winter port for the British squadron under Lord Richard Howe.

Lord Howe commanded a fleet of 73 warships by the end of 1776. He had arrived in New York that summer with instructions to wage an aggressive war at sea. But it became quickly apparent that he lacked adequate ships to conduct independent naval operations and to support the army as well. The squadron was concentrated in New York, with stations at Quebec, Halifax, Nova Scotia, and St. Augustine. To meet the army's needs the Royal Navy was required to convoy transports, halt enemy communications by water, carry dispatches, protect Canadian fisheries, and cut off rebel supplies. The last of these proved to be most difficult. No more than 15 ships were ever available to cruise against rebel privateers and to blockade the Atlantic coast from Maine to Georgia.

The blockade was rendered ineffective by the vigorousness of enemy privateers and by the coastline itself. Southern stations, from which colonial staples were exported to the West Indies to pay for arms, ammunition, and clothing, were spread out. Adequate patrol of this area was impossible. Since Howe could not protect the Delaware River until November, rebel supply ships sailed smoothly into Philadelphia. The route from the West Indies to the colonies was so poorly guarded that by the end of the year the Americans had imported more than 80 percent of the gunpowder they would require for the first two and one-half years of the war. Moreover, rebel seamen discovered early in the war that the profits far outweighed the risks of privateering. "Their ships come fast to us richly laden," remarked financier Robert Morris. In 1776 American privateers captured 350 prizes worth several million pounds. Over the same period, fewer than 200 rebel prize ships fell into British hands (80 in November and December when Howe's blockade strength increased).

On November 29, 12 British warships and 51 transports, commanded by Sir Peter Parker, left New York and sailed up the Sound to Newport, arriving on December 8. On board were 7,000 British and Hessian soldiers under Maj. Gen. Henry Clinton. The appearance of the British off the Rhode Island coast had sent seven enemy ships fleeing up the bay ("rebel privateers, commonly called the Continental fleet," according to Parker). They remained trapped while Parker gloated at having "put an effectual stop to any further mischief from that nest of pirates."

When the British troops disembarked at Weaver's Cove, the Americans had already abandoned their defenses and retired to Bristol Ferry at the northern end of the island. A British detachment was sent to obstruct the escape, but only a few prisoners and two cannon were taken. Clinton began quartering his troops in great haste since the temperature had dropped and a winter storm threatened. He then issued orders against plundering and warned his men that misconduct would not be tolerated. Clinton was particularly afraid of fire breaking out—Newport was built almost entirely of wood. The inhabitants, most of them Quakers, were relieved that the town had not been taken by force, and they were inclined to be hospitable (although one resident suggested that the Hessians might be sent back aboard ship).

Before Clinton left New York, Maj. Gen. Howe rejected his suggestion that the Chesapeake would be a finer winter port than Newport. The excellent roadstead at Newport appealed to Lord Howe. When Maj. Gen. Howe wrote to Clinton advising a move against Providence, Clinton refused, believing that no raids on the mainland could be conducted amidst the dangers and ravages of winter. In January, 1777, Clinton sailed to England on leave, and the command at Newport passed to Lord Hugh Percy.

Maj. Gen. Howe anticipated an excellent supply of forage from his seizure of Long Island in August. But either because the Americans had destroyed the fields and stores or because Howe's expectations were too high, the island at first proved a disappointment. In September cavalry horses and wagon animals were being fed on reduced rations, and even on the navy's oatmeal. Forage obtained during the British invasion of New Jersey in late November and December provided some relief, but by January Howe requested Percy to send forage from Newport. The prospect of great quantities of forage there also proved illusory. Discouraged by the scarcity of fresh provisions and fuel as well, Percy had difficulty collecting hay and distrusted a commissary's estimate of the amount of forage at Newport. Percy was reluctant to deprive the neutral inhabitants of hay for their livestock. An unfortunate letter from the commissary at Newport prompted Howe to chastize Percy for holding back forage for his own use. Percy angrily threatened to resign from the army and departed for England as soon as he was granted permission.

The first winter at Newport was bitter. A full regiment of 612 men plus officers required 949 cords of wood to get through the season. By spring the British had exhausted the tree supply on the island. This necessitated weekly expeditions to other localities to cut timber. In addition, peat was burned and an attempt made to locate coal mines at Newport. The British occupation lasted three years. Food and fuel continued to be less than adequate; but the hay supply did increase, and army horses were transported to Newport to feed during subsequent winters.

The map was made in 1774 by a British army surveyor, Charles Blaskowitz. This copy, with the grid intact, was probably used by Clinton in 1776. The "Cove" is Weaver's Cove, where the British disembarked. Windmills shown on the map were used as power for grinding corn since there were no creeks or streams on the island.

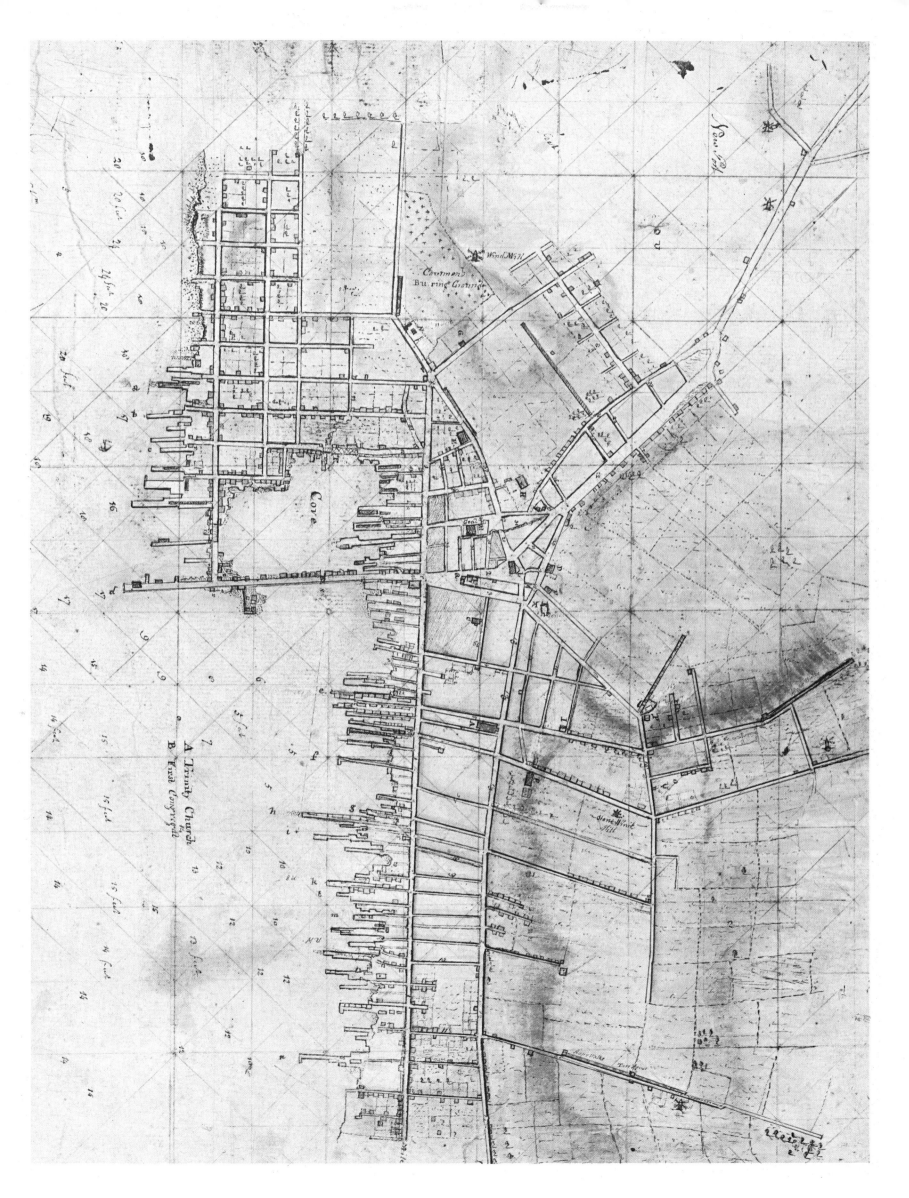

Lake Champlain

The American army which evacuated Canada in June, 1776, was in miserable condition. Casualties of 5,000 had been left behind. Of the survivors who reached upper New York State, 2,000 suffered smallpox, and the remaining 6,000 were described by John Adams as "defeated, discontented, diseased, naked, undisciplined, eaten up with vermin." Actually, they barely escaped capture.

On June 14 the British divided their pursuit of the Americans between a force under Maj. Gen. John Burgoyne which marched south along the Richelieu River and another under Maj. Gen. Guy Carleton which was to sail 50 miles southwest up the St. Lawrence River, disembark opposite Montreal, and rendezvous with Burgoyne at St. Johns (see map on page 13; Richelieu River is labeled "River Sorel"). Two days after the expedition separated, Carleton's transports had progressed only 15 miles because of weak winds. They abandoned their boats, and marched toward the union at St. Johns arriving three days later. The pincer, however, had closed too late to snare the Americans.

From this point, the British advance was marked by further delay. Part of the problem was the need to assemble an adequate reserve of food. By the end of June food ran short because one of the four supply ships assigned to Burgoyne's army of 10,000 had caught fire and sunk in the English Channel two months earlier. It took time to develop an alternative supply network within Canada, and the commissary general assigned to the task was inexperienced. In addition to procuring food, Carleton was burdened with the construction of vessels in which to move his men and provisions onto Lake Champlain. The lake was a 125-mile segment along the principal artery between Canada and the 13 colonies. However, it was only 14 miles across at its widest point and blocked to navigation at both ends. Because of the unnavigable northern stretch of the Richelieu River, flowing north from Lake Champlain, boats destined for the lake had to be transported overland from Montreal to St. Johns; the alternative was to construct vessels on the spot.

The American commanders held a council of war on July 5 and decided to abandon their position at Crown Point and withdraw ten miles to Fort Ticonderoga at the south end of Lake Champlain. There, the remnants of the forces from Canada were to be reinforced by militia and three regiments of Continentals. Ticonderoga was well supplied with 120 cannon of various sizes, but short of mounts, ramrods, powder, and other necessities. This vital equipment was not to reach them until October 6, only five days before the battle at Valcour Island.

The lack of ships was another problem. The patriots had seized three schooners and a sloop the previous year but more would be needed to repel a British squadron. Standing timber had to be cut, and abandoned sawmills reopened. Tools and craftsmen were imported at exorbitant prices. Brig. Gen. Benedict Arnold, who had argued against a retreat to Albany, was given overall charge of construction. He eventually built four ten-gun galleys with exotic lateen rigged sails and eight three-gun gondolas with two square sails. Morale and hunger gradually lifted from the Americans, and by the end of August 5,500 effectives could be counted in the area.

Gunships and transport vessels were a problem for the British also. All that could be obtained from England were 14 gunboats mounting a single cannon each and 10 flat-bottomed landing craft. Two schooners of 12 and 14 guns were disassembled on the St. Lawrence and brought overland 15 miles to be reconstructed on the Richelieu. Lt. William Twiss, Corps of Engineers, and aide-de-camp to Maj. Gen. William Phillips, was assigned to build support craft. In all, 560 flat-bottomed transport boats were constructed, and an additional 120 were brought from other parts of Canada. A huge 16-gun sailing scow was also built on the spot. Yet Carleton did not feel safe until the 18-gun sloop *Inflexible* joined the contingent. Its reassembly took 28 days and delayed the sailing until October 4.

The plan opposite indicates that some consideration had been given to the order of procession on the lake. The arrangement differs somewhat from a plan in the Marburg archives not showing the gunboats in front lettered *A*, and with the position of the *Carleton* and *Inflexible* reversed. The British had been strengthened by the arrival of several German regiments in September to bring their total force to 13,000, plus 700 sailors.

Arnold maneuvered the American squadron 50 miles north of Fort Ticonderoga and anchored behind Valcour Island. He awaited the arrival of the British flotilla and lured them into an attack on his position on October 11. Unfortunately, the decoy schooner ran aground attempting to beat back against the wind. The 12-gun British schooner moved up to disable it but sailed too close to the American line and could not get back. A general engagement then ensued at a range of 350 yards as other British gunboats came up in support. American fire concentrated on the schooner and damaged it. Total British firepower was twice as great as that of the Americans, and toward evening, the *Inflexible* sailed in to batter them with point blank broadsides. A heavy fog moved in with darkness which enabled Arnold to guide his squadron single file past the unsuspecting enemy. At dawn the outraged and outwitted Carleton sailed after the fleeing Americans. A fresh wind aided pursuit. He bore down on Arnold's craft and dispersed them with superior firepower. Yet Arnold managed to beach the wrecks and escape with 200 men. He had lost 11 of 16 vessels en route, but his resourcefulness provided the margin of time needed stop Carleton.

The British advanced to Crown Point, but Carleton felt unprepared for a prolonged siege at Fort Ticonderoga. It might have succeeded. That year the St. Lawrence remained ice-free until December and lines of communication could have been held open. Yet Carleton feared the onset of winter and withdrew his forces back into Canada where provisions were available. Delay had cost the British their advanced position, and Burgoyne was forced to repeat the whole operation the next year.

The Order of Battle in crossing Lake Champlain.

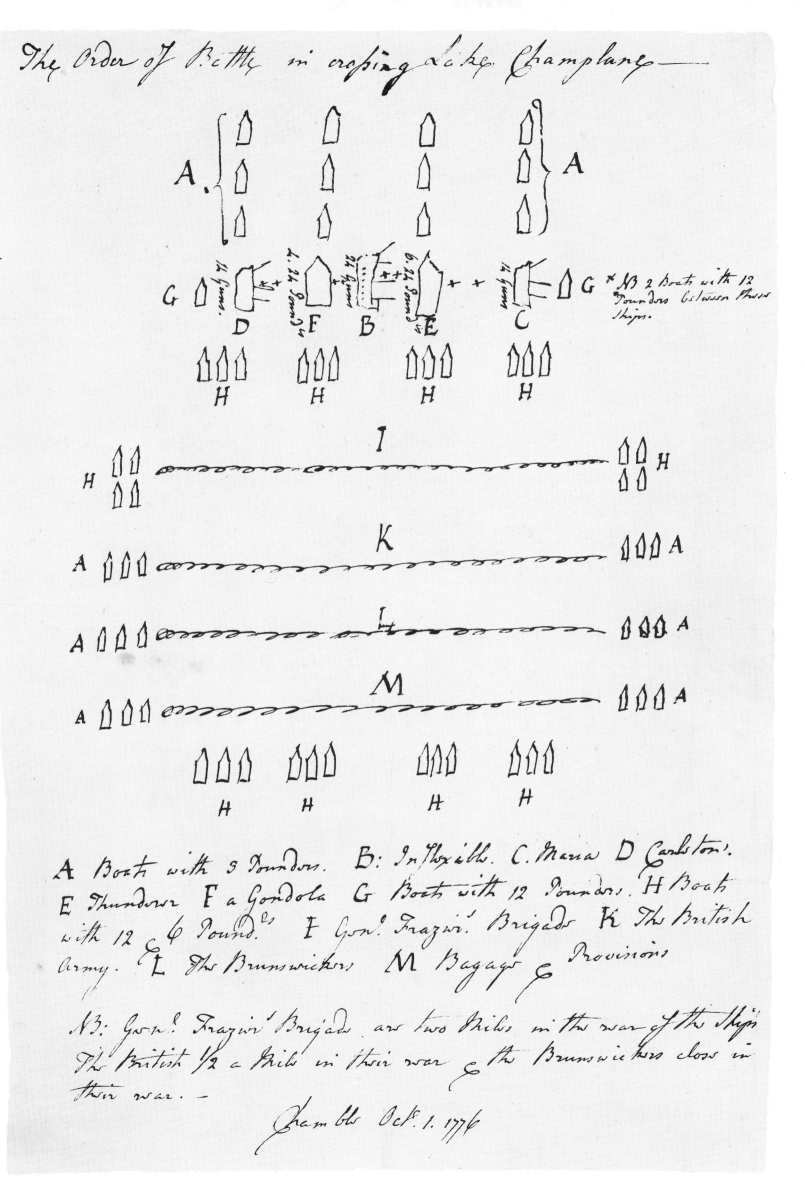

A Boats with 3 Pounders. B: Inflexible. C. Maria D Carleton.
E Thunderer F a Gondola G Boats with 12 Pounders. H Boats
with 12 & 6 Pound.ᵉˢ F Genˡ. Frazier' Brigade K The British
Army. L The Brunswickers M Bagage & Provisions

NB: Genˡ. Frazier' Brigade are two Miles in the rear of the Ships
The British 1½ a Mile in their rear & the Brunswickers close in
their rear. —

Chamble Octˡ. 1. 1776

New Jersey Invasion

As soon as Fort Lee was abandoned, Washington began to withdraw his army across New Jersey toward Philadelphia. About 5,000 Americans left Hackensack on November 21, 1776, and retired without casualties 100 miles to safety behind the Delaware River on December 7. But the troops suffered a want of clothing and a sense of defeat which quickly translated into high sickness and desertion rates. It was a demoralized army that unraveled in retreat. Even their stoic commander despaired over "a noble cause lost," and wrote to his brother, "I think the game is pretty near up."

The British followed on their heels. The advance guard under Lord Cornwallis came close to intercepting the Americans at Newark, New Brunswick, Princeton, and Trenton. Yet what could have been accomplished in five days took three weeks. By burning bridges en route and securing all boats to the far bank of the Delaware, Washington had enough time to delay pursuit. This last action stranded the British at Trenton where they prepared to settle into winter quarters.

One explanation for this dilatory progress can be drawn from Sir William Howe's priorities. The British commander said he needed to provision the army from the farms of New Jersey (an army of 35,000 men and 4,000 horses consumed 37 tons of food and 38 tons of fodder per day). Howe also must have considered Trenton as the site to quarter his troops for the winter since one-fourth of New York City had been destroyed by fire in September. Thus, if the capture of Philadelphia and Washington's army could not be accomplished any earlier, it might well be delayed until spring. Meanwhile, Howe had perceived from deserters that the Americans were in a weak, dissipated condition; he also learned that Congress had fled from Philadelphia to Baltimore. It was time to extend the olive branch. In exchange for a signed oath, Howe promised to pardon revolutionary supporters and return forfeited lands. Within two weeks the measure attracted perhaps 3,500 pledges of loyalty to the king throughout New York and New Jersey, including those from 1,500 militiamen on Long Island. Patriot resistance appeared to be dissolving.

Yet things were not as they seemed. The occupation of New Jersey did not win long-term friends for the British. Since there were no barracks, soldiers lodged among villagers in unwelcome familiarity. In some towns as many as six officers shared a room, even though their rank entitled each to a single room. Residents complained when their guests refused to practice a moral standard in common with their own. Hessians were particularly objectionable. Unfamiliar with the language, the German mercenaries frequently failed to distinguish loyalists from patriots. Livestock and household goods were taken without promise of payment. Incidents of rape were reported. Thus, partisan sympathy for the army steadily eroded.

The establishment of British logistical outposts across New Jersey assumed that the American army was de-

teriorating, or at least that it would hibernate soon. Once winter set in, eighteenth-century armies seldom moved. This map was drawn by Capt. John Montresor, then serving as a staff officer under Howe. It shows the dispersal of British troops in New Jersey. Although patriot gunboats checked the occupation of Burlington, the left flank of the army was anchored with about 1,500 German troops at Bordentown and 1,300 at Trenton. They were 30 miles from Philadelphia. Howe and Cornwallis retired to headquarters in New York and left corpulent Maj. Gen. James Grant in charge. Grant held a seat in the House of Commons, as did six other general officers then in America, and in a speech the year before stated, "The Americans could not fight." Literally, he was in for a surprise.

The American command feared that the British would advance over the Delaware as soon as the river froze. However, patriot hopes were bolstered by the arrival of 2,000 Continentals from the command of Maj. Gen. Charles Lee. Their number had been reduced from 5,000 regulars and militia that had started out from positions above New York. The loss included the difficult Lee, who was captured at a New Jersey inn. Washington began planning what was to be his boldest stroke of the war. He would recross the Delaware at night and descend from the north on Trenton with a force of 2,400. Col. John Cadwalader, with 1,800 men, was assigned to distract the German garrison at Bordentown. Christmas night was chosen.

The crossing was made under severe conditions. Winds, floating ice, and rain impeded their progress. But Col. John Glover's Massachusetts fishermen ferried the troops safely to the opposite shore. On the subsequent eight-mile march into Trenton, sleet glazed the roads and dampened powder and flints. Halfway to their destination, the force was divided between Maj. Gens. John Sullivan, assigned to attack from the road along the river, and Nathanael Greene, instructed to circle the town from the northeast. Washington accompanied Greene.

As the Hessian pickets were driven back into town, their musket fire awakened most of the defenders. It was 8:00 A.M. Many Hessians, including their commander Col. Johann Rall, had spent the previous evening celebrating the holiday and were in no condition to assemble quickly. The barrage from patriot artillery chief Henry Knox prevented them from forming ranks in the streets. Rall ordered a withdrawal to an open field nearby, but was killed attempting to carry it out. By 9:30 A.M. the three Hessian regiments had struck their colors. Casualties amounted to 23 killed, 84 wounded, and 918 taken prisoner; perhaps 300 escaped. Only two Americans were killed and four wounded.

Washington's heartening victory spoiled Howe's best prospects for a negotiated peace. Henceforth, even in winter, the Americans had to be considered an active force in the field.

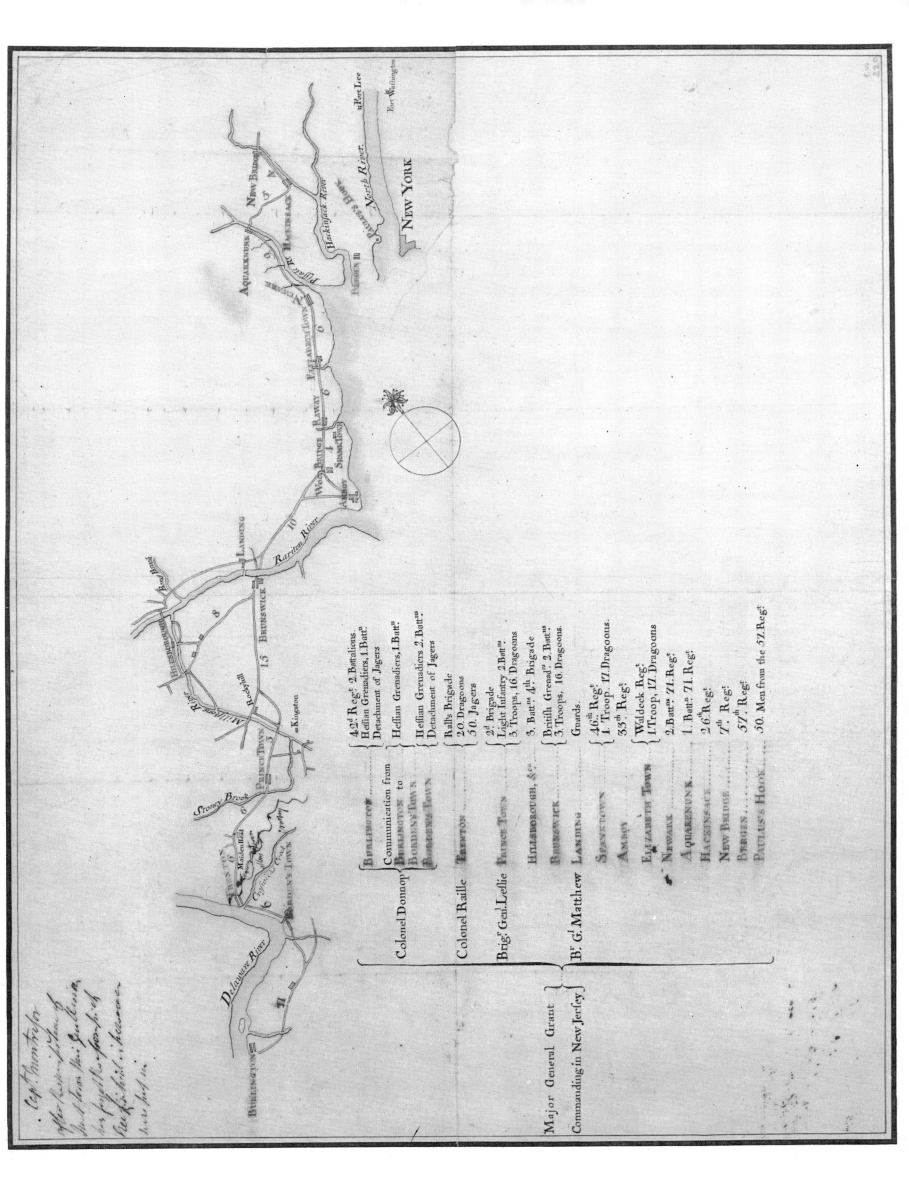

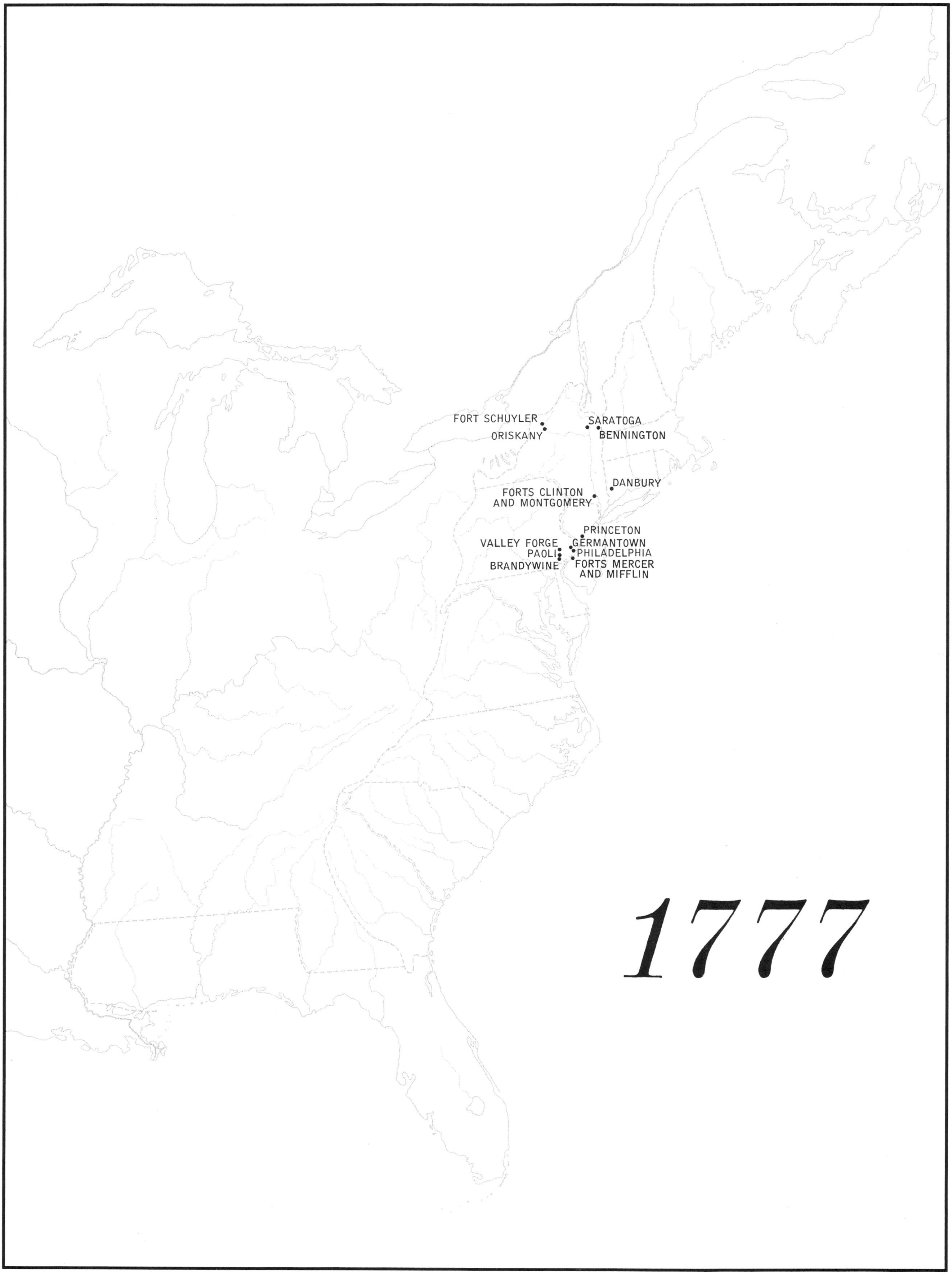

FORT SCHUYLER •   SARATOGA
                         •
ORISKANY •   • BENNINGTON
                •

                              • DANBURY

FORTS CLINTON •
AND MONTGOMERY

                    • PRINCETON
VALLEY FORGE • • GERMANTOWN
         PAOLI •• PHILADELPHIA
BRANDYWINE • • FORTS MERCER
                AND MIFFLIN

1777

On February 12, 1777, Capt. James Wallace of the *Experiment* arrived in London with news of the defeat of the Hessians at Trenton. It quickly ricocheted around the stunned British ministry that the rebellion would not soon disintegrate, but indeed would require a plan of operations for the spring. Unfortunately, it came on the heels of such encouraging reports as the advance across New Jersey, the capture of Rhode Island, and the success of the loyalty oaths.

The ministry eventually endorsed two plans for the operation of the army in the next campaign season. Maj. Gen. John Burgoyne had successfully promoted his idea for a northern invasion to sever New England from the other colonies along the Hudson River. Lt. Gen. William Howe proposed to invade Philadelphia while holding his bases in New York and Newport. Both projects were approved without any effort to coordinate them.

At British headquarters in New York, the effect of the Trenton attack was dissipated by the normal pursuits of an army at rest in winter quarters. There were social obligations to the loyalists, entertainments for the younger officers, and celebrations of the queen's and king's birthdays. Sir William Howe, knighted for his New York campaign, was preoccupied with romancing Mrs. Joshua Loring, wife of his commissary of prisoners. By spring, many officers were optimistic that patriot resistance would soon crumble. Capt. John Montresor predicted that the raid on Danbury would be the war's last campaign.

American resistance had been seriously underestimated. But who could foresee that a whole army would arise from nothing to defeat Burgoyne? Some officers had revised their conception of American capabilities after Trenton. Lt. Col. William Harcourt spoke for the revisionists: "Though they seem to be ignorant of the precision, order, and even of the principles, by which large bodies are moved, yet they possess some of the requisites for making good troops, such as extreme cunning, great industry in moving ground and felling of wood, activity and a spirit of enterprise upon any advantage . . . though it was once the fashion of this army to treat them in the most contemptible light, they are now became a fashionable army."

The Americans spent a less pleasant winter in garrisons at Morristown, Middlebrook, and the Hudson Highlands. From these points, they could deny the British access to farm produce in New Jersey and New York. Although fresh meat was obtainable, forage became a particular problem for the British. In order to open the campaign season, an adequate reserve had to be collected or else the horses would need to graze—in which case the opening of activities would be delayed until edible sprouts were available in the field. The collection of fodder that winter became complicated by American resistance. The frequency and size of the foraging expeditions increased. Six times in January and February and ten times in March, major British detachments were forced into the New Jersey countryside. Units of 500 men and sometimes 2,000

were required for these operations, and casualties of 60 and 100 were not uncommon. To requisition these foodstuffs and return safely to the garrisons at New Brunswick or Amboy required knowledge of local topography—and the British maps were not reliable for these activities.

On January 8, 1775, Lt. Gen. Thomas Gage had issued regimental orders for anyone capable of drawing maps to report to headquarters. The wording seemed extraordinary to Lt. John Barker who commented that the commander must have "doubted whether there were any such." This same dispatch prompted Lt. Frederick Mackenzie to remark that "not many officers in this army will be found qualified for this service. It is a branch of military education too little attended to."

Part of Gage's problem was the small size of the official military organization trained in cartography—the Corps of Engineers. The corps numbered only 47 officers in 1775 for service in England and all the colonies except Ireland, which maintained a separate organization. Even with the immense obligations imposed by the war, its staff was expanded to only 75 officers by 1782. Moreover, the principal duty of this service was the conduct of sieges and the construction and maintenance of fortifications, bridges, and roads. Cartography was a tertiary consideration, and not all members of the corps were proficient in drawing and surveying.

During the French and Indian War some line officers had been given engineer duties to remedy the shortage of skilled labor. They were titled "assistant engineers" and paid an additional five shillings per day from the Extraordinary Account of the British army. Many were Dutch or Swiss Protestants who had been trained in their native countries. Among the 20 or so who served in America, Samuel Holland was the most prominent. Yet all but one had resigned from the army by the time of the Revolution. When Gage attempted to commission others at Boston in 1775, the new assistant engineers were "laughed at for their ignorance."

As the war progressed, the volume of work continued to exceed the available engineer talent. Returns from the summer of 1777 indicated that while eight members of the Corps of Engineers were assigned to the main army at New York, their services were supplemented by a staff of eight assistant engineers. Assistant engineers were also assigned to the British armies in Canada and Nova Scotia. In some instances, they were appointed by the commander of a garrison when no member of the Corps of Engineers was available. At other times, assistant engineers were commissioned by the commander in chief upon recommendation by the senior member of the Corps of Engineers in America. After 1778 the proportion of established engineers in relation to assistant engineers declined rapidly. Robert Morse listed himself and three other members of the Corps of Engineers at New York in 1782 with no fewer than 13 assistant engineers. Eight of the fifty British maps in the *atlas* were drawn by officers commissioned as assistant engineers.

Princeton

The success of the swoop on Trenton was encouraging to the Americans. Was it mere luck? Could it be repeated? Washington still had the boats and a confident corps of veterans; and militia were coming in. Besides, Col. John Cadwalader, who had been unable to pass the Delaware on December 25, had crossed two days later and and occupied Burlington. With more aggressiveness than other militia commanders, he wanted to join forces with the Continentals and pursue the Hessians and British northward in New Jersey. Washington concluded that more was to be lost by inaction than by action.

Only a lack of food restrained the Americans. When the commissary wagons began rolling in on December 29, Washington started his men recrossing the Delaware the next day, despite six inches of snow. By the time the main army reached Trenton, Cadwalader's brigade had moved up to Bordentown, six miles to the south (see preceding map). The Germans there had withdrawn northward in panic. But another danger threatened the Americans as the enlistment terms of most of the soldiers expired on December 31.

Unaccustomed to pleading, Washington nevertheless began a program of addressing each regiment, urging the men to reenlist, even for just six weeks, offering a bounty of ten dollars and promising better care and more opportunities for glory. He sent Brig. Gen. Thomas Mifflin, an eloquent speaker, to harangue Cadwalader's brigade. By the end of the day they had won over two-thirds to three-quarters of the whole army.

Cadwalader had been useful in another way. He forwarded a spy's sketch of Princeton (opposite) to Washington. It showed the streets of the small town, the tavern, the college building (Nassau Hall), two batteries on either side of the road running south over the bridge above Stony Brook, and the enemy headquarters of the garrison. It also revealed another road, parallel to the main road, but farther east. This caught Washington's eye.

Meanwhile, on New Year's Day, 1777, the commander laid out a line below Trenton and behind Assunpink Creek. His men began digging in as if to make a stand. They were joined late in the day by Cadwalader's reinforcement and other militia. Washington sent a few regiments up the road halfway to Princeton to meet the British advance that was sure to come.

Denied his winter leave to go home to England, a disgruntled Maj. Gen. Charles Cornwallis was ordered to Princeton to take command of the British and German regiments and recapture Trenton. His Lordship pushed into Trenton at dusk on January 2 with a column of 6,800 regulars. Their advance was slow, having to fight their way against a brigade under Col. Edward Hand who knew how to organize a delaying action. Washington needed this precious time. It was then too late in the day to mount an attack against the American line, but Cornwallis was sure he could strike the next morning with

rested troops. Their army retired for the night.

Before dark Washington held a council of his officers. They agreed that a set battle would be disastrous. The alternatives were a dangerous night retreat southward, or an attempt to recross the river. Brig. Gen. Arthur St. Clair, who knew the area, mentioned a back road northward to Princeton, the road Washington had noticed on the map. It lay to the east, and a quiet night march would take the Americans around Cornwallis and up to Princeton by daylight. That was it!

Behind bright campfires and the clamor of men still digging, Washington sent his baggage wagons back to Burlington and peeled off his men noiselessly to the east. The artillery wheels of the 40 guns were muffled with cloth shrouds. Far up the creek they crossed the Quaker Bridge and followed a frozen road straight up toward the college town, a distance of 11 miles. By morning they were in sight of Princeton. When Cornwallis bestirred himself and looked out across the smoldering campfires, he saw only a vacant campsite, a few piles of dirt, and a pastoral landscape beyond the creek.

Meanwhile, two British regiments, the 17th and 55th, under Lt. Col. Charles Mawhood, marching out of Princeton to support Cornwallis suddenly saw Americans in an orchard on their left. The British turned off the main road to face a detachment of 350 Virginians under Brig. Gen. Hugh Mercer. Washington had ordered these men to destroy the Stony Brook bridge on the main road. The rest of his column was marching on to Princeton where the British 40th Regiment remained on guard. The action in the orchard turned against the Americans at first, but Washington gathered some of Col. Daniel Hitchcock's brigade—which was at the rear of his column —and led them to Mercer's support. Their fire forced the British to flee, but Mercer, Col. John Haslet, and 21 others were killed and about 20 wounded. British losses were higher, amounting to 28 killed, 58 wounded, and 129 captured. The bridge was then destroyed.

Washington continued his march into Princeton. The British fled northward, except for a few who holed up in Nassau Hall and quickly surrendered. The Americans had two hours in the town to gather up British supplies before word came that Cornwallis's troops were racing back from Trenton. Washington's army was too weary for another battle and marched northward missing a chance to bag the £70,000 British pay chest at New Brunswick. The frustrated British reentered Princeton "in a most infernal sweat—running, puffing, and blowing, and swearing at being so outwitted," as Brig. Gen. Henry Knox learned. They continued all the way to New Brunswick; their extended winter line had been suddenly rolled back more than 60 miles. Washington's army then settled into winter quarters at Morristown where he could threaten all of eastern New Jersey, which served as a base for British supplies.

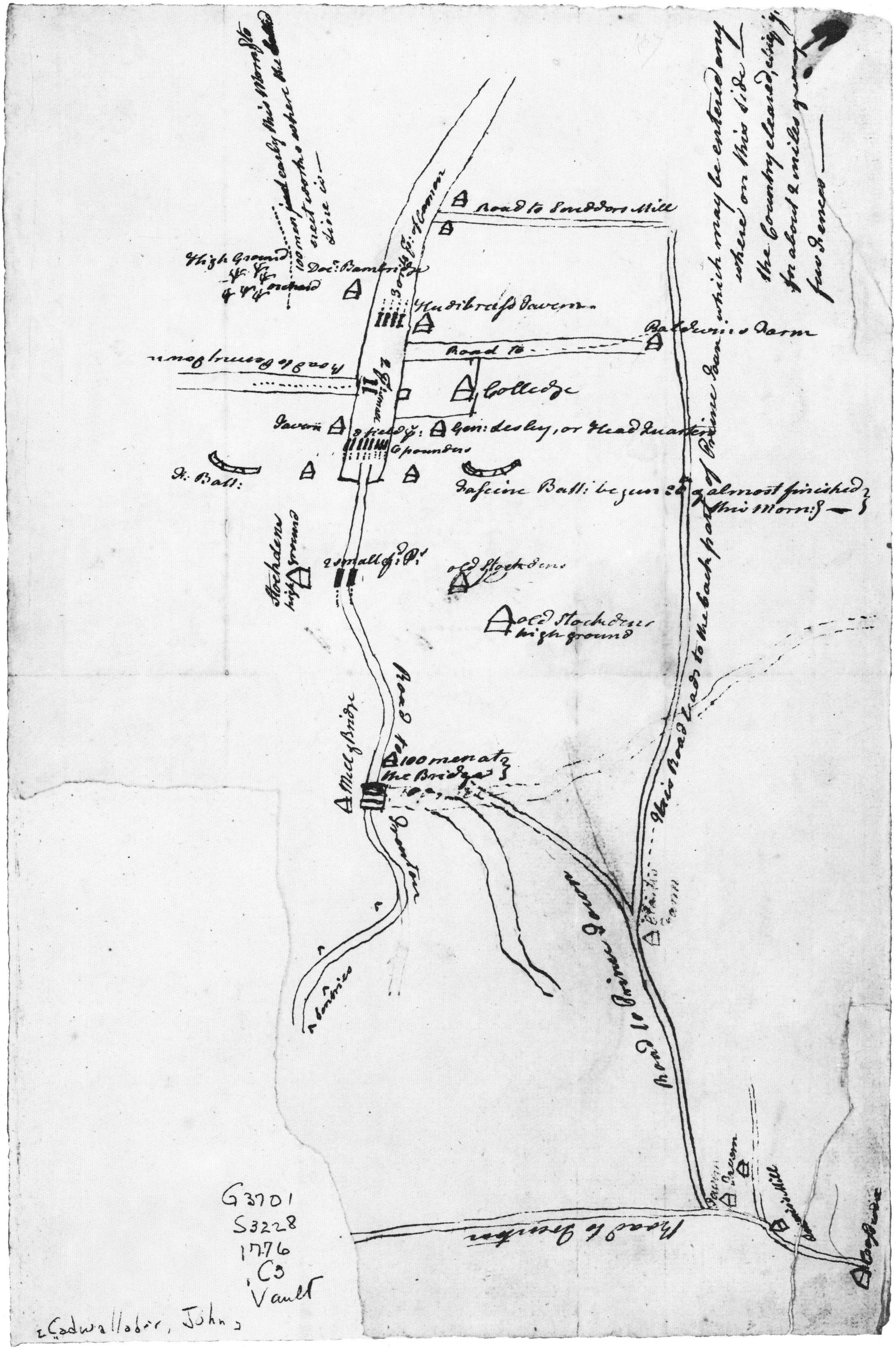

100 men just early this Morning erect works where the Road is —

High Ground 4 4 4 4 orchard

Doc.r Bainbridge

Road to Scudders Mill

Hudibrass Tavern

Baldwins Tavern

the Country cleared, excep.s where otherwise on this side. the Country cleared, excep.s for about 2 miles round — fine fences

Road to Bennig Town

Colledge

Road to

Tavern

8 field p.s

Gen: Lesley, or Head Quarters

6 pounders

Dr. Ball:

Fascine Ball: begun & almost finished this Morn.g

Stockders high ground

2 small fd: p.s:

old Stockders

old Stockders high ground

Mill Bridge

Road

100 men at the Bridge

Quarter

sentries

this Road leads to the back part of Princetown

Road to Princetown

Road to

Tavern

Road to Trenton

Stoney Brook

Danbury

The Sound separated American logistical bases in Connecticut from British bases on Long Island. It provided two forms of contact between belligerents—contraband trade and supply raids. The mercantile aspect developed out of shared needs and became known as "London trading"; American agricultural produce was exchanged for British finished goods. A fleet of oared 30-foot boats operated along the length of the Connecticut coast (see map on page 21). They regularly darted across the Sound loaded with provisions. In fact, the trade became so endemic that it fostered a parasitic colony of privateers who plundered friend and foe alike.

The Sound was also an avenue by which to launch raids on supply bases. Almost as soon as the British established control on Long Island, they were subject to whale-boat warfare, as it came to be known. Ambrose Serle reported that in October a party of 400 men from New London, Conn., seized cattle, provisions, and forage on Long Island. The number of sheep taken alone exceeded 17,000. The raids necessitated constant protection by guards and sentries. This threat of intervention kept the British from developing the resources of the largest territory in America under their possession.

Brig. William Tryon, the deposed governor of New York, probably suggested the plan to attack the American supply base at Danbury. The 1777 plan was conceived as a punitive raid, despite the British shortage of fodder and foodstuffs. Brig. James Agnew was assigned coleader with Tryon of the expedition, but the command seems to have devolved on Brig. Sir William Erskine. Earlier that winter Erskine had led a foraging expedition to New Jersey in which "he routed the rebels with great slaughter; he took no prisoners."

Twelve transports, a hospital ship, and some small craft embarked on April 22 with about 2,000 troops, 300 of them loyalists. Simultaneously, a diversionary force of frigates sailed up the Hudson. The ships on the expedition to Danbury were under the command of Capt. Henry Duncan. They passed into Long Island Sound and anchored for the night about 10 miles past Hell Gate. For two days the troops waited out a headwind in discomfort aboard ship before they could proceed the remaining 30 miles. Their destination was Cedar Point, a position on the Connecticut shore about 4 miles east of Norwalk and 8 miles west of Fairfield. They landed at 5:00 P.M. on April 25 at a stretch of beach which Duncan called "exceedingly unfavourable," but they quickly took possession of Compo Hill and Bennet's Rocks. In a light rain the supplies were brought ashore and by 11:00 P.M. the troops were on the march by the Reading road to Danbury.

The British column reached Reading 12 hours later— a distance of 20 miles. Moving through the uneven terrain and the passes at Gilbertown and Jump Hill, they encountered only scattered resistance. The fatigued troops reached Danbury at 5:00 P.M. and drove off 150 Continentals who had been attempting to remove supplies. Seven patriot snipers stayed behind and opened fire from a house in town. Two companies of regulars charged and put the dwelling to the torch with the men inside. The high ground about the town was secured.

Before their departure early the next morning, the British destroyed 4,000-5,000 barrels of pork, beef, and flour; 5,000 pairs of shoes; 2,000 bushels of grain; and 1,600 tents, among other supplies. Nineteen houses and 22 storehouses were burned. The British left by the western road toward Ridgefield.

Meanwhile, a force of 500 militia and 100 Continentals was hurrying toward Danbury under Brig. Gen. Gold Selleck Silliman. He was joined by Brig. Gen. Benedict Arnold. With 400 of the troops they reached Ridgefield after a forced march at 11:00 A.M. and cut off the British line of advance. Brig. Gen. David Wooster took the balance of the Americans and charged the British rear guard. In what was termed "smart skirmishing" near Ridgefield, Wooster was mortally wounded. Arnold held the front for about an hour against three cannon, had his horse shot out from under him, and killed a soldier who ran up to take him prisoner. The uncoordinated British attack in three waves under Erskine eventually dispersed the Americans. But the patriots regrouped 15 miles farther south at the bridge over the Saugatuck River and were joined by reinforcements. The British encamped on the battlefield that evening.

At daybreak on April 28 the British column set off again, but it was molested by irregular gunfire from rebels in the undergrowth beside the road. The British outflanked a group of Americans at the Norwalk River Bridge by crossing on a route farther upstream as marked on the map. The same strategy was used again at the Saugatuck River. Arnold had collected 500 troops above the bridge to the south, but the British crossed 3 miles north and headed over Finch's Hill to their ships. Silliman with another 500 troops and two cannon skirmished at the British rear guard until they reached Compo Hill. There the British turned on their pursuers, and with bayonets fixed, four regiments charged. Despite their exhaustion after a day's march, they drove back the Americans a mile and one-half. Duncan prepared a defense for the reembarkation and loaded 1,000 troops in ten minutes. The remainder soon followed and the fleet got under way at 6:00 P.M. for the voyage back to New York.

The British loss was 140 killed and wounded, with about 20 prisoners. A British officer claimed an American return showed 100 killed and 200 wounded, but American reports estimated between 60 and 100 casualties. Washington ordered supply depots moved beyond a one-day march from the coast; the tents he had lost were virtually irreplaceable. Col. Return Jonathan Meigs crossed the Sound from New Haven in whaleboats on October 23. He burned ships and supplies at the British base in Sag Harbor, returning with 90 prisoners.

The map corresponds precisely to the account in Capt. Lt. Archibald Robertson's diary. It may be assumed that Capt. John Montresor made this copy of it.

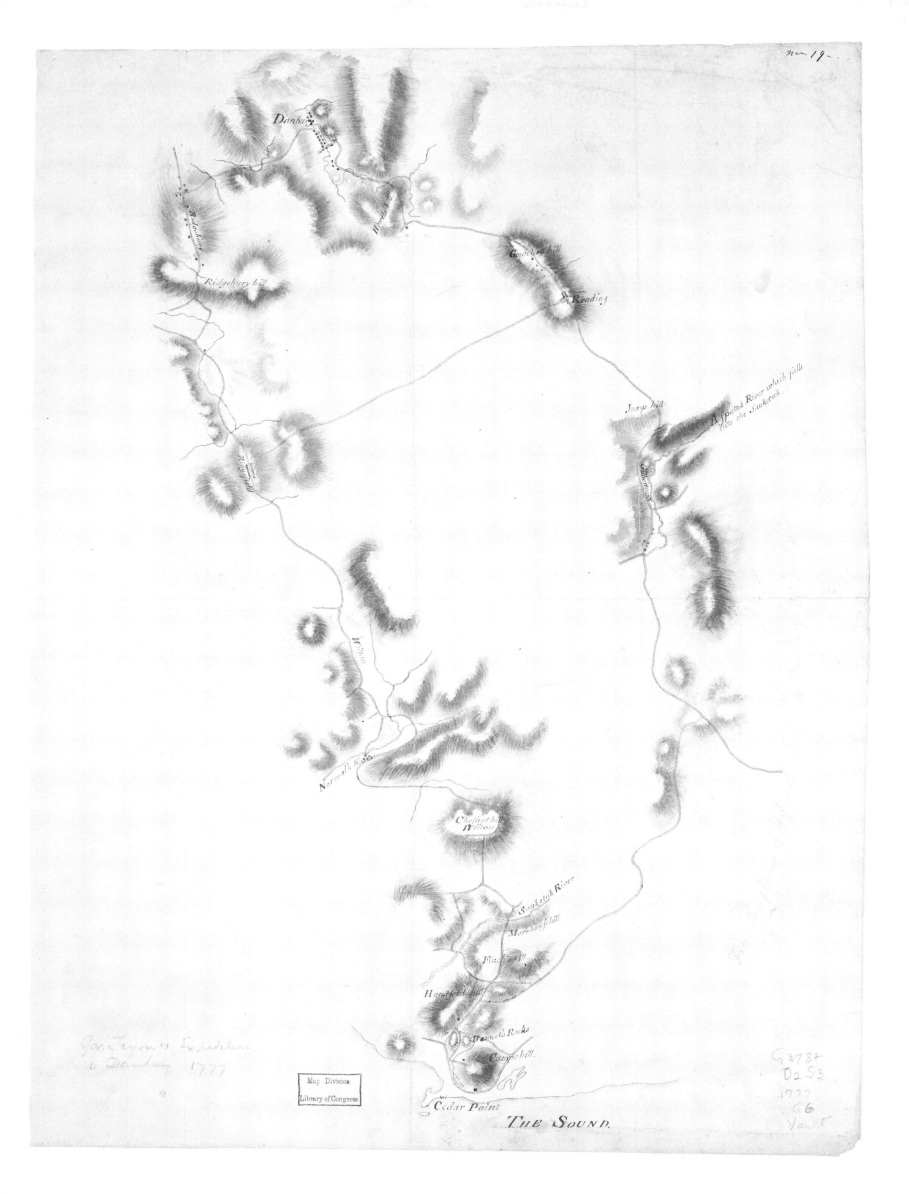

Danbury

Honochill

Gowchi hill

Reading

Riderbury

Ridgebury hill

Jump hill

A Spatuk River which falls
into the Sauketuk

Gilberteus

Wilton

Norwalk River

Chesint hill
Wilton

Sauketuk River

Morehouse hill

Finch hill

Hauilyerth hill

Bennel's Rocks

Camp hill

Cedar Point

THE SOUND.

Gen Tryon's Expedition
to Danbury 1777

Map Division
Library of Congress

nn 19
266

G3784
.D253
1777
.S6
Vault

Fort Schuyler and Oriskany

Maj. Gen. John Burgoyne's advance into New York State in 1777 included a diversionary expedition under Lt. Col. Barry St. Leger. He was to proceed to Oswego, N.Y., march eastward through the Mohawk Valley, and finally link up with Burgoyne at Albany. St. Leger commanded a motley force of 1,700 men: one-half of them were Indians, mostly Mohawks and Senecas; 340 were regulars; the rest were loyalists—many of them former inhabitants of the Mohawk Valley.

The main obstruction in the British route was Fort Schuyler (old Fort Stanwix at modern Rome, renamed a year earlier in honor of Maj. Gen. Philip Schuyler). The fort had been an elaborate structure during the French and Indian War, but in the spring of 1777, its state was such that a French engineer wrote, "It is absolutely necessary that I make it intirely new." Col. Peter Gansevoort and later Lt. Col. Marinus Willett were sent to garrison and repair the fort. By the time St. Leger arrived, it was in remarkably improved condition—more so than St. Leger anticipated.

On July 30 a friendly Oneida reported to Brig. Gen. Nicholas Herkimer that St. Leger was approaching Fort Schuyler. Herkimer immediately raised 800 militia, and on August 4 (two days after St. Leger had invested the fort), he marched the troops to within ten miles of Fort Schuyler and encamped for the night. Herkimer sent messengers to urge Gansevoort to make a sortie as the relief column approached.

Molly Brant, sister of Mohawk Chief Joseph Brant, learned of Herkimer's advance on the evening of August 5 and informed St. Leger. He prepared an ambush six miles from the fort (two miles west of modern Oriskany), a site later named Battle Brook. Four hundred Indians under Brant hid themselves in the woods along a narrow corduroy causeway in a ravine. Maj. John Butler with loyalist troops waited to hit the head of Herkimer's column as it came through. St. Leger kept his regulars firing on Fort Schuyler.

Herkimer's little army was strung out for a mile. The commander rode far into the trap before the enemy fired at about 10:00 A.M. on August 6. The rear guard of 200 militiamen turned and ran. In the first volley 16 officers fell, either killed or wounded. A shot killed Herkimer's horse and seriously wounded Herkimer in the leg, but he continued to direct the battle seated on his saddle on the ground. The militia spread out and tried to take cover. But because they fought as individuals, the Indians were able to rush a soldier after he fired and kill him before he could reload.

After three-quarters of an hour, a heavy downpour halted all action. When the battle resumed an hour later, Herkimer had his men fight in pairs to protect each other. In the meantime his messengers had finally penetrated Fort Schuyler and persuaded Gansevoort to order a sortie. When the rain ceased, Willett burst from the fort with 250 men, scattered the enemy regulars temporarily, looted the loyalist camp of Sir John Johnson (who fled in his shirt-sleeves), and destroyed nearly everything that belonged to the Mohawks.

Although he suffered severe casualties, Herkimer's valiant militia were giving such a good account of themselves that the Indians were ready to quit. Butler received a small reinforcement of loyalists whom he tried to disguise as troops from Fort Schuyler coming to Herkimer's aid. The deception failed when a militiaman recognized a former loyalist neighbor; a rough hand-to-hand fight followed. In midafternoon the Mohawks withdrew and forced the loyalists to break off combat. The Americans lost 71 killed and carried off about 75 wounded. Herkimer died of his wound ten days later.

The Indians, who had been promised much loot for little fighting, now found they had borne the brunt of the action and suffered the loss of their possessions left in camp. However, that night two of St. Leger's officers who had been captured in the day's sortie told Gansevoort what had happened at Oriskany and advised capitulation. Gansevoort refused to surrender but agreed to a three-day truce. After dark, he slipped Willett and another officer out of the fort; they headed for Schuyler's headquarters at Stillwater. When Maj. Gen. Benedict Arnold heard their story, he offered to lead a relief force. He picked up 1,000 volunteers in a few days and hurried westward through the woods.

Arnold enlisted the cooperation of Hon Yost Schuyler, who was well known to the Mohawks as a lunatic and, therefore, held by them in some awe. As a ruse, he was instructed to go on ahead and tell St. Leger's Indian troops that an American force as numerous as leaves on the trees was marching on Fort Schuyler. The already discouraged Indians believed Schuyler's story, which was corroborated by several other Indians whom Schuyler had cunningly sought to support him. St. Leger resolved to retire that night, but the Indians, as he wrote to Burgoyne, "grew furious and abandoned; seized upon the officers' liquor and clothes, and became more formidable than the enemy we had to expect." The loyalists, of no mind to face their infuriated neighbors, followed the Indians' retreat.

St. Leger's expedition was thus reduced to the small detachment of regulars. He had no choice but to give up the siege on August 22 and return to Oswego. Arnold reached the fort two days later. Gansevoort immediately set out in pursuit of St. Leger, but only a few laggards and deserters were captured.

The map was made presumably later in the year by Capt. Francois de Fleury, a French engineer who volunteered his services in America and was commissioned by Congress in May, 1777. He distinguished himself in action around Philadelphia during the autumn of that year. Fleury presented his sketch to Gansevoort to commemorate his firm stand. Willett's sortie into the loyalist camp is indicated at the lower right corner of the map. The ambush at Oriskany is off the map to the right.

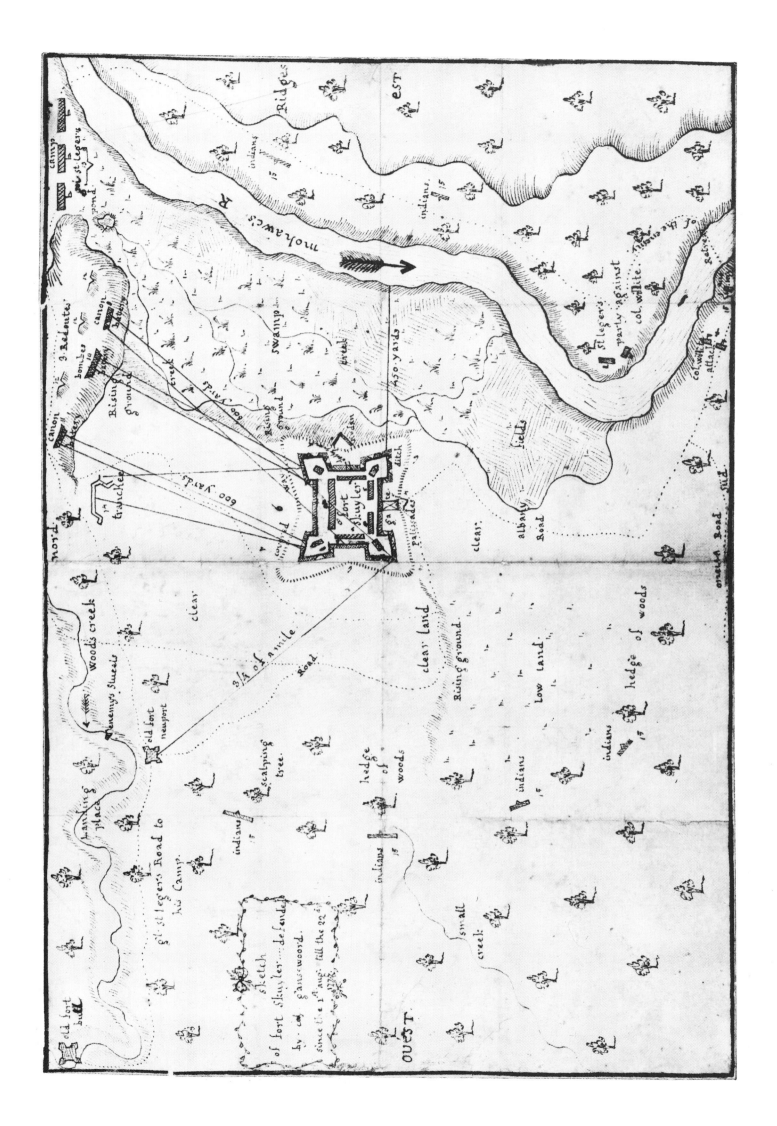

Bennington

Maj. Gen. John Burgoyne arrived in Canada on May 7, 1777, after spending the winter in England. He had received permission to take an army south along the familiar Richelieu River-Lake Champlain-Hudson River corridor to New York City. His objective was Albany. Burgoyne began his march with 7,300 carefully chosen infantrymen (one-half of them crack regulars and one-half Germans), accompanied by 600 artillerymen. It was regarded as a magnificent army. The force was supplemented by 650 Canadians and loyalists, 400 Indians, and 1,000 noncombatant transport men, commissariat personnel, and women camp followers.

Burgoyne was known as an aggressive and talented officer who had married well and in leisure wrote plays and a military treatise. He had earned his military reputation as a cavalry officer in the Seven Years War, where he developed an appreciation for swiftness of movement, surprise attacks, and artillery support. He also possessed the ability to change his mind tactically. Unlike many of his contemporaries, he came to respect the Americans' military skill after Breed's Hill. Unfortunately, he modified this insight for the campaign of 1777 and regarded his own force as invincible. In planning for his expedition he seemed to ignore the fact that the transport of heavy artillery would impede swift, bold movements, although he futilely admonished his officers to lighten their baggage in order to carry out such operations. The number of female camp followers was cut from a norm of six per company to three, and this may have influenced the proportionately higher desertion rates.

When Burgoyne's expedition embarked from St. Johns on June 12, it was powerful but greatly encumbered. He had estimated that 400 horses would be required to transport 138 pieces of artillery and another 1,000 to pull the 500 hastily constructed carts loaded with provisions and baggage. But his calculations could not be met. Horses were scarce in Canada, and the supply for transport was further lessened by soldiers who requisitioned their own mounts. By the time the train departed only a portion (probably one-half) of the necessary number of horses had been procured. Foraging was not common practice for armies on a route march in the eighteenth century, but Burgoyne assumed he would be able to find additional horses and fodder along the way.

The British sailed in a large flotilla up the Richelieu River and onto Lake Champlain. There were few settlements along the route to Albany, and the first conflict was expected to be at Fort Ticonderoga. When the expedition reached Crown Point on June 27, it was only eight miles from the fort (see map on page 13).

The American defense force of the Northern Department, weak and faction-ridden, was commanded by Maj. Gen. Philip Schuyler. His main strength was 2,500 Continentals under Maj. Gen. Arthur St. Clair at Ticonderoga. In addition there were militia detachments farther south at Skenesboro (modern Whitehall), Fort Anne, and Fort Edward. St. Clair decided he could not stand a siege with insufficient troops. On July 5 he abandoned the fort, withdrawing to Fort Edward. Burgoyne moved triumphantly into Ticonderoga. Leaving a garrison of nearly 1,000, he pushed on to Skenesboro on July 9. But two significant skirmishes occurred between the British and the rebels. On July 7 at Hubbardton (east of Ticonderoga) a British detachment under Brig. Simon Fraser missed a chance to capture the entire American rear guard, but took 228 prisoners nonetheless. At Fort Anne two days later, the rebels attacked and temporarily surrounded a British detachment, which managed to escape with only a few casualties.

Burgoyne had a choice of two routes south of Lake Champlain. Lacking sufficient boats to carry both troops and supplies over the water route of Lake George, he sent only his artillery (42 cannon, the rest had been left at Crown Point and Ticonderoga). He then settled down at Skenesboro while his troops cleared the longer and more difficult land route to Fort Edward. Along the stretch of densely wooded and swampy country, American militiamen had destroyed 40 bridges, felled huge trees to block the road, and flooded a creek. When Burgoyne's train began to move again with insufficient transport, it took 20 days to travel the 22 miles to Fort Edward, which they then found abandoned. On July 27, two days before the British arrived, an incident occurred that further confounded Burgoyne.

A party of British-allied Indians had carried into camp a distinctive scalp. One of the loyalist officers with shock recognized it as that of Jane McCrea, his fiancée who had been on her way to meet him. Although outraged, Burgoyne decided not to punish the alleged murderer for fear the Indians would leave. News of the atrocity spread swiftly through New York and New England, and became a means of propaganda to call out large numbers of militia. The story was especially effective among the frightened settlers on the frontier.

Burgoyne's logistical difficulties now became critical. His supply line back to Montreal was 185 miles long, and few transport wagons were dispatched from St. Johns to rendezvous with the train en route. Expecting to meet with loyalist inhabitants who would furnish horses and fodder, Burgoyne instead found burned fields and deserted farms in the thinly populated territory. The British were now unable to advance more than three miles without waiting eight or ten days for the overworked horses and supply wagons to catch up.

Burgoyne was therefore amenable to a proposition by Baron Friedrich von Riedesel, commander of the German troops, to send an expedition east to the Connecticut valley to collect horses, cattle, and wagons. A force of 800, including 50 British marksmen, 300 loyalists and Indians, and 400 Germans, was assembled under Lt. Col. Friedrich Baum, who spoke no English. The German detachment included a horseless regiment of dragoons, who plodded through the dense woods in 12-pound, thigh-high boots, their long sabers catching in the brush. Altogether, it was

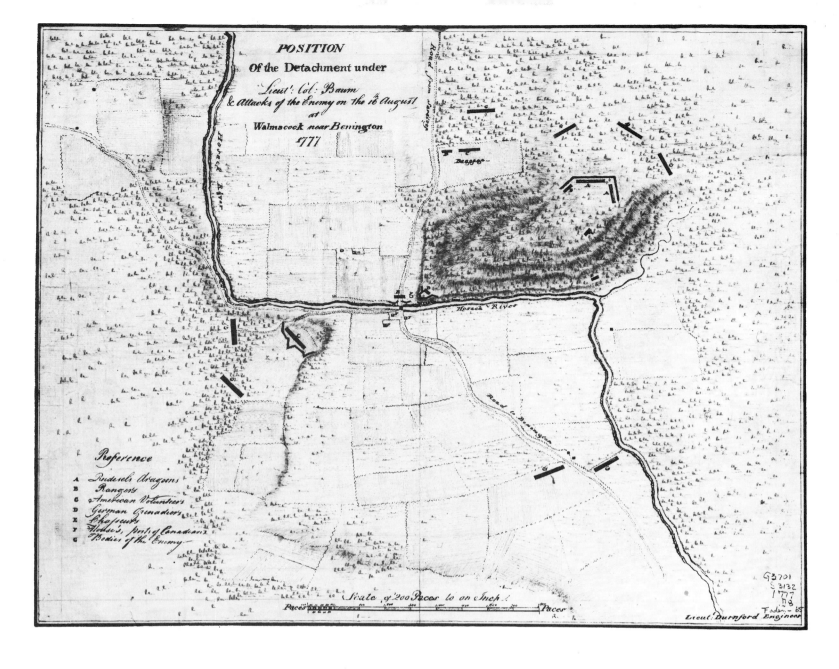

not the most appropriate force for a sweeping supply raid. Before they marched out from Fort Miller (south of Fort Edward) on August 11, Baum received new orders to proceed southeast to Bennington, where reportedly a rebel supply depot was guarded by only 400 militia. Baum advanced slowly, and soon received a report that there were 1,800 militia in Bennington.

This information was essentially correct. Brig. Gen. John Stark, commissioned by the state of New Hampshire after resigning his Continental rank in a huff, had just raised 1,500 men and called for Col. Seth Warner to join him with 350 Vermont troops. Ignorant of Baum's approach, Stark intended to strike at Burgoyne's rear. He then learned of the nearby enemy and on August 14 moved north to Sancoik's Mill where he first encountered brief resistance, and then proceeded four miles farther to the bridge across the Walloomsac River. On the map this is labeled the Hosack (Hoosic) River, which is a tributary of the Walloomsac. In an open space where the river turned south, Stark waited; his encampment is not shown. (C "American Volunteers" means the loyalists.)

While halted at the bridge, Baum sent for reinforcements and foolishly scattered his small force at several posts on both sides of the river. Rain postponed action the next day. On the afternoon of August 16 Stark advanced, still without Warner. His infantrymen overran the detached outposts and closed in on Baum's main redoubt,

marked A on the map. The German held his ground for about two hours and at 5:00 P.M. he fell, mortally wounded.

A tired reinforcement of 600 Germans under Col. Heinrich von Breymann was less than four miles away, hurrying to relieve Baum. Stark was in a desperate state when Warner caught up with him. A second battle developed along stationary lines and lasted almost until sunset when Breymann ran out of ammunition and ordered a retreat. The New Hampshire and Vermont men swarmed over the Germans, causing panic and surrender. Although wounded, Breymann managed to get two-thirds of his men away in the dark; only nine of Baum's escaped.

The Germans lost 207 killed and 700 captured. Stark reported only 14 killed and 42 wounded, but both figures are considered too low; Stark's casualties were closer to 80.

This defeat, coupled with the news that Lt. Col. Barry St. Leger had decamped following the impressive show of New York militia at Oriskany, brought home to Burgoyne the hard facts of irregular warfare in America. "Wherever the King's forces point, militia to the amount of three or four thousand assemble in twenty-four hours," wrote Burgoyne to Lord Germain. Although many patriots were unwilling to join the Continental army and spend three years in distant parts of the country, they would not hesitate to take up arms for the protection of their own areas of settlement.

Saratoga

If the defeat of the German detachments near Bennington was a blow to Lt. Gen. John Burgoyne, it was compounded within a week by the sobering news of Lt. Col. Barry St. Leger's withdrawal from western New York. Still, Burgoyne was not pessimistic, and the morale of his hand-picked troops was high despite sickness and desertions. Most of his Indians had gone home and were not missed. The American force in front of him was yet too small to do more than cause delay. Brig. Gen. John Stark posed no threat on his flank because Stark was immobile, his militia disintegrating. Sir William Howe, on his way to take the rebel capital of Philadelphia, was thereby occupying Washington's army. Sir Henry Clinton held the lower Hudson.

Burgoyne's fatal miscalculation was the belief that his opponent, Maj. Gen. Philip Schuyler held the maximum defensive force that could be assembled. True, volunteers from New England joined the American army slowly, and Congress finally sent Maj. Gen. Horatio Gates to take command. Washington gave him two New York regiments stationed at Peekskill and Col. Daniel Morgan's newly formed regiment of riflemen. Maj. Gen. Benedict Arnold brought back the detachment he had led against St. Leger. Gates set about placating the touchy Stark; and a mollified New England began answering his call for reinforcements, reflecting strong resentment over British use of Indians and the Jane McCrea atrocity. Burgoyne posed a threat, but there was some optimism that if the German regiments could be beaten, the British regulars could be handled as well.

The response was beyond all expectation. A *second* American army began to materialize. Gates moved northward across the Mohawk River, as far as Stillwater, on September 8. The Polish engineer Col. Thaddeus Kosciuszko laid out entrenchments on Bemis Heights (outlined by the white area above the British line on the campaign map following). The Americans occupied the heights on September 12.

Burgoyne's advance was slowed by his need to accumulate a 30-day supply of food by inadequate means of conveyance from Montreal. After Ticonderoga was captured, the movement of 42 guns tied up transport and further impeded his progress. Finally on September 13 he crossed the river below Fort Miller to the hamlet of Saratoga (now Schuylerville). The crossing occupied two days. Then his troops, reduced to slightly over 6,000, started south. On September 18 he made contact with Gates's advance and halted, unaware that he now faced a foe of 7,000.

Burgoyne divided his force into three attacking columns. Brig. Simon Fraser led 2,200 men in a westward sweep. Maj. Gen. Baron Friedrich Adolph von Riedesel commanded about 1,200 Germans who hugged the river road. The center was nominally under Brig. James Hamilton, though Burgoyne went with him. It was composed of four incomplete British regiments, amounting to about 1,200 men. Artillery batteries accompanied each column.

The remainder of Burgoyne's troops guarded baggage and boats.

On September 19 the center column moved forward in a southwesterly direction to draw closer to Fraser. An advance guard emerged from the woods onto the abandoned fields of a farm owned by Isaac Freeman. Gates ordered Arnold to send Morgan's riflemen, augmented by others under Maj. Henry Dearborn, through the woods on the south side of the fields to meet this thrust. When Morgan saw Hamilton's advance in the clearing, his men aimed for every officer present. It was 1:00 P.M. The rest of the picket fled back followed by the riflemen across the open field. They ran into Hamilton's main body, supported now by Fraser, and were repulsed. Morgan feared his corps had been lost, but his turkey call rallied them again. Burgoyne fired a signal gun that indicated he was advancing and moved up to Freeman's farm in force.

Arnold brought up seven regiments to support Morgan. In the open, the British could not withstand the rifle and musket fire, and fell back into the woods. Then, when the Americans charged into the open field, they were blasted by British cannon. Thus the conflict seesawed for several hours. Finally Burgoyne sent for Riedesel who brought reinforcements and won the day. Darkness began to fall. Burgoyne camped on the field, considering the engagement a victory, although he reported casualties of 556 killed, wounded, and captured. Gates suffered 80 killed, 200 wounded, and 36 missing, but he still occupied his strong position.

Burgoyne planned another strike on September 21 principally utilizing Fraser's column. Then he received a letter, dated September 12, from Clinton in New York, saying that in ten days he would start up the Hudson to attack Forts Clinton and Montgomery, above Peekskill. Burgoyne decided to await the effect of this diversion.

The map on the overleaf shows the British position after the engagement. Riedesel remained next to the river. Adjacent to him was Burgoyne's center, here considered part of the right wing, and to the west was the true right wing under Fraser. The cleared fields of Freeman's abandoned farm are evident in the center of the British line. The map is oriented with south at the top where the American defenses on Bemis Heights were located. It was drawn by a British participant, Lt. William Wilkinson, and gives a feeling of the dense undergrowth and broken terrain.

From the first battle of Freeman's farm and subsequent desertions, Burgoyne's strength declined to 5,000. The invaders waited. On September 28 Burgoyne wrote to Clinton asking him for instructions on whether to attack or retreat, thus deftly shifting responsibility. Clinton replied that he would not presume to give any orders to another commander. Yet he had launched a diversion and seized Forts Clinton and Montgomery from Maj. Gen. Israel Putnam, whose troops had been reduced by the two regiments sent to Gates. Clinton said nothing about sailing farther north, and understandably refused to do so without reinforcements. A sketch of the British positions in relation to West Point is shown here.

As the days passed Gates's strength increased substantially. Maj. Gen. Benjamin Lincoln brought in his 2,000 troops, while Schuyler forwarded ammunition and supplies from Albany. Two thousand New Hampshire militia had moved toward Fort Edward. Thirteen hundred Massachusetts militia were marching on Saratoga. By October 7 Gates had 11,000 men.

Still in the dark about Clinton's thrust, Burgoyne launched his second drive on October 7. He formed a 1,100-yard line across Freeman's farm, manned by only 1,500 troops. Each end reached into woods. On the west, 600 men under a Capt. Fraser were sent into the hills. Gates dispatched Morgan to deal with them, and sent Brig. Gen. Enoch Poor's brigade to strike the east end of the British line that was under Maj. John Acland. Brig. Gen. Ebenezer Learned's brigade was to try the center, where Riedesel commanded. Poor rolled up the British left, capturing the wounded Acland. Morgan routed Fraser's men, and one of the Pennsylvania riflemen killed Brig. Simon Fraser. Arnold dashed back into action and participated in an unsuccessful attack on the Balcarres's redoubt in the British center. He then gathered up Morgan's regiment with three others to seize the stronghold of Col. Heinrich von Breymann on the right. The frenzied Breymann, who had sabered four of his own men, was killed by a fifth.

The second battle ended. Burgoyne's entrenchments were now useless with Breymann's redoubt gone. He pulled back to an earlier position and counted his losses —250 captured, perhaps 350 killed and wounded, and 10 cannon taken. Gates never reported his casualties; it is believed he had about 30 killed and 100 wounded.

The Americans now occupied Freeman's farm, but Gates did not pursue his enemy. There was some cannonading on October 8, and Lincoln was wounded by a sniper. Late that night Burgoyne started his retreat northward, leaving his sick and wounded behind. He moved up to within three miles of Saratoga where Brig. Gen. John Fellows's militia lay sleeping. It rained all of the next day, and when Burgoyne finally marched in late afternoon, his wagons stuck in the mud. Fellows recrossed the river before Burgoyne arrived at Saratoga. The latter took refuge in Schuyler's mansion on the south side of Fishkill Creek. On October 10 he sent two regiments under Lt. Col. Nicholas Sutherland up the west side of the Hudson toward Fort Edward to bridge the river.

Gates followed the same day and reached the south side of Fishkill Creek. Burgoyne burned Schuyler's house before crossing into the village. Gates did not attack Burgoyne in his strong defensive position, but instead captured Burgoyne's supply boats. On October 12 Morgan and Learned crossed the creek to the west of

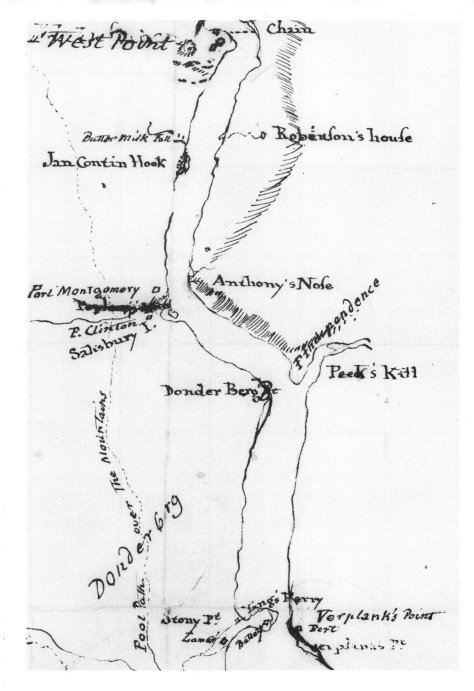

Burgoyne and moved up even with him. The British now were enveloped on three sides.

Burgoyne called a council of war and laid five proposals before it: to stand fast; attack; retreat in force; retreat without the artillery and baggage; or strike toward Albany again, if Gates shifted his strength westward. Riedesel urged making a run for Fort Edward that night, and this was decided. But at 10:00 P.M. Burgoyne cancelled the plan. He had just learned that Stark had crossed the Hudson four miles north and shut off that escape route.

The next day Burgoyne called another council. It unanimously advised negotiating for honorable terms. Gates, however, demanded unconditional surrender. The British refused, and Burgoyne proposed that his arms be surrendered, but that the men be allowed to return to England and not serve again in America. Gates agreed, uncertain of how quickly the British rescue operation was moving up the Hudson. Meanwhile, Clinton had sent out Maj. Gen. John Vaughan who burned Kingston on October 16 in an effort both tardy and too feeble to help Burgoyne. At the last moment Burgoyne tried to stall, but on October 17 he signed the convention giving up his whole force.

PLAN of the

RIVER HUDSON

Scale of Yards.

...sition of the Army under the command of Lieut. Genl. Burgoyne near Still Water;

...in which it encamped on ye 20th Septr. 1777.

Presented by
Colonel Sir Augustus Frazer.
K. C. B.

RENCES.

try } Brig. Genl. Frazer Advanced Corps.

...ne composing the Right Wing.

...nswickers } German Line composing ye Left Wing.
...nau

...17th Regt. attached to ye Store Provisions &cr.

...n.

...ssels Dragoons.
...nced Corps.
...rials.
...nadian Companies.
...y.

RENCES.

Brandywine

While Maj. Gen. John Burgoyne was meeting resistance in upper New York—which led to his surrender at Saratoga—Lt. Gen. Sir William Howe was opening his campaign to capture Philadelphia. Lord George Germain, the colonial secretary, had given his approval to Howe for a land operation after launching Burgoyne on his ill-fated expedition. Germain assumed that Howe would be successful in time to support Burgoyne if necessary. His assumption was wrong. Sir Henry Clinton, Howe's second in command in New York City, thought the move against Philadelphia was both foolish and dangerous and that a division of the army would weaken all parts.

The British objective to occupy cities rather than destroy the rebel army delayed the outcome of the war. Howe believed that if he could seize the capital and control the settled areas, it would defeat the American army by segmenting its base. It would also support the loyalists there. Howe evacuated New Jersey and put his expedition of 12,500 men and several hundred horses on board ship in sweltering weather. Finally, on July 23, 1777, he sailed out of New York harbor. Burgoyne had taken Fort Ticonderoga and seemed destined for victory on Lake George.

Washington stood at Middlebrook, N.J., unable to comprehend the intelligence brought to him about Howe's grand departure in 264 ships. Surely Howe must be heading up the Hudson in a pincer movement with Burgoyne. A week later the ships were seen off New Jersey. They entered Delaware Bay where Howe was urged to disembark his troops by Capt. Andrew Hamond, commander of a small squadron in the bay. Hamond carried the faulty intelligence that Washington was near Wilmington. But Howe could not be persuaded by the enemy's nearness; to the amazement of his shipweary men, he put back to sea.

Washington felt reasonably certain that Howe was not going to Charleston, S.C., but his real destination remained a puzzle. The American had another cause for comment: "Genl Howe's in a manner abandoning Genl Burgoyne, is so unaccountable a matter, that till I am fully assured it is so, I cannot help casting my eyes continually behind me."

It took the British a month to make a one-week voyage, owing to contrary winds, thunderstorms, and intense heat. The cavalry mounts were decimated; 170 died en route and another 150 left the ship unfit for duty. Finally on August 22 Howe's transports turned into Chesapeake Bay and sailed to the north end. He disembarked near Head of Elk, Md., on August 25 and 26, more than 50 miles southwest of Philadelphia. Washington had put his troops in motion the last of July, but was unsure in which direction to move. In search of the British army and navy, Maj. Gen. Nathanael Greene complained, "We are compelled to wander about the country like the Arabs." After the British appeared in the Chesapeake, Washington turned south and marched through Philadelphia on August 24 to await Howe below Wilmington. He had 11,000 men in four divisions, including that of Maj. Gen. Benjamin Lincoln (who was absent). Commanding the forces were Greene and Maj. Gens. John Sullivan, William Alexander (Lord Stirling), and Adam Stephen.

Howe began marching slowly northward on August 28. The weather continued hot and rainy. As he approached, Washington shifted his troops to new positions on the east side of Brandywine Creek, about 25 miles southwest of Philadelphia. Brandywine was normally too deep for wading, but several fords crossed it. It seemed reasonable to Washington that as the British moved up the Great Valley Road parallel to the creek, they would try to cross at Chadds Ford. He concentrated two divisions there, and the others lay on the right as far as three miles north. However, there were five other fords lying northward about a mile apart.

Howe's tactics resembled his advance on Long Island the year before. The troops moved in two columns on September 11. Brig. Wilhelm von Knyphausen with 5,000 men was to try to cross Chadds Ford, but this was designed as a diversionary attack. Lord Cornwallis, leading the second column of 7,500, was to continue marching north to Jeffries Ford, the last of the five, cross there, and turn back south toward Birmingham Meeting House to get behind the Americans and deliver the main blow. Washington's intelligence was so faulty and incomplete that Howe's strategy worked.

Knyphausen reached Chadds Ford at 10:30 A.M. and began cannonading the left bank. When he did not cross, Washington began to suspect that Cornwallis might show up farther north—unless he was in hiding behind Knyphausen. He ordered two divisions, Stirling's and Stephen's, back to Birmingham as a precaution and decided to attack Knyphausen with his other three divisions. When he heard that Cornwallis had not been seen farther north, he rescinded both orders. This inaccurate intelligence reinforced his suspicion that Knyphausen was acting as a decoy because of his concealed strength. Then at 2:00 P.M. Washington learned that Cornwallis, long out of sight, had indeed crossed the Brandywine at distant Jeffries Ford and was nearing Osborne's Hill, halfway back to Birmingham Meeting House. Immediately he dispatched Sullivan toward Osborne's Hill, and Stirling and Stephen to Birmingham.

Two hours later Washington heard firing to his right and rear. At the same time Knyphausen stepped up his shelling as if he meant to cross then. Washington waited perhaps 40 minutes, then decided to gamble against the Germans. He led Greene's division in a fast run to reinforce Sullivan.

Sullivan was falling back from Osborne's Hill toward Plowed Hill, next to Birmingham where Stirling and Stephen had deployed their troops. The three divisions stopped Cornwallis's advance temporarily. The British began concentrating on both ends of the American line as Greene's division came up. Washington left Sullivan in charge and rode along the line to encourage his men. The four divisions held the enemy force at bay until about

6:30 P.M. and then began retreating toward Chester. Cornwallis stopped; his men had marched 17 miles, fought for several hours, and were exhausted.

Knyphausen did cross Chadds Ford against the slight opposition of Lincoln's division. Two other brigades fell back before him and took the road to Chester, linking up finally with the other divisions. Knyphausen joined Cornwallis after dark, and Howe established headquarters at Dilworth, east of Birmingham. It was a solid British victory in clearing the route to Philadelphia, but again a trap had failed to close on the Americans.

As nearly as can be estimated, Washington lost about 200 killed, 500 wounded, and 400 captured, along with 11 cannon. Howe had 90 killed, 448 wounded, and 6 missing.

The map (overleaf) was made by an engineer with the Hessians, Capt. Reinhard Jacob Martin. He was the principal mapmaker for the Hessian army in America. Most of the Hessian maps which survive in the archives of Marburg are copies of British maps. Some are not; and this map of Brandywine apparently has no British antecedent. It was the custom of German officers to communicate military or diplomatic intelligence in French. The textual matter explaining the map is herewith translated:

Battle of the Brandywine, Sept. 11, 1777, won by the British army under General Howe, against the Rebels. *A* General Knyphausen's column. *B* First skirmish of this column's advance guard. Having forced the enemy to quit the defile *C*, Knyphausen's column widened at *D*. The enemy reinforced its outposts, *E*. General Knyphausen attacked with the Queen's Rangers and Ferguson's riflemen, followed by the rest of the column, which, after forcing the enemy to retire behind the Brandywine at *F*, positioned itself at *G* to await the attack by General Cornwallis. Cornwallis's column passed the first branch of the Brandywine at 11:00 A.M. and halted at *H*. At 2:00 P.M. it again began to march, passed the other branch of the creek, *I*, and stopped once more at *K* to reconnoiter the enemy's position, *L*. General Howe formed three columns and advanced at 4:00 P.M. by the route *M*. Arriving at *N*, he formed a line and commenced the main attack. The Guard Brigade, the Hessian Grenadiers, the 1st Battalion of English Gren-

adiers, and the 1st Battalion of Light Infantry took after the enemy, who, having been forced from the battlefield, was fleeing along *O*. The riflemen of the 2nd Battalion of Light Infantry, the 2nd Battalion of English Grenadiers, and the 4th Brigade followed the route *P*. The right wing of the enemy established a second position at *Q* and was driven out by the riflemen and the 2nd Battalion of Light Infantry. The retreating enemy met the 2nd Battalion of English Grenadiers, which had advanced too quickly and without support. Forming some brigades at *R*, the rebels fell upon the battalion at *S*, but the 4th Brigade arrived and forced the enemy back. The 2nd Battalion of Light Infantry, the 2nd Battalion of English Grenadiers, and the 4th Brigade found another enemy corps at *T*, positioned there to cover the retreat. They attacked and forced the rebels' withdrawal as daylight ended.

At 4:00 P.M. General Knyphausen took up his march at *U*, placed four cannon at *V*, and crossed the Brandywine at *W* in the following order: the 2nd Battalion of the 71st Regiment, the 4th Regiment, riflemen, Queen's Rangers, and several other troops in the order of their brigades, excluding Donop's Regiment. The latter was sent to reinforce the two other battalions of the 71st Regiment, commanding the artillery. The enemy positioned itself at *X*, with redoubts at *Y*. The head of General Knyphausen's corps, having crossed the river, attacked at *Z* and pursued the rebels along *a*. The rest of this corps marched by way of *b*. The enemy retreated, leaving four cannon at *c*, and overtook the main route to Chester by nightfall. Prevented by darkness from following the rebels, the army moved to *d*.

e The sites chosen by the enemy, facing the head of Knyphausen's column. *f* The army's camp, occupied on Sept. 12, 1777.

The 3rd Brigade was the reserve corps of General Cornwallis's column and followed as the latter advanced.

New York, January 6, 1779.
Martin
Captain, Corps of Engineers

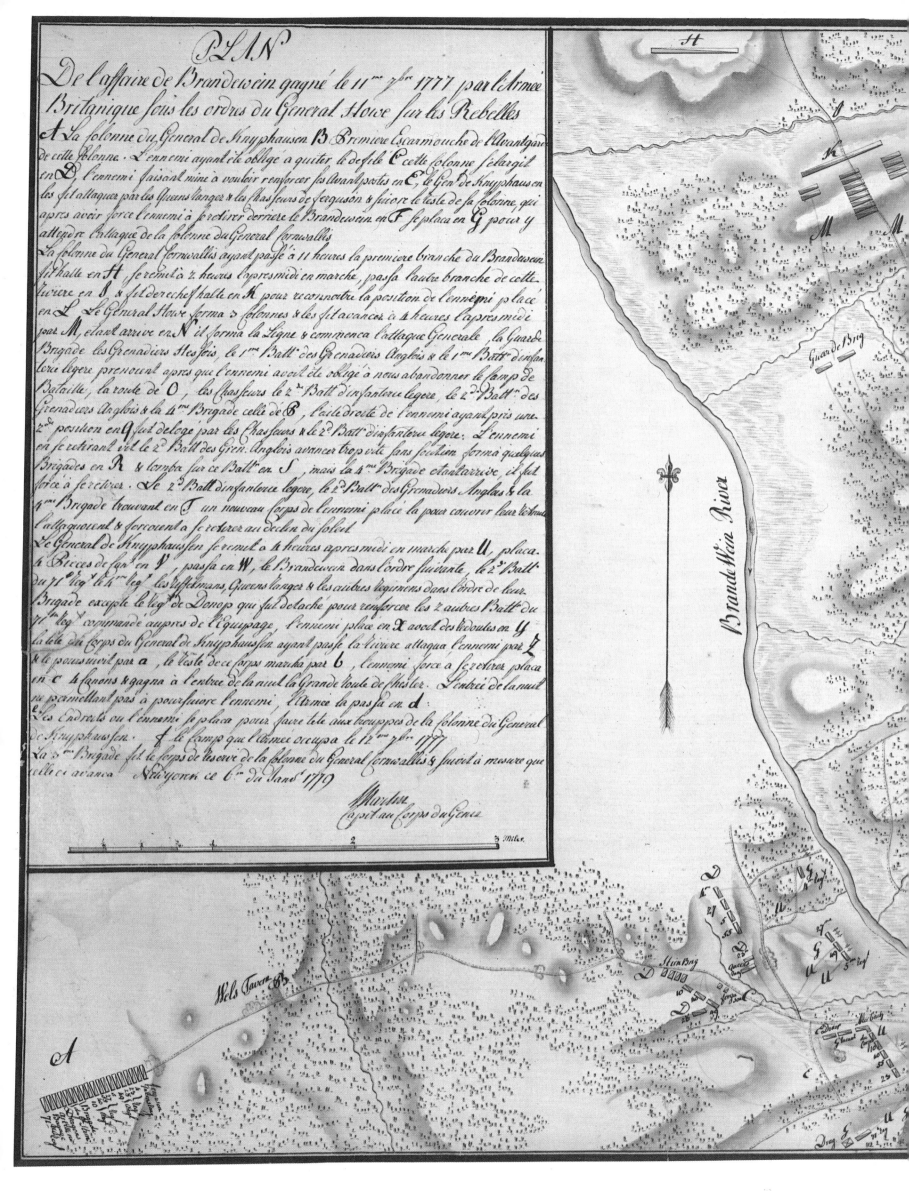

Chemin pour Lancaster

Chasseurs

Gnarde Angl
& Inf leger

Dellworth

Chemin pour Chester

Chemin pour Wilmington

Chemin pour Wilmington

Paoli and Philadelphia

Lt. Gen. Sir William Howe's plan for the reconquest of Pennsylvania was to prove ultimately untenable. After the engagement at Brandywine Creek, he defeated the Americans again, but the Continental army continued intact with reinforcements. Howe could not so easily replace his losses; his plan depended on raising units of loyalists to garrison his conquered territory.

Yet after he had disembarked at Head of Elk, Md., in late August, he found empty houses and deserted farms. Along their march northward the British sighted clouds of smoke from stores and fields set afire by the retreating inhabitants. The mirage of loyalist support was growing apparent, just as another old problem began to plague Howe. Neither sentence of death nor flogging could deter his troops from plundering the colonists' homes. Indeed, the inhabitants had fled from the hearsay horrors of Hessian marauding in New Jersey a year earlier.

Following the Brandywine victory, Howe spent several days dispatching his wounded to Wilmington. On September 16 Howe thrust his troops north in order to cut off Washington's sudden movement west. But within five miles of the enemy, Howe's intended assault was thwarted by torrential rains. The next encounter was small, but lethal.

Washington had drawn his forces slowly east, then north, and finally crossed the Schuylkill River near Germantown on September 19, 1777. He then moved northwestward to Swede's Ford. He left Brig. Gen. Anthony Wayne's division south of the river as a rear guard to harass Howe's steady advance. With about 1,500 men Wayne took up a hidden position in a woods about two miles southwest of Paoli Tavern. Because he had grown up in the area, he knew the region well. From this spot, about 12 miles west of Philadelphia, he believed he could dash out and strike at any enemy column that passed.

The location of Wayne's campsite was promptly reported to the British by local loyalists, and Howe decided to try a night attack. He selected Maj. Gen. Charles Grey to lead the assault with three regiments. He was to be supported by two other regiments later, but they did not participate in the action. Grey's men were not allowed to fire their muskets; if they could not unload them, they removed the flints. Thus the enemy would be identifiable in the dark as those who were firing. (These instructions earned Grey the nickname "No-flint.") For the British it was to be a bayonet attack, not easily undertaken at night.

Soon after midnight on September 21, Grey approached through the woods and sighted Wayne's campfires. His troops struck suddenly. Four sentries fired and then ran. The Americans turned out immediately, but in much confusion. Those silhouetted against the fires were easy targets, and many were bayoneted. They fled in panic through the woods, although Wayne did manage to drag off his four cannon.

Wayne never reported the number of his casualties. Another American officer somehow picked up the figure of 364 killed, wounded, and captured. Howe reported that the enemy had suffered 380 casualties. Local residents buried 53 mangled bodies, but these may not have been all of the dead. The true figures are not known. The British lost only 6 killed and about 23 wounded. Grey achieved a dubious distinction from what was called the "Paoli Massacre." Wayne was charged with failing to take "timely notice" of British intentions. He asked for a court-martial and was acquitted "with the highest honors."

Howe proceeded to the river at Valley Forge and then swung westward away from Philadelphia. Washington feared he was heading for the new supply depot at Reading and he hurried northwest to shield it. This was exactly what Howe intended him to do. That night Howe reversed his march to go downstream and crossed the Schuylkill at Flatland Ford. The British now stood between Washington and Philadelphia. Howe encamped at Germantown. On September 26 Cornwallis led a column into Philadelphia "amidst the acclamation of some thousands of the inhabitants, mostly women and children."

But the crowds' cheers proved hollow. From late August through September Howe had issued proclamations intended to identify loyalist strength. But his various pardons with land options in exchange for service in a provincial regiment were ineffective. The people of Pennsylvania, noted one observer, "are now almost satiated with British clemency, and numbers. . .will shortly put themselves out of British protections." Howe's reliance on loyalist support was privately ridiculed by his officers who were certain that only a clean sweep of the Continental army would win back the colonies.

Howe's great campaign had reached its goal. Yet the countryside around Philadelphia teemed with rebels, and the enemy-held Delaware River defied Howe's secure possession of the capital.

The map opposite was made by Capt. John André, a talented aide to Grey. It reveals the whole area and traces the movement of Howe's army from its landing in Elk River north to the Schuylkill and down the north side of that river to Philadelphia. The clashes en route are shown at Aiken's Tavern, Brandywine, and Paoli, along with two more to come at Germantown and the Delaware River forts.

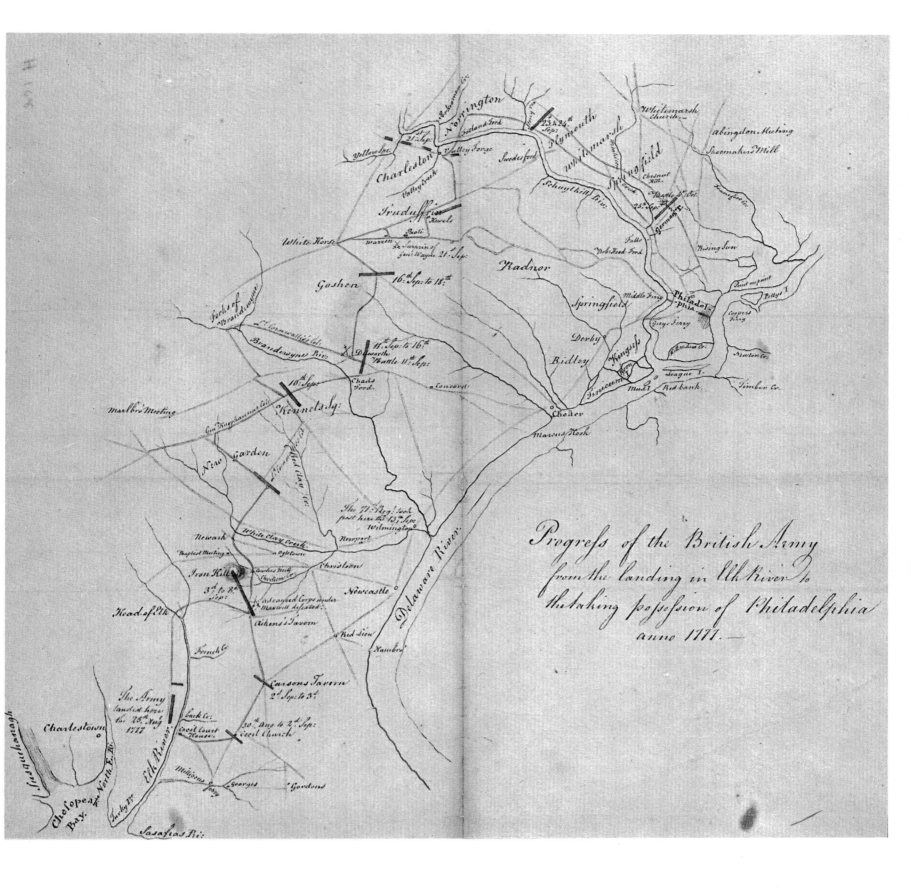

Progress of the British Army from the landing in Elk River to the taking possession of Philadelphia anno 1777.

Germantown

American intelligence reports of the divided British army dared Washington to plan an assault on Germantown. Lt. Gen. Sir William Howe, obsessed with securing uninterrupted access to the Delaware River, had dispatched some troops to take Billingsport, a vulnerable river fort near Chester. He diverted another unit to escort supplies up from Head of Elk. In Philadelphia a large detachment was left under Lord Cornwallis. Howe's main body of 9,000 troops was encamped at Germantown, five miles north of the city.

In early October Washington still had 11,000 Continentals and militia dispersed along several miles north of Germantown. Four roads led south to the village, suggesting to Washington a classic plan of battle. It was simple in conception—the convergence of four columns—but its execution was intricate, demanding exact, coordinated timing. Maryland and New Jersey militia under Brig. Gen. William Smallwood and Col. Samuel Forman were to move down the easternmost road. Pennsylvania militia under Brig. Gen. John Armstrong would occupy the western or Manatawny Road near the Schuylkill River. In between these two lines were three divisions under Maj. Gen. Nathanael Greene, representing two-thirds of the total American forces. They would proceed down the Limekiln Road to strike at what was believed to be the stronger British flank on the right. Maj. Gen. John Sullivan's column of three brigades on the Skippack Road was to head directly into Germantown, followed by Maj. Gen. William Alexander's (Lord Stirling) division. The maneuver began on the night of October 3.

If the coordination had been maintained, all four columns would have struck the British within a few minutes of one another early in the morning. But in the night march Greene's guide lost his way and delayed the strongest column by half an hour. Following rough roads, the militia units on the east were also slow to arrive at the scene. The Pennsylvania militia on the west made contact with the British left and gave battle immediately. The main strike came from Sullivan's corps. Under cover of a heavy early morning fog, he drove in the enemy pickets and rolled back Howe's light infantry and the 48th Regiment. With no immediate help on either side, especially to the east, Sullivan was forced to spread his troops sending Brig. Gen. Anthony Wayne to the extreme left.

The British fell back more than two miles. But Lt. Col. Thomas Musgrave, also shielded by the fog, sent six companies of the 40th Regiment into the Chew House, a large stone dwelling, and used it as a fort. American momentum ground to a temporary halt as Washington called a hasty staff conference to consider the problem. Some officers favored pressing forward and leaving a regiment behind to deal with the Chew House impediment. A solution was offered by 27-year-old Brig. Gen. Henry Knox, who remembered that no occupied garrison of the enemy should be left behind a forward advance. Knox had owned a bookstore in Boston before the war, and his wide reading and authority in military literature was recognized. Washington finally concurred.

The plan resulted in a one-half-hour delay. This gave Greene's force time to catch up; they came along to the east just as part of Sullivan's command concentrated its fire on the Chew House. Then, without orders, Maj. Gen. Adam Stephen led his division back westward toward the sound of battle. He blundered into Wayne's men in the fog and fired upon his fellow soldiers. Believing that the British were about to enfilade, Wayne's troops ran back, and their panic infected the rest of Sullivan's force. Despite Washington's attempt to rally his men, the attack began to fall apart. An uncontrollable retreat ensued as Greene assaulted Luken's Mill (Lewiss Mill on the map), east of the Chew House. In a dash from Philadelphia, Cornwallis appeared with a British reinforcement of three regiments. He did not pursue the exhausted Americans vigorously, and by midmorning the battle was over.

In his report to Congress, Washington blamed the fog and the Chew House "annoyance" for the collapse. Stephen was court-martialed, found guilty of drunkenness, and dismissed from the army. Greene's unfortunate tardiness was perhaps the biggest factor in blunting the attack. It may be that Washington's strategy was too sophisticated for field officers who lacked tactical experience; and, there were many new, raw soldiers among both the Continentals and the militia. What snatched victory from Washington's grasp were these imponderables. The Americans believed they had nearly succeeded at Germantown, and this lifted morale, despite losses. Washington suffered 152 killed, 521 wounded, and over 400 captured (many of these were probably counted as wounded).

Howe reported 537 killed and wounded and 14 captured. He recognized, after his narrow victory, that he could not string out his troops as he had done without courting attack. A few weeks later he evacuated Germantown and reestablished his troops in a line of forts north of Philadelphia.

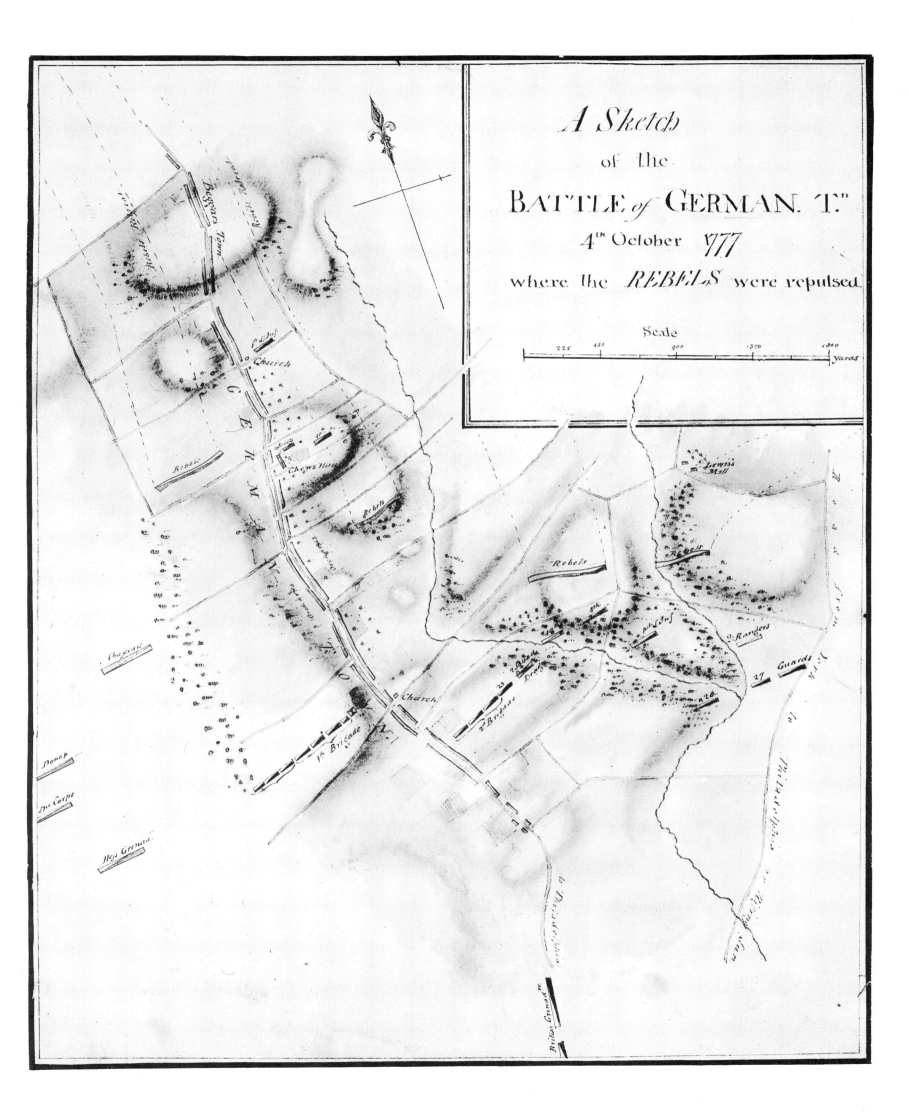

A Sketch
of the
BATTLE of GERMAN. T.
4.th October 1777
where the REBELS were repulsed.

Scale

225   450   900   1350   1000
yards

Forts Mercer and Mifflin

The British entrance into Philadelphia on September 26 did not signify complete control of the rebel capital. To properly supply and fully protect the port the British navy required access up the Delaware River to the city's docks. Yet the Americans were still in control of the river's navigation by means of a series of forts and *chevaux de frise*. The latter were sharpened stakes sunk about four feet from the water's surface and pointed downstream. In addition, the Americans had a considerable naval force, including 14 fire ships and 13 row galleys (small armed boats). These defenses were jointly under the command of Washington and the Navy Board of Congress.

The key posts stood about three miles southwest of Philadelphia where the Delaware River was deflected into two channels by marshy islands. Fort Mifflin on Port Island and Fort Mercer across the river at Red Bank, N.J., commanded the main river channel. Between them ran a triple line of 30 *chevaux de frise*. Fort Mifflin held a garrison of 450 men under Lt. Col. Samuel Smith; its four blockhouses contained four guns each, and there was a battery of 10 other cannon. Fort Mercer was a larger, stronger earthwork holding 14 cannon and a garrison of about 400 Rhode Island troops under Col. Christopher Greene. After it was inspected by a French engineer, the fort was declared too big for its garrison, and a new north wall was built inside the fort to reduce its size.

Howe's first offensive was against a vulnerable, unfinished fort at Billingsport, some five miles downstream from the key defenses. On October 1 the British took the fort without resistance and began breaking a channel through the underwater barricades there. Howe then concentrated his efforts farther upstream. In mud up to their knees, his men dragged heavy artillery onto swampy Province Island at the mouth of the Schuylkill River and almost opposite Fort Mifflin. These guns started bombarding the fort intermittently on October 15, but to no effect. The return fire from the island almost destroyed the British batteries.

Frustrated by the failure of his artillery, Howe sent Col. Carl von Donop across the river to New Jersey. He was to circle around and assault Fort Mercer from the land side. Donop approached the fort on the afternoon of October 22 and demanded surrender, threatening to show no mercy to the garrison if he was refused. Greene defied him and promised no quarter in return. That night the Hessians attacked in two columns against the north and east walls—but without scaling ladders. The column at the north wall managed to climb over and to their dismay found themselves confronted by another wall. After both wings had hunched against the walls, Greene's men showered them with musket fire at close range. Donop and several other officers were fatally wounded. The Hessians withdrew, formed again to approach the south side, and there met a similar torrent of fire plus cannon shelling from the row galleys in the Delaware River. Shattered, the enemy retreated. They suffered 153 killed and more than 200 wounded, many of whom were captured along with

20 uninjured men who feared to retreat. Greene lost 14 killed, 23 wounded, and 1 captured.

The road map of New Jersey shows Cooper's Ferry where the Hessians crossed the Delaware from Philadelphia on October 21. They followed the road to Haddonfield and encamped there for the night. Their progress the next day was delayed by a detour where a bridge was out (possibly sabotaged). It may have been Clements Bridge, above "Strawberry Farm or Isaac Ballinger's" on the map. This road led directly to Red Bank.

The British navy finally cleared some gaps in the river obstructions at Billingsport, and six vessels sailed through. They came in sight of Fort Mifflin on October 23. American cannon immediately opened up on them. Additional firepower came from gunboats near the island. The British ships took a battering. Two ran aground and were destroyed by magazine explosions with a loss of 400 men. The others retreated down the river. Two victories in two days were encouraging to the Americans, but Washington knew the delay obtained was temporary.

The large map of the river channel has one island missing. Mud Island is shown as the site of Fort Mifflin, and that identification has continued in many accounts. Actually the fort was on Port Island, between Hog Island downstream and Mud Island upstream. The map was probably drawn at the time of the final capture, even though the date is omitted from the "Plan" in the lower right-hand corner.

For the past two months Howe's supply line had been the long and vulnerable overland route from the head of the Chesapeake where he had disembarked in late August. Since the British had taken Philadelphia, supplies were becoming critically low. Howe could not rely on the overland route to provision his Philadelphia quarters through the winter. Furthermore, he required direct water communication with both New York and England. If he failed to open the Delaware soon, he would have to abandon the hard-won city.

Howe's next assault on Fort Mifflin began on November 10. For several weeks amidst severe storms he had built up heavier artillery on Province Island and constructed a floating battery of 22 cannon. The British bombarded the fort for six days. Washington considered sending troops to attack the artillery on the British island, but could not manage it. The stubborn garrison answered the enemy fire as best it could, but gradually the fort guns were knocked out. Smith was wounded and carried over to the New Jersey shore. On November 15 British warships (including the *Vigilante* and *Somerset* on the map) reappeared and swung in so close to the island that marines could fire down into the fort. Only two cannon could be used, and then they were hit. That night Maj. Simeon Thayer ordered evacuation of his reduced garrison, and under cover of darkness the men were rowed to Fort Mercer. At least 20 had been killed and 40 wounded. British officers landing on the island after the withdrawal were stunned by the damage the old fort had sustained.

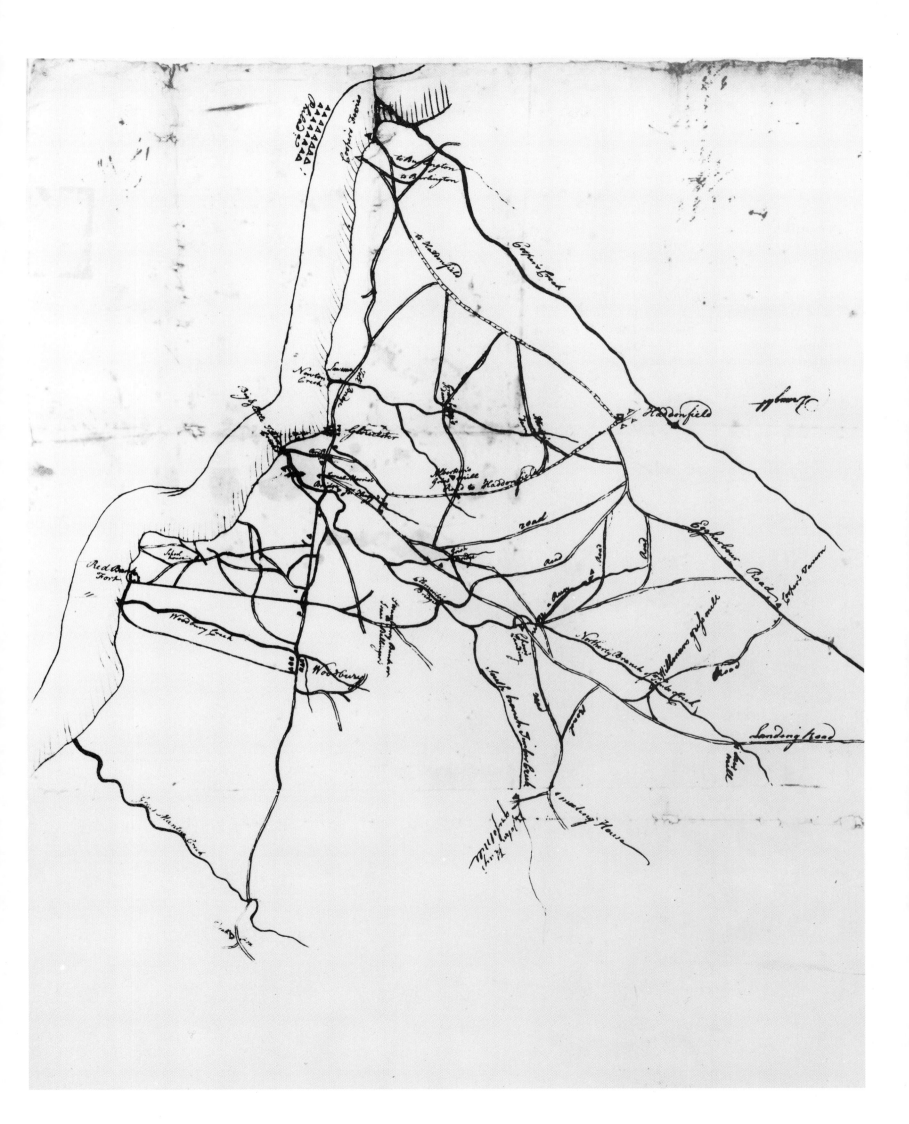

Lord Cornwallis now moved into New Jersey to prevent any support from reaching Fort Mercer. As he approached Red Bank, Greene decided he could not endure a siege. On the night of November 20-21 he abandoned the fort. At last the Delaware River was open to the British.

The campaign of 1777 was now concluded. The invasion from Canada had failed completely; Burgoyne's army was captured. Howe had occupied Philadelphia after three battles, but its value to the British was negligible. Washington's army was still in the field. It would be ready to resume combat in the spring. Sensing his own failure to achieve either peace or victory, Howe had submitted his resignation on October 22.

References.

A. Battery of two 32 p.rs
B. Battery of Six 24 p.rs one
   8 Inch Mortar, & one 8 Inch
   Howitzer.
C. Battery of one 8 Inch Mortar
   & one Howitzer do.
D. 13 Inch Mortar.
   Reference to Mud Island &
E. Water or Grand Battery of
   30 pieces of Cannon, mostly
   dismounted before the General
   attack.
E.E.F. Block Houses 4 pieces of
   Cannon each.
G.G.G. Line of Pickets for Musq-
   ry.
H.H.H. Troup de Loups.
I. Traverses.
K. Barracks.

The Schuylkill.

Block
House

Battery to defend the
entrance of the Schuyl-
kill. 2.18 p.rs

18 p.r never fired.

REEDY ISLAND.

Red Bank

32 p.r

Rebel Shipping
under Cover of
the Works on the
Bank.

NIUD ISLAND.

2.12 p.rs

Wharf

Sloop 4.18 6.rs

Vigilant 16
24 p.rs

Rebel Ships to Cover the Gondolas.

Rebel Gondolas heavy Guns
firing on the Somerset.

B Attacking the
Vigilant & Sloop.

Gondolas firing on the
Ships that attacked a Two
32 p.rs Battery on the Jersey
Shore.

HOG ISLAND.

Chevaux de Frize

The Somerset
64 Guns, only fired her
Bow Chase during the
attack.

Course of the Vigilant coming in

PLAN.
of the General attack
on
Fort Mifflin the   of

The Rebels evacuated it
and burnd the Barracks
and Line of Pickets about
11 'clock at night, taken in
Possession early next Morning.

Valley Forge

When Washington moved into winter quarters in December, 1777, he chose a location between British-held Philadelphia and the Continental Congress at York. Valley Forge, 18 miles northwest of Philadelphia and on the south side of the Schuylkill River was not a town, nor hardly a settlement. Maj. Gen. Baron de Kalb thought it must have been chosen on the advice of a traitor, a speculator, or a council of ignoramuses. Yet it had some military advantages. The so-called valley was a good defensive spot hemmed in by a river, two creeks, and hills. It provided an abundant water supply and ample wood for fuel and the construction of shelters.

Washington and his men arrived there on December 19. He had left two Maryland brigades at Wilmington, some small detachments at Lancaster and York, one regiment in New Jersey, and nine regiments stationed on the Hudson. About 15,000 officers and men went with him to Valley Forge, but 2,500 were "ineffective" from sickness and lack of clothing. All troops lacked outer coats, and one-half had no blankets. One-third were without shoes or breeches. Almost no medicines were available for the sick, and worst of all was the extreme scarcity of food. In order to build huts they had to find hammers, axes, and saws; nails could not be procured.

However, it was not primarily the snow and cold that paralyzed the camp, but military mismanagement, civilian indifference, and graft. Commissary General John Trumbull, who was responsible for obtaining food, became sick and returned to Connecticut leaving an onerous job to his deputy. Thomas Mifflin, the quartermaster general in charge of procuring military supplies and blankets, was simply unequal to the task. Clothing was either not ordered or not made up; civilian contractors bought grain and flour to sell to the British and loyalists in New York and New England; in New Jersey, pork spoiled for lack of transport to camp.

The effects of neglect, shortages, and frustration hobbled the desperate army. Huts, each measuring 14 x 16 feet, were not ready until the latter part of January. The men without clothes had to wrap themselves in blankets, and those without shoes were unable to leave their crowded huts. Frostbite and scabies were commonplace; smallpox spread rapidly. The records kept by the adjutant general reveal some mournful figures. At the end of December the army had 2,087 sick in camp and 5,008 absent because of sickness, a total of 32 percent of the paper figure of those 22,000 men in and around Valley Forge. The number declined in January, 1778, but in February there were 3,201 sick present and 3,680 sick absent, or 35 percent of a reduced force of 19,400. The ill dropped two percentage points in March and declined a little more in April and May. As for deaths, there were 90 in December, no figure was recorded for January, 292 occurred in February, 431 in March, 414 in April (including the Hudson River contingent), and 390 in May.

Still, the winter was not all gloom and stagnation. Late in February, Baron Friedrich von Steuben, a former staff captain and aide to Frederick the Great, arrived in camp and was soon made temporary inspector general to train the Americans as soldiers. Benjamin Franklin had slyly represented him as a Prussian lieutenant general, and he was received by Congress with deference, especially when he volunteered to serve without pay. Speaking French to an interpreter who translated his shouted orders, Steuben began to train the ragged troops in formations and movements. Drill methods were practiced from 9:00 A.M. to 5:00 P.M. with one meal break. At night Steuben composed a manual which was translated and copied for use by officers. With Steuben's influence Washington intended to challenge the British army with conventional methods of warfare. He had spurned the radical ideas advocated by Maj. Gen. Charles Lee for a war of raids and welcomed Steuben's efforts to develop the Continentals into competitive professional forces.

In early March Mifflin was replaced by Maj. Gen. Nathanael Greene, who at first greeted the news with a disappointed "who ever heard of a quartermaster in history as such?" But he acted vigorously, and foraging expeditions soon ranged into New Jersey and Delaware as well as central Pennsylvania. By the end of March food and clothing were in comparative abundance; the crisis had passed. In addition, Steuben's training had produced a disciplined, increasingly professional army with more resilient fighting capabilities.

The map opposite is an anonymous sketch that came into the possession of Sir Henry Clinton. On the verso is the title: "Plan of Washingtons position," and a notation: "Mr. Parker late a Mercht in Virginia now at Philadelphia." North is at the bottom of the map, as Valley Forge lies south of the river. Washington's headquarters was in a stone house belonging to Isaac Potts. The other marked triangles are apparently private residences, except for "B Meetg," which is the Baptist meeting house. The bridge across the river was built by troops under the direction of Maj. Gen. John Sullivan.

The map is an indication of British efforts at reconnaissance on Valley Forge. Still, the Americans' position was too strong for a frontal assault and a winter campaign seemed unorthodox. Since his resignation was awaiting action in London, Sir William Howe may not have wanted to risk an action.

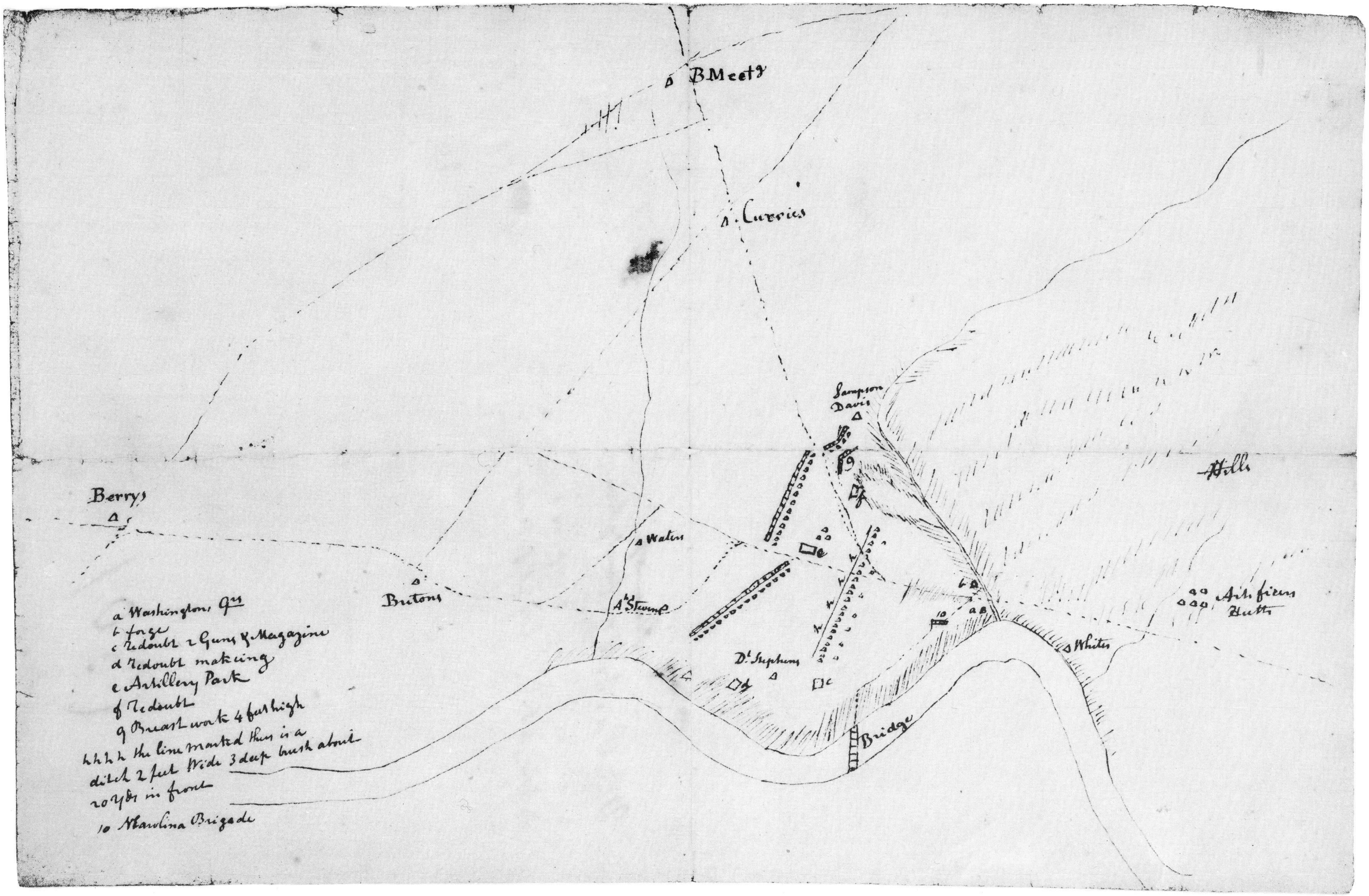

Hill

Ash field
Bratton

White

Bridge

Sampson
Davis

Dr Septum

Weston

A.S. Trump

Bratton

Curries

B Meet?

Berrys

a Washingtons Gut
b Forge
c Redoubt 2 Guns & Magazine
d Redoubt mounting
e Artillery Park
f Redoubt
g Breastwork 4 feet high
h.h.h. the line mounted then in a
ditch 2 feet Pede 3 deep bush about
20 feet in front
10 Carolina Brigade

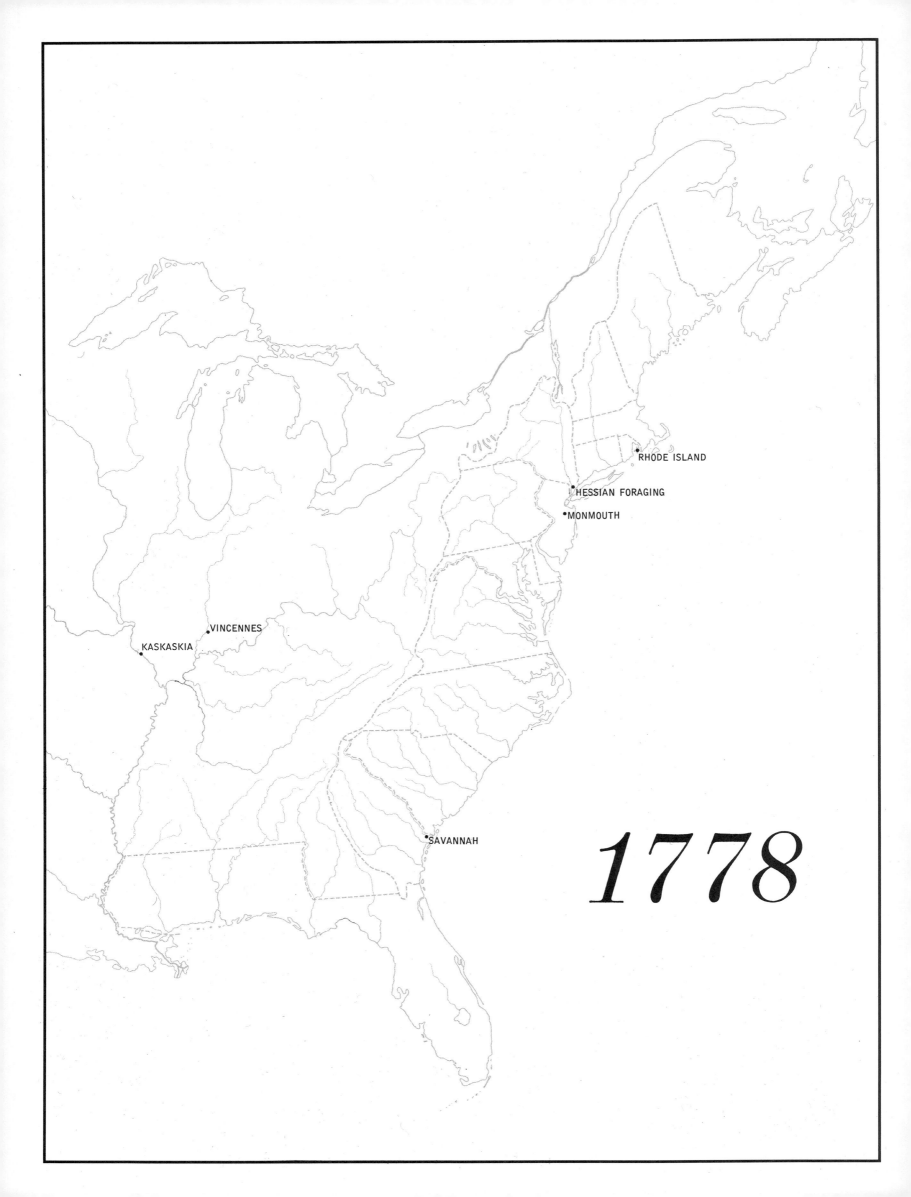

RHODE ISLAND

HESSIAN FORAGING

MONMOUTH

VINCENNES

KASKASKIA

SAVANNAH

1778

For the British army in America, 1778 was a year of retrenchment and defense. The vast effort of the previous year to secure territorial dominion in Pennsylvania and New York was not to be repeated. Instead, the French declaration of war in support of the American cause predicated a revision of British strategy.

Throughout the war, British bases in America depended on access to the sea. French intervention jeopardized this relationship. At the beginning of 1778, the British held only Philadelphia, Rhode Island, and New York harbor within the area of rebellion. These posts were protected by about 25,000 troops and a naval fleet of six ships of the line (averaging 64 guns each) and three ships of 50 guns. They opposed equivalent American forces at Valley Forge, Providence, and the Hudson Highlands and were challenged by a French fleet of eleven ships of the line (averaging 74 guns each) and one of 50 guns.

The French intervention also opened the war to a global perspective and committed available British troops to other theaters. In the minds of eighteenth-century European statesmen, the sugar-rich West Indies were a higher priority than North America. The British cabinet ordered 5,000 troops withdrawn from the three occupied stations and sent them to invade St. Lucia. The protection of garrisons in East and West Florida diverted another 3,000. Clearly, the initiative for war in America was no longer with the British.

In order to fulfill the larger commitments of empire, the British ministry decided to abandon Philadelphia. One-half of the forces were to be sent to Florida and the West Indies, while the remainder went overland to New York. Concurrently, a peace commission was dispatched from London with instructions to negotiate virtually everything short of independence. Offensive statutes were to be repealed and offenders pardoned. Yet from all perspectives the effort was futile. The London delegation was sent to Philadelphia without being informed that the city was to be abandoned. Independence was the only issue on which the Americans would negotiate and the commissioners were not prepared to grant this concession. And it was not a matter of dealing from strength. The British army had been humiliated at Saratoga and the preeminence of the Royal Navy was about to be threatened by the entry of the French. No one gave peace much hope.

When Sir William Howe sailed for England on May 25, control of the army in America passed to his second in command, Sir Henry Clinton. Clinton had important political connections in England and was momentarily popular. His prickly nature was known but his military ability was also highly regarded. To him fell the burden of organizing the withdrawal from Philadelphia and dispensing one-third of his army to distant commands. Ten days after the evacuation began on June 18, he was confronted by the American army at Monmouth. Clinton had hoped for a major battle to draw out and defeat the Americans but the topographic conditions were unfavorable. His successful rear-guard action enabled the British to reach Sandy Hook on July 1. There they were met by transports, and the last units reached New York five days later. Not a moment too soon. The powerful French fleet was sighted off New Jersey on July 7. Had the British army taken the water transit from Philadelphia they would have been lost. Had the keels of the French ships been higher in the water they might have crossed the bar into New York harbor and done considerable damage. Instead the attack was diverted to Rhode Island where a poorly coordinated operation with the American army was defeated by a resourceful British commander.

The precariousness of the British position in America had been rescued only by good fortune and prudent leadership. By the end of the year the strength of the army had declined to about 14,000 effectives and the commander had submitted his resignation—not to be accepted. The focus of war dissolved south to St. Lucia, where a British convoy and transports raced and beat the superior French fleet running parallel; and also west to the Wabash and Mohawk rivers, where American expeditions wrenched control from the British and Indian alliance.

In terms of cartography, the year produced no effort to systematically survey occupied territory. No large-scale triangulations were attempted despite the presence of 21 members of the Corps of Engineers. Returns for 1777 indicate that four persons were paid as chainbearers. But after Capt. John Montresor's survey of the Philadelphia vicinity they must have been inactive. Montresor had evolved a separate engineer command in Philadelphia at the time that he obtained a staff appointment under Sir William Howe. With evacuation from the American capital, all engineer activities were reconcentrated in the New York drawing room.

Surveying required different skills from the drawing of maps. It was the responsibility of the Drawing Room in the Tower of London to assign draftsmen to the various military commands throughout the empire, but no allotment was made to America. Even though the London office employed between 38 and 52 draftsmen during the war, it was contended that none could be spared. The expansion of the Corps of Engineers was intended to provide for this service, but of the 15 engineers taken into the corps from the Drawing Room after 1775 none was put on the American establishment. The shortage of drawing talent was answered by improvisation. Montresor's son was paid as a draftsman, but it is likely that the position was a sinecure since no maps can be attributed to him. Two draftsmen who appear on an engineer return for June, 1777, must have been paid from the Extraordinary Accounts for the army. Finally, John Hills may have been attached to the drawing room in New York while he served as a volunteer waiting to obtain an officers commission. He constructed a series of route maps of the movement of the British army across New Jersey in 1778.

Monmouth

After the French alliance with the Americans was confirmed early in 1778, King George III accepted the resignations of Lord Richard and Sir William Howe and took more active charge of British strategy in America. He ordered Sir Henry Clinton to assume command and to abandon Philadelphia. A detachment of 5,000 troops was to attack the French West Indian island of St. Lucia, and 3,000 more men were to be sent to Florida.

Clinton journeyed to Philadelphia in May, 1778, bade goodbye to William Howe, and made plans for pulling out of the city. Ships that were in the Delaware River were needed to transport heavy equipment, the wounded, and 3,000 loyalists who felt obliged to leave the city. The 10,000 British troops were, therefore, to march across New Jersey to reach New York City.

At Valley Forge a gaunt winter had given way to a warm spring of renewed American morale founded on improved training and adequate supplies. When Clinton crossed the Delaware into New Jersey on June 18, Washington, who had been waiting for an indication of the enemy's plans, detached Maj. Gen. Benedict Arnold to occupy abandoned Philadelphia. He then took off northeastward with 13,000 troops in pursuit of the British.

On June 24 Washington called a council of war to decide whether the army should merely harass the retreating British or seek a major engagement. Maj. Gen. Charles Lee argued emphatically for a passive role by magnifying the risk of committing unsophisticated American troops against British regulars on the latter's terms. Two generals sided with him. Favoring a major offensive in varying degrees were five other commanders. Lt. Col. Alexander Hamilton characterized the council as doing "honor to the most honorable body of midwives and to them only." A compromise was reached to avoid a general action, but to advance a force of 1,500 to "act as occasion may serve." However, when Washington learned that Clinton was heading away toward Monmouth Court House (the local name for Freehold), he decided to raise the advance detachment to 4,000 and give the command to the Marquis de Lafayette. Lee claimed its leadership as second in command of the army. Washington accommodated him, despite Lee's stated opposition to the proposed engagement.

Clinton reached Monmouth on the afternoon of June 26 after a tiring march of 19 miles in suffocating heat. He took a strong defensive position and chose to rest there the next day and resume the march early on June 28. Washington's men had arrived at Cranbury, ten miles west of Monmouth, on June 26. The following day, Lee's advance force approached Englishtown, six miles west of the enemy camp. His new orders were to attack as soon as Clinton began leaving Monmouth.

Before dawn on June 28, Brig. Wilhelm von Knyphausen began moving 10 battalions and the army's 1,500 wagons on the road to Middletown. Cornwallis followed with another division of troops. A rear guard of 1,500 to 2,000 remained behind.

Lee's approach from Englishtown passed through three ravines formed by Wemrock Brook and its tributaries. This terrain had not been reconnoitered by either Washington or Lee. Lee launched his attack on the rear guard's flank beyond the farthest ravine. Clinton, who had expected the assault, sent his rearmost division back along the road against the Americans. The action from this point on became confused and complex. Lafayette and Brig. Gens. Anthony Wayne and Charles Scott, all in the front lines, apparently were unsure of Lee's plan of operation. A series of orders and counterorders carried by mounted messengers further perplexed the officers. There was some danger that a part of Lee's force would be trapped in one of the ravines. Then, a backward movement by Scott and Wayne was construed by other units as a retreat, and all organization dissolved.

Riding in from Englishtown, Washington heard the sounds of battle and received a report that Lee's troops were retreating in confusion. In disbelief, Washington rode forward and confronted Lee. There occurred a heated exchange of words. Washington turned away to rally the men. He established a temporary defense until his main body formed a solid line.

Clinton, encouraged by Lee's retreat, reorganized his troops for a general engagement. But he was checked when he came up against Washington's line. Clinton tried to get around the American left under Maj. Gen. William Alexander (Lord Stirling) but was repulsed. Cornwallis then struck at the American right under Maj. Gen. Nathanael Greene and was stopped. Beneath a scorching afternoon sun, Wayne's troops, in the center, managed to turn back three attacks. Soon after 5:00 P.M., Clinton realized that victory was hopeless, and he began withdrawing his forces. Washington ordered a counterattack, but the thirsty and exhausted troops began to collapse after an advance of a few hundred yards. Clinton rested his men as dusk fell and then resumed his march at midnight. His army reached Middletown on the next morning, and on June 30 proceeded to Sandy Hook. During the next several days the British were transported to New York.

Washington lost 69 killed, another 37 dead of sunstroke, 161 wounded, and 95 missing. Clinton's losses are uncertain; he reported 147 dead, 170 wounded, and 64 missing. But evidently he did not count his German allies, for the Americans buried 251 of the enemy.

Monmouth was the last major revolutionary battle in the North between the two armies. And, it was the last time that Lee would command American troops. He demanded a court-martial and was tried and convicted on three counts: disobedience of orders, making an unnecessary retreat, and disrespect toward the commander in chief. Whether he was guilty of the first two is a matter of conjecture, but his letters disproved any innocence of the third. Sentenced to a one-year suspension of command, he was dismissed from the service entirely after writing an insolent letter to Congress.

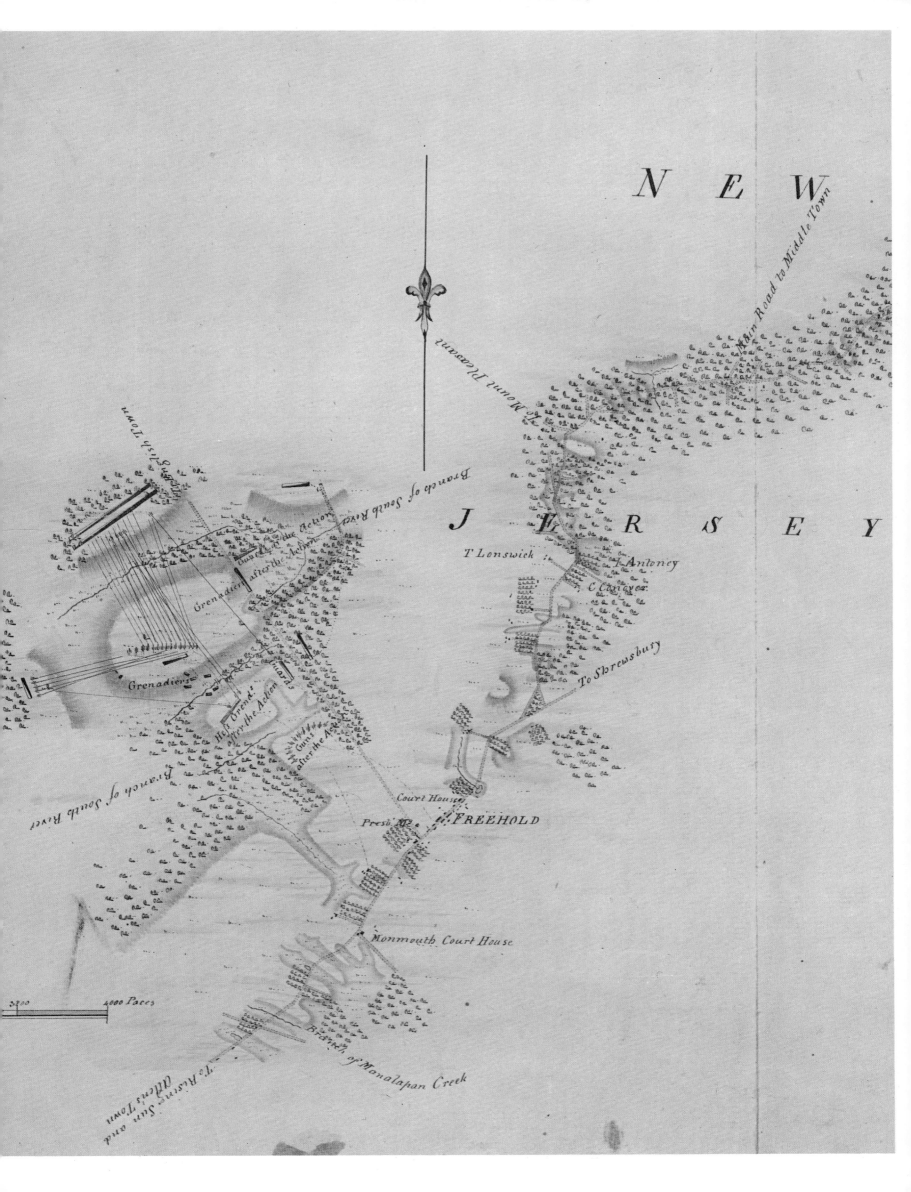

N E W

J E R S E Y

Main Road to Middle Town

To Mount Pleasant

Branch of South River

To English Town

Guards after the Action

Grenadiers after the Action

Grenadiers

Hess Grend: after the Action

Guards

Guns after the Action

Branch of South River

T Lonswick

J. Antoney

C Conver

To Shrewsbury

Court House

Presb. M.

FREEHOLD

Monmouth Court House

3800   4000 Paces

To Rising Sun and Allens Town

Bridge of Monalapan Creek

Hessian Foraging

The procurement of fuel, livestock, and especially forage preoccupied the troops of the British army in America. Foraging required ceaseless exertions, for the most part on a small scale, and wore down men and equipment. Supply ships from England imported 5,840 tons of oats annually, but the requirement to transport food and stores prevented the shipment of hay. A daily ration per horse consisted of 20 pounds of hay and 9 pounds of oats. In desperate times, as in the winter of 1776, the ration was reduced to 14 pounds of hay and 10 pounds of oats for cavalry mounts and 8 pounds of hay and 10 pounds of oats for wagon horses. After 1779, rough rice from the South was transshipped as a partial supplement in place of unobtainable hay. Multiplied by the average complement of 4,000 army horses, the consumption level reached incredible proportions requiring 18 tons of oats and 40 tons of hay every day.

The ministry had high hopes to develop America as a reliable source of supply but these expectations were never fully realized. Commanders felt comfortable to plan initiatives only when they had a substantial reserve of provisions. The recommended level was a six-month margin, and when it fell to two months, evacuation was seriously considered. Yet the minimum supply was reached for an agonizing total of 16 months during the first six years of British military presence in America. In the last half of 1778, a shortfall developed through the contract system and man and beast alike were to suffer. A provision crisis of the first magnitude enveloped the army.

The presence of the French fleet in American waters jeopardized reliance on Britain as a source of supply. When the Comte d'Estaing first appeared off Sandy Hook in July, 1778, there was considerable fear that the anticipated convoy of provision ships would be captured. As it turned out, the British ships had been routed to Philadelphia, uninformed that the army had left, and did not reach New York until September. Throughout the summer, food for the troops had been so scarce that they lived a virtual hand-to-mouth existence. In August, the army was down to a 22-day supply of flour and a 33-day ration of meat. By January, 1779, after the provisions of the last convoy had been exhausted, commodities were down to a desperate 4-day level. Only the providential arrival of more supply ships staved off a collapse of the army at New York.

Raids were designed to supplement the import arrangement. In September, Maj. Gen. Charles Grey took a force to Martha's Vineyard and obtained 10,000 sheep and 300 cattle. While these figures appear large, they answered the army's meat requirement for a period of only two weeks. But the principal area of foraging activity was the perimeter of New York City after Philadelphia had been evacuated in May. The territory between American bases in the Hudson Highlands and the entrance to Manhattan Island at Kingsbridge was patrolled by both sides. Lt.

Col. John Graves Simcoe, who commanded the loyalist Queen's Rangers, estimated that 1,500 American troops were foraging in the area that summer. He described their tactics as patterned after the Indians and that they mislabeled their patrols, "in their antiquated dialect, *scouting*." The American units averaged about 30 men per patrol.

Simcoe described the terrain as, "irregular, intersected with woods, and so broken and covered with stone walls as to be most liable to ambuscades; the inhabitants were, by no means, to be trusted." This countryside formed a no-man's land and was frequently contested by both sides. On August 31, Simcoe intercepted 60 Stockbridge Indians who were under treaty to aid the American army and killed and wounded 40.

The British launched a major expedition to Valentine's Hill on September 24. Brig. Wilhelm von Knyphausen and Maj. Gen. James Grant marched 4 miles north from Kingsbridge and deployed along a front between the Hudson River and the Bronx River, as shown on the map. The provincial units under Simcoe formed a flying camp to the east of the Bronx River. This show of strength was not seriously contested, although Maj. Henry ("Light Horse Harry") Lee ambushed a patrol of 15 mounted Yägers.

Meanwhile, Lord Cornwallis took a force of 3,000 men to the Jersey shore under Grey and Maj. Gen. Edward Mathew. These troops successfully foraged in the Hackensack area. According to Maj. Carl Leopold Baurmeister, "It was General Clinton's intention to procure all these necessities either by paying for them outright or by giving receipts." The British were opposed by American militia under Brig. Gen. Nathaniel Heard, and a plan was devised to send the 71st Regiment and the Queen's Rangers across the Hudson and encircle the Americans from the north. Simcoe and the British used 25 flatboats to float across the Hudson on the night of September 27, which required considerable knowledge of tidal patterns and shoals. The American forces, however, had changed their position and the envelopment failed. Simcoe's units rounded up cattle and returned to the east shore the next evening.

The effort at foraging in the vicinity of Valentine's Hill came to nothing. Only 50 tons of hay were found at Mamaroneck and the "destitute population allow no surplus." British and Hessian forces were withdrawn back to Kingsbridge on October 10. Cornwallis was more fortunate; he obtained an unexpected abundance of provisions. In a single day, 30 sloops returned with full loads to New York.

The map is oriented with northeast at the top, and the deployment is consistent with the entry in the journal of Baurmeister, who served as adjutant to the Hessian commanders. His entry for Sept. 24 reverses the order of the Minnigerode and Lengerke regiments and places the 63rd and 71st regiments between the 49th and 4th.

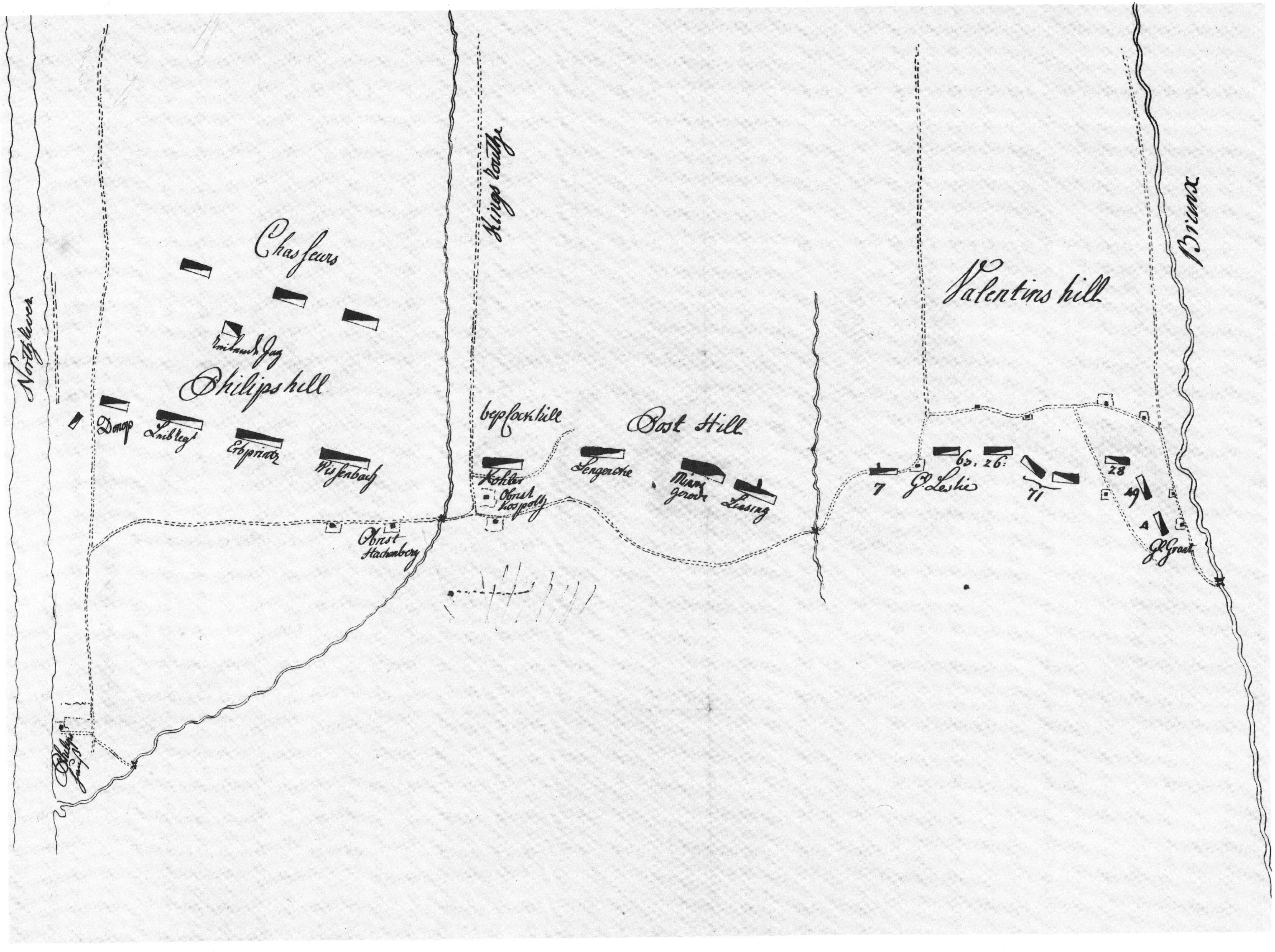

Chasseurs
Philipshill
Donop
Leibregt
Erbprintz
Wissenbach
Kings bridge
Kohler
Post Hill
Valentins hill
Bronx
7
Gl. Leslie
63. 26.
71
28
49
4
Gl. Grant

Rhode Island

After the seizure of Newport in late 1776, the British occupation of the port over the next one and one-half years was comparatively routine. The troops spent most of this time on guard duty and in building and repairing the island's fortifications. Occasionally rebels on the mainland provoked the British outposts to return artillery fire, or rebel ships from Providence attempted to elude the enemy batteries and sail out to sea. The British were content to maintain an alert defense rather than to expand their perimeter onto the mainland. Yet vigilant intelligence operations were conducted. In October, 1777, for example, the Americans at Providence detained a British sloop that had sailed upriver under a flag of truce; the ship's commander had used the maneuver to take a sketch of the river, with soundings. His espionage was uncovered by the rebels.

In July, 1777, the British commander at Newport, Col. Richard Prescott, was captured in a daring raid (a year later he was exchanged for Maj. Gen. Charles Lee). Now and then British regiments would be ordered elsewhere; by mid-1778 the garrison had been reduced from 6,000 to 3,000. However, these events and the normal process of collecting provisions and fodder did little to relieve the tedium of the garrison's life. Desertions were common and suicide not unknown. One officer noted that "We attempt nothing against the enemy by which [the men's] minds might be engaged. Their present inactive state, while all the rest of the army is in motion, naturally leads some to gloomy reflections." But in the summer of 1778 Newport became the focal point of the war. This operation marked the first appearance of the French army on behalf of the American cause.

In early July a French fleet of 16 warships, with transports carrying 4,000 soldiers under the command of the Comte d'Estaing, arrived off Delaware Bay. Unable to cross the bar at Sandy Hook with his deep-draft ships to attack the smaller British fleet in New York harbor, d'Estaing sailed northeast. He had agreed to combine operations against Newport with an American land force under Maj. Gen. John Sullivan.

Sullivan, whose force of 1,000 Continentals had been threatening the post since March, was authorized by Washington to call up the New England militia. In addition, Maj. Gen. Nathanael Greene, a native of Rhode Island, and the Marquis de Lafayette were sent to support Sullivan with two veteran brigades under Brig. Gens. James Varnum and John Glover. On July 29, the French fleet reached Point Judith, near Newport, where Sullivan and d'Estaing conferred. It was decided that d'Estaing would land his troops on the west side of the island of Rhode Island (Newport was on the island's southern tip—see map on pages 72–73). Sullivan would march his men from Providence and cross over to the east side of the island. Plans were delayed until the arrival of the militia—6,000 strong under command of Maj. Gen. John Hancock, a former president of Congress—on August 5. Sullivan now assumed the field with a troop strength of 8,500.

The American command believed this attack to be a foregone victory. The allied force was several times larger than the British garrison. Moreover, two of the French ships had already created panic by sailing up the east, or Sakonnet, channel. The British garrison of 3,000 was under the resourceful command of Maj. Gen. Robert Pigot. Ever since Sullivan began preparations that spring, Pigot had conducted raids on his supply depots. Four British frigates were burned to prevent their capture. Two other ships and several transports were scuttled to block the French from the passage.

Yet relations between d'Estaing and Sullivan soon threatened to disturb the offensive. Finding the northern tip of the island abandoned, Sullivan moved his men across ahead of the French landing. D'Estaing resented this breach of etiquette, but before he could embark more than a small portion of his force, he sighted British sails to the south.

In New York Vice Adm. Richard Howe had received a reinforcement of four warships as the first installment of Lord John Byron's squadron. On August 1, he departed for Newport with a fleet of one 74-gun man-of-war, seven 64's, five 50's, six frigates, and nine smaller vessels. Troop transports were refused; the French fleet was to be the only objective.

During the night of August 9-10, the southern winds shifted to the north, and in the morning d'Estaing abandoned Sullivan and crowded sail to confront Howe. The outgunned British fleet declined to take the initiative of entering the harbor. When d'Estaing came out, the two fleets maneuvered for position for a day and a half. On the second night a gale blew up and scattered both. As a result, several ships were damaged and others met singly in combat without decisive results. Howe turned back to New York to refit. D'Estaing gathered his battered fleet and returned to Newport on August 20.

Meanwhile, on August 15 Sullivan had moved close enough to the Newport fortifications to dig parallels and begin siege operations. Initially encouraged by the reappearance of the French, he soon learned that d'Estaing intended to sail to Boston for repairs. To Sullivan's consternation Lafayette supported these objections; when d'Estaing insisted on going, he was urged to at least leave his 4,000 men. Without these troops, it was argued, the attack would falter. But d'Estaing's officers reported that the troops would fight only under their French commander. There was no resolution. On August 22 the French sailed away. Lafayette, chagrined by his compatriot's action, rode to Boston in seven hours for a last attempt to persuade d'Estaing to return to the Americans' aid. He failed.

News of the French withdrawal had frightened and dismayed the militia, and in a few days one-half deserted. Sullivan complained indelicately in general orders of the "sudden and unexpected departure of the French fleet." He then made an effort to reassure his men that because they still outnumbered the enemy, they could yet achieve victory. However, on August 28, he received word that British reinforcements were on their way from New York. The American forces retreated north.

Pigot now moved out in pursuit. Sullivan's rear guard kept the enemy at a distance until Butts Hill opposite the ferry was fortified. The British established themselves on two hills to the south. On August 29 their right wing attacked the brigades of Varnum and Glover under Greene and was driven back. Pigot shifted his assault to the American right under Sullivan, who sustained three attacks before forcing the British to retreat in disorder. A new regiment of Rhode Island blacks, both slave and free, distinguished itself in the action under Col. Christopher Greene.

Pigot returned to Newport on August 30 to bring up more artillery. But Glover's brigade of Massachusetts fishermen had begun ferrying the American army across the channel to Tiverton and to Bristol. Only a few hours later, Sir Henry Clinton reached Newport with 4,000 reinforcements after contrary winds had becalmed the transports for several days. He was too late to prevent Sullivan's escape and unfairly criticized Pigot for a preemptory advance that sprung the trap.

Losses were about equal for both sides. Thirty Americans and 38 British were killed. Sullivan reported 137 wounded and 44 missing; of Pigot's force, 210 were wounded and 12 missing.

D'Estaing was blamed for the disrupted offensive. Sullivan and several of his officers had signed a letter of protest, referring to the stain on "the honor of France." Lafayette felt obliged to defend his countryman. Despite Washington's tactful efforts to restore harmony with the allies, the citizens of New England, at least, remained hostile to the French for over a year.

Newport continued under British control until its evacuation late in 1779. Its value as a winter naval station and a source of forage and provisions had begun to pale in the face of the increasing French superiority at sea. Initially, Clinton had advised against the occupation of Newport and within the following year, many British officers came to believe that the port was inconsequential. Its function to block commerce on the Narragansett had been eclipsed as the war moved south and the troops were required elsewhere. Moreover, the appearance of the French fleet in American waters isolated all British outposts and threatened their lines of communication. Fourteen months after its successful defense, Rhode Island was permanently abandoned.

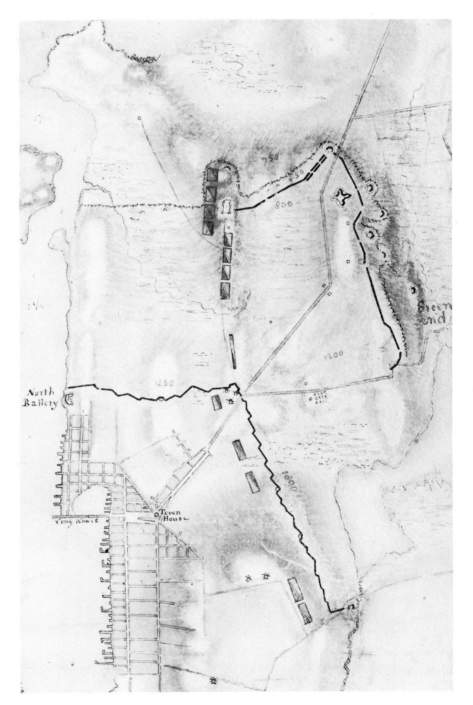

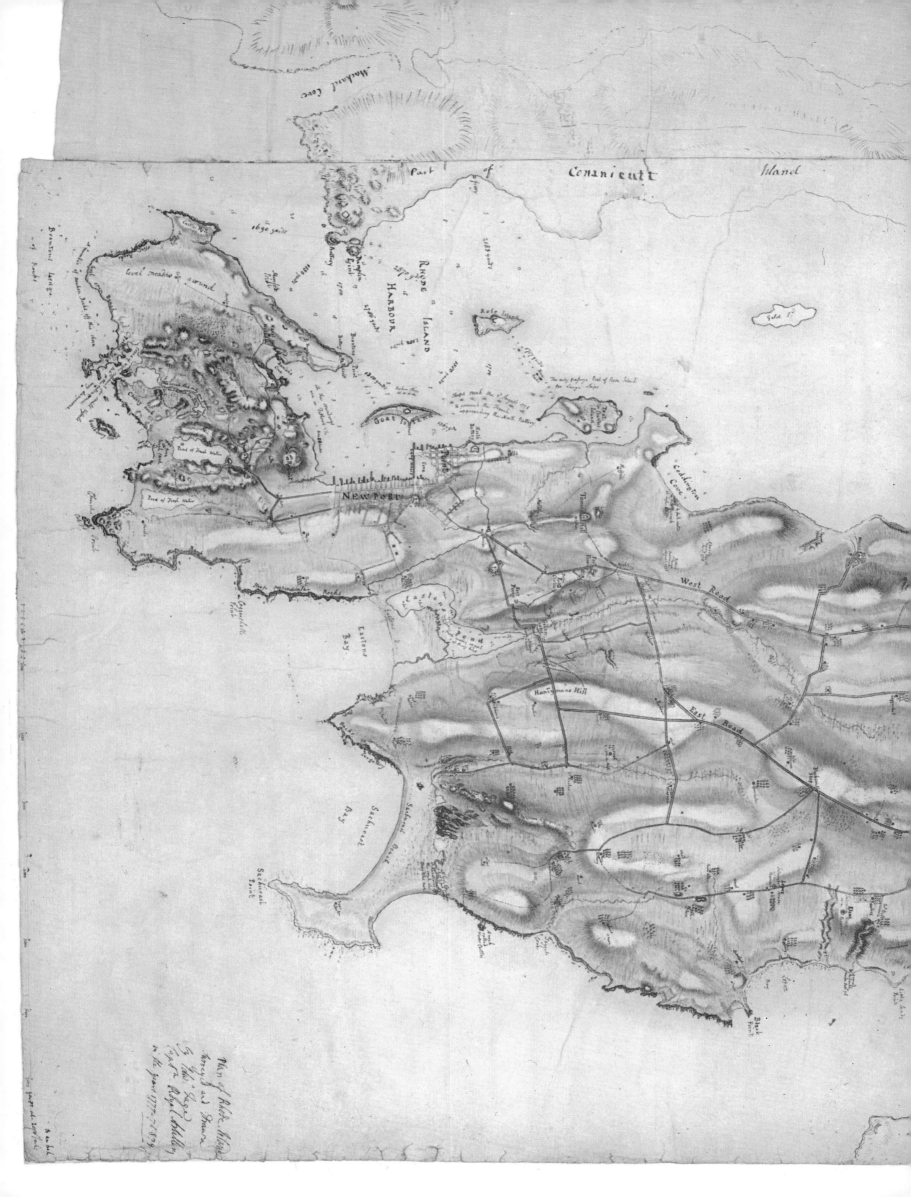

Kaskaskia and Vincennes

The western campaigns of the Revolution along the sparsely settled frontier were conducted on a smaller scale than those elsewhere; and no permanent strategic advantage was to result for either side. Here, Indians were influential in the balance of power between the Americans and British. Their tactics depended on lightning marches over incredible distances, foraging off the land, surprise, and ambush. In their more brutal application, they employed the use of torture, pillage of isolated settlements, scalping, slaying of noncombatants, destruction of crops, and exhumation. The settlers adopted retaliatory tactics.

Enemy encounters on the frontier during 1777 were particularly violent. Late in 1776 British-allied Indians were raiding Kentucky settlements which were organized as a county of Virginia at about this time. George Rogers Clark, a delegate from Kentucky to the House of Burgesses, concluded that the way to stop the raids was to capture the centers of British authority in the West. These were Kaskaskia and its satellites in the Illinois country, Vincennes on the Wabash River in modern Indiana, and Detroit. In 1776, however, British troops had been withdrawn from Illinois and redcoats were found only in Detroit and Michilimackinac.

Clark was only 24 years old, a tall, rugged, redheaded surveyor with a resourceful and diplomatic flair. In 1777 he presented his bold plan to Gov. Patrick Henry for authorization and aid. At the end of the year in Williamsburg, Clark was commissioned a lieutenant colonel and empowered to raise seven companies and to draw supplies from Fort Pitt. Ostensibly, Clark was raising a defense force to protect Kentucky from the Indians; his secret orders were to capture Kaskaskia and, if feasible, to move against Detroit.

Clark had considerable trouble recruiting companies for his hazardous mission. Finally, on June 26, 1778, he set off with 175 men. Moving in flatboats down the Ohio River, they stopped at the mouth of the Tennessee River on the Illinois side and began a difficult march of 120 miles northwestward to Kaskaskia. The French town had a population of about 900 and stood on the west bank of the Kaskaskia River, about three miles east of the Mississippi. The British had left Sieur de Rocheblave in charge of the town. His house was surrounded by a stockade garrisoned by a few local militia.

Clark's force reached the town July 4. That night he divided his men, one column marching boldly into the streets, the other moving quickly into the fort through its open gate. When awakened, Rocheblave immediately surrendered. Clark's announcement of the Franco-American alliance to the inhabitants was greeted with enthusiastic acceptance of the American cause.

The following day Clark sent a delegation of soldiers and civilians to Prairie du Rocher, 16 miles northwest, and to Cahokia, 60 miles north. Both settlements were won over without bloodshed. A priest at Kaskaskia and a town doctor were entreated to lead a delegation eastward to Vincennes. There on July 20 they persuaded the isolated French to shift their allegiance to Virginia. Capt. Leonard Helm and a handful of American soldiers were then dispatched to Vincennes.

Despite his small force and inadequate supplies, Clark had enjoyed genuine success. With the help of Oliver Pollock, a New Orleans merchant who shipped supplies up the Mississippi, Clark was able to maintain his position. He next prevailed upon the British-allied Indians to accept the change of flags. In a series of conferences and treaties Clark "flattered, cajoled, and threatened" the chiefs into a promise of neutrality and good behavior.

The commandant in Detroit, Lt. Col. Henry Hamilton, was not long in learning what had happened in his jurisdictional backyard. Hamilton had acquired an unsavory reputation for dispatching British-led Indian raids on frontier settlements; and it was rumored that Hamilton paid for scalps. He met Clark's threat by mustering a few regulars and some French militia, 175 altogether, and 60 Indians and setting out for Vincennes on October 7. His route was by water to Lake Erie, up the Maumee River, and down the Wabash. For an incredible 71 days he traveled, increasing the number of Indians en route. He entered Vincennes 500 strong on December 17, and Helm then surrendered.

At Kaskaskia Clark learned that Hamilton intended to spend the winter in Vincennes with only 35 regulars. Clark's force had also been reduced to about 100. Nevertheless, he wrote to Henry on February 3, 1779, "Great things have been effected by a few men well conducted." After enlisting French volunteers, he raised a force of almost 200. On February 6, with no tents and little food, they started for Vincennes, 170 miles away. Eleven days later at the Embarras River they found the whole area flooded by an early thaw. Wading from mound to mound, they finally crossed the Wabash, two miles from town, during the night of February 20-21.

Clark sent instructions into Vincennes for "the friends of the States" to stay in their houses and for those of British sympathy to go to the fort. Hamilton had antagonized many of the townspeople by his haughtiness, so that most of them remained in their homes. Clark advanced during the night in order to conceal his meager strength. The British withstood Clark's attack all night. The next day, February 24, Clark hastened his opponent's surrender by having four Indians (who had been captured with white scalps swinging from their belts) tomahawked in sight of the fort and their bodies pitched into the Wabash. Hamilton, fearing for his own life, plus 79 men and a detachment of 40 who had returned from patrol were taken prisoner. Clark never realized his dream of capturing Detroit, but his singular exploits enabled the Americans to claim the Indiana-Illinois country.

The map by Lt. Philip Pittman was made for Lt. Gen. Thomas Gage before the war. The fort which is shown on a bluff across the river burned after the map was made. _D_ is the commandant's house, and after 1778 was enclosed by a stockade.

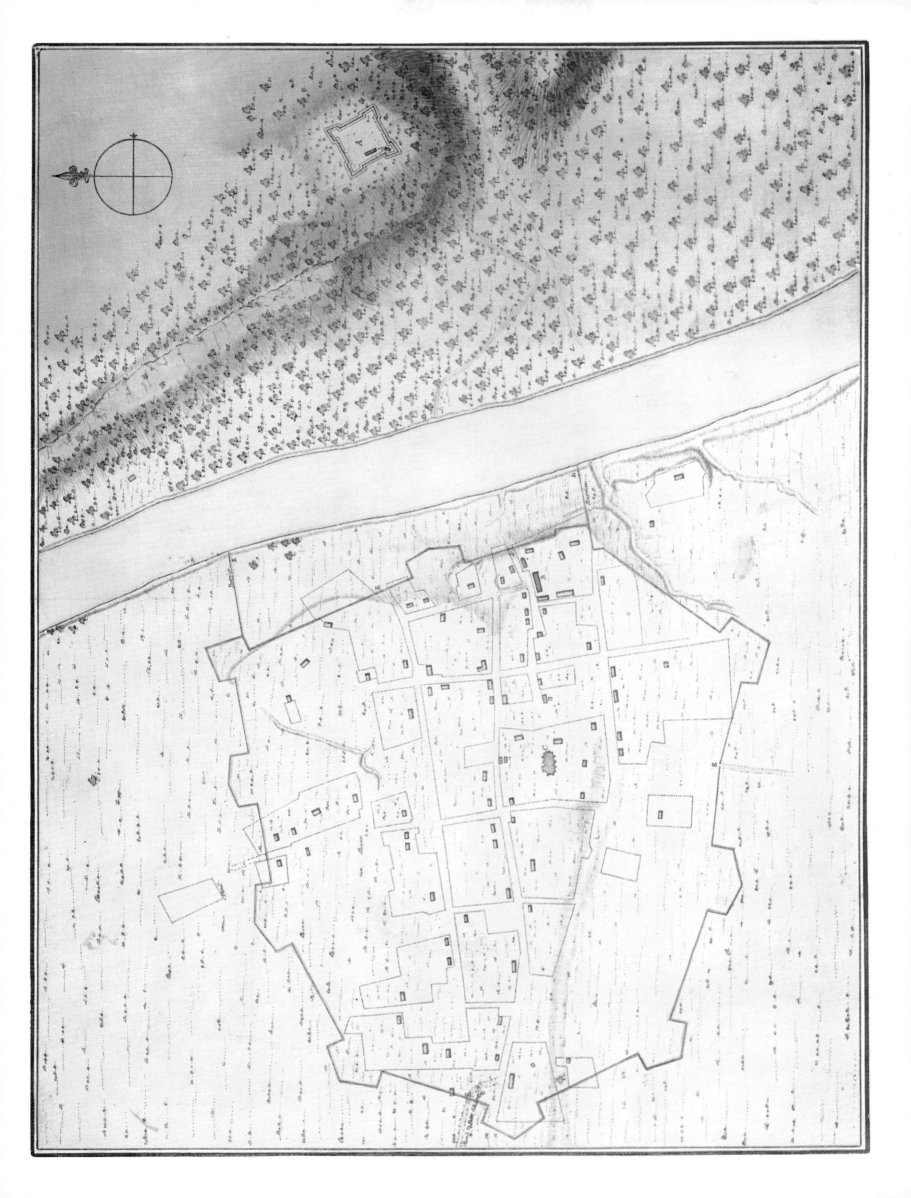

Savannah

From early 1776 when they had been forced by patriots to leave, the deposed British governors and lieutenant governors of Georgia and South Carolina began presenting their plans to the government in London for the return of their colonies to British control. The officials argued that in both areas loyalist support remained strong but subdued by rebel command. The presence of British forces, they maintained, would allow loyalists to resume regulation of the colonies' exports— exports currently paying for rebel military supplies. In addition, restoration of loyalist control of Charleston and Savannah would ensure control of the entire province.

By early 1778 the British government had decided that loyalist control of Georgia and South Carolina was indeed essential. Sir Henry Clinton was directed to capture Savannah and, as soon as troops were available, Charleston. He was further advised that a campaign in the South would be easier in the winter than in other seasons in which malaria, heat, bad weather, and spoiled provisions could affect the outcome of the British efforts. In addition forces which would otherwise be idled by the northern winter could be put to use.

British chances for a successful southern campaign were increased by Clinton's withdrawal from Philadelphia to New York in June, 1778. He could spare more than enough troops to seize Savannah, move up the Savannah River to Augusta, and then capture rebel strongholds in South Carolina before they would be needed for the spring campaign in the North. The offensive operation was considered "comparatively easy." Clinton placed Lt. Col. Archibald Campbell in command of 3,500 troops which set sail from New York on November 27. According to Clinton's plans, Campbell would join forces with Maj. Gen. Augustine Prevost's troops moving north from St. Augustine; but the reduction was almost complete before Prevost's arrival. Prevost had been delayed by the need to reprovision en route. Rations were sent north in boats to rendezvous with troops marching by land. Connections were missed and the soldiers ate what could be salvaged from the sea—at one inlet oysters, at another, alligator which they washed down with Madeira seized from a wreck.

As the British forces converged on Savannah, patriot defenses were in disarray. Troops in Georgia were garrisoned on the frontier against the Indians. Officers and soldiers deserted to look after their families and property once it was confirmed that the British were in Savannah. And it was difficult to provide the munitions. While in command of the South, the American Maj. Gen. Robert Howe had convinced Georgia officials that he intended to usurp the prerogatives of the Georgia militia leaders' defense of their own lands. Howe lamented that "It is impossible for me to give an account of the confused, perplexed way in which I found matters in this state, nor has it been in my power to get them . . . in a better train."

Despite advance warning of British movement toward Savannah, the disorganized patriot leaders failed to oppose Campbell's December 27 landing at Tybee Island —the most obvious landing place and a site visited by Howe the day before. Savannah at the time of the landing was, moreover, without an organized defense force. Howe, some 30 miles south at Sunbury, Ga., advanced on Savannah to do what he could to repel the British. His forces were reduced to 850 men when he left 200 to defend Sunbury. Approaching Savannah only hours before the British landing, Howe posted 50 Continentals at the Girardeau plantation, about two miles below the city. With the remaining 800 men he established a defense line across the road one-half mile southeast of town. The road was actually a raised causeway that passed over a shallow stream and was flanked on both sides by rice swamps. On the left were Georgia militia and one cannon, on the right Continentals, and on the far right more militia commanded by Col. George Walton.

On the morning of December 29, Campbell's British forces completed their journey from the mouth of the Savannah River. Their landing party encountered firing from the 50 Americans left behind at Girardeau's plantation. The first volley killed three British soldiers, including the leader of the landing party, and wounded five more, but failed to retard the assault. The American defenders retreated to rejoin Howe with Campbell's forces following them to within 1,000 yards of the American line.

After surveying his position, Campbell with the assistance of an elderly black guide discovered a path through the wooded swamp around the American right— a morass which Howe deemed impassable. Campbell dispatched Capt. James Baird and the New York Volunteers along this path to flank the American right.

Howe began shelling the enemy's front line. The British did not respond. Upon hearing fire on his far right, where Baird had surprised Walton's militia and put them to flight, Campbell ordered a charge against the American left. Attacked on both sides, Howe was obliged to retreat (see map on pages 78–79). The whole force withdrew around Savannah and escaped into South Carolina. Campbell entered Savannah but did not pursue the patriots any farther.

The British had lost only another 4 killed and 14 wounded in the second engagement. The Americans suffered 83 killed, 11 wounded, and 453 captured.

In the wake of the afternoon battle, Campbell had succeeded in capturing a military and political foothold from which British authority could be restored throughout Georgia and South Carolina. Upon Prevost's arrival in Savannah, Campbell advanced his plan for winning complete control of the province and thus became, as Campbell put it, the first officer "to take a stripe and star from the rebel flag of Congress." Within a month of his triumph at Savannah, Campbell with about 1,000 troops secured Augusta—a British victory won without the loss of a single man. Before he left Savannah, however, Campbell issued a proclamation stating that British military presence evidenced the crown's determination to protect loyal subjects in southern provinces. The proclamation urged Savannah residents to reaffirm their loyalty since protection would be based upon their future allegiance rather than on their past disloyalties. Although the immediate response was mixed, many Savannah loyalists eventually joined the British army.

As for Howe, the general retreated up the Savannah River into South Carolina where he relinquished his troops to Maj. Gen. Benjamin Lincoln who succeeded to the command of the Southern Department. Never fully understanding how he had lost or even knowing how many men he commanded during the defense of Savannah, Howe was, nevertheless, cleared of particular blame when he faced a court of inquiry.

The loss of Savannah did not, as the British had hoped, signal the end of patriot resistance in Georgia. Campbell was soon compelled to withdraw from Augusta in the face of numerically superior North Carolina troops. After several raids were organized by each side, Lincoln and the Comte Charles d'Estaing, commander of the French fleet in American waters, led a joint offensive to retake Savannah.

For four days in early October, 1779, d'Estaing's artillery bombarded the city. Finally, on the fifth day d'Estaing could wait no longer and stormed the British lines at the head of the combined French and American forces. The vastly outnumbered forces under Prevost stood their ground, however, and the French and the Americans retreated their separate ways. The defenses had been organized by Capt. Lt. James Moncrief, Corps of Engineers, whose distinguished efforts during the siege were recognized and rewarded by his commander.

The entreaties of the deposed British governors proved wrong in arguing that loyalist control of Savannah would ensure control of all of Georgia, but the British victory at Savannah in 1778 permitted loyalists to remain in control of the colony until 1782. Thus Georgia became the only state in the union in which a legislative body was convened under the crown.

The map on the following pages, by John Wilson, assistant engineer with Prevost, is oriented with north at the bottom. The British "Landing Place" is plainly shown. *A* is the higher ground of Girardeau's plantation where the first resistance was encountered. The dotted line is the obscure path through the wooded swamp that brought Baird's men against Walton's militia at *F*, while Howe's main body was in line at *G*. *H* marks the retreat of the Americans around Savannah. The plan below by Maj. Patrick Ferguson is representative of defense installations for urban field defenses.

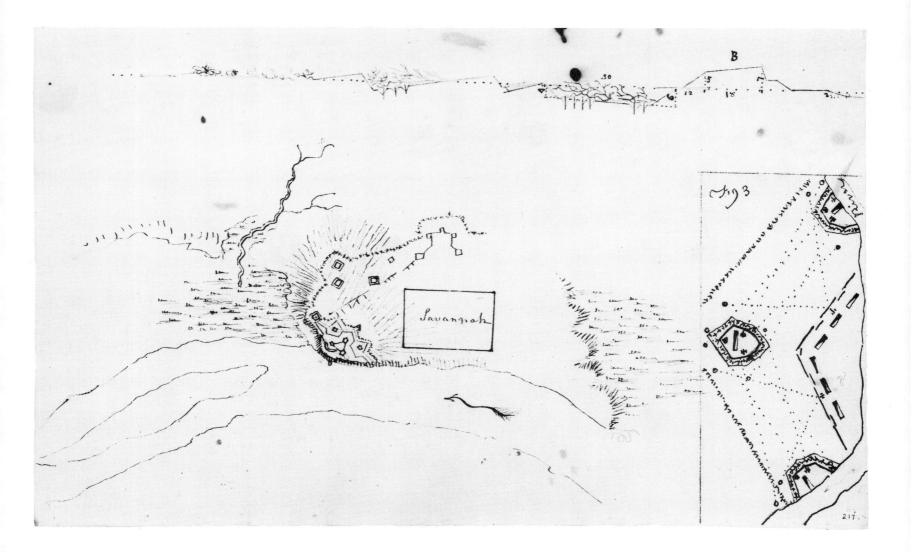

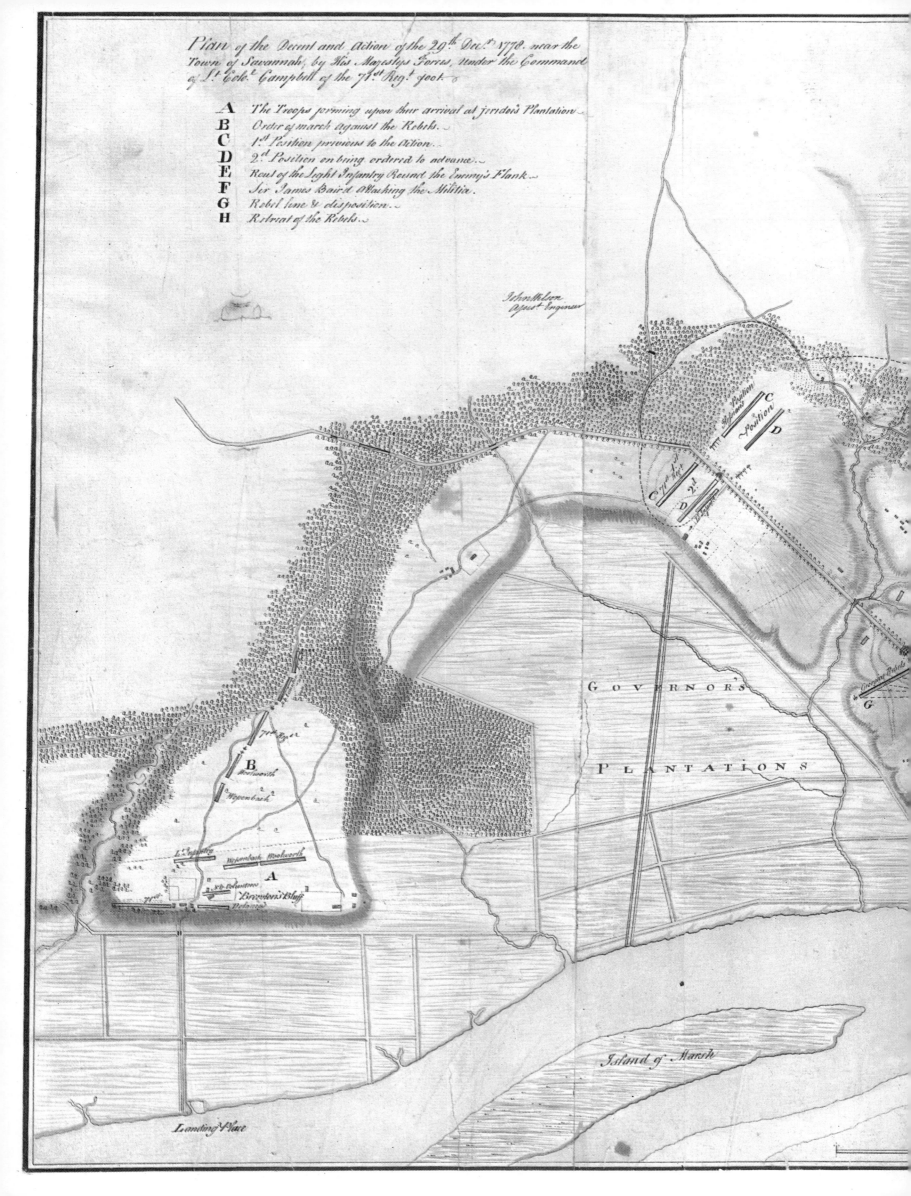

Plan of the Decent and Action of the 29th Decr. 1778. near the Town of Savannah, by His Majestys Forces, under the Command of Lt. Colo. Campbell of the 71st Regt. foot.

A   The Troops forming upon their arrival at Jeridoe's Plantation.
B   Order of march against the Rebels.
C   1st Position previous to the Action.
D   2d Position on being ordered to advance.
E   Rout of the Light Infantry Round the Enemy's Flank.
F   Sir James Baird Attacking the Militia.
G   Rebel line & disposition.
H   Retreat of the Rebels.

John Wilson
Assist Engineer

G O V E R N O R'S

P L A N T A T I O N S

Island of Marsh

Landing Place

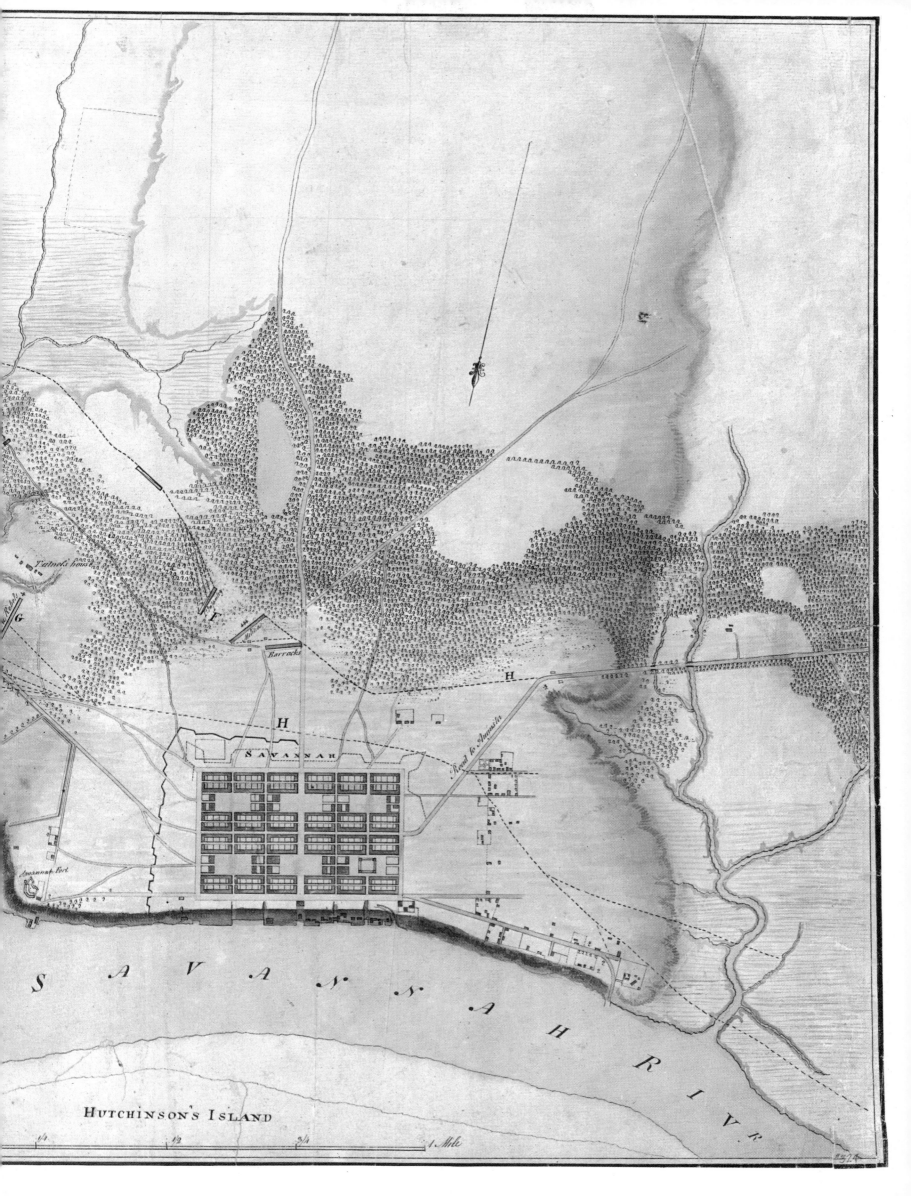

Valnet's hous.

F

G

Mills.

Barracks

H

H

A

SAVANNAH

Road to Augusta

Savannah Fort

S A V A N N A H   R I V E R

HUTCHINSON'S ISLAND

1/4   1/2   3/4   1 Mile

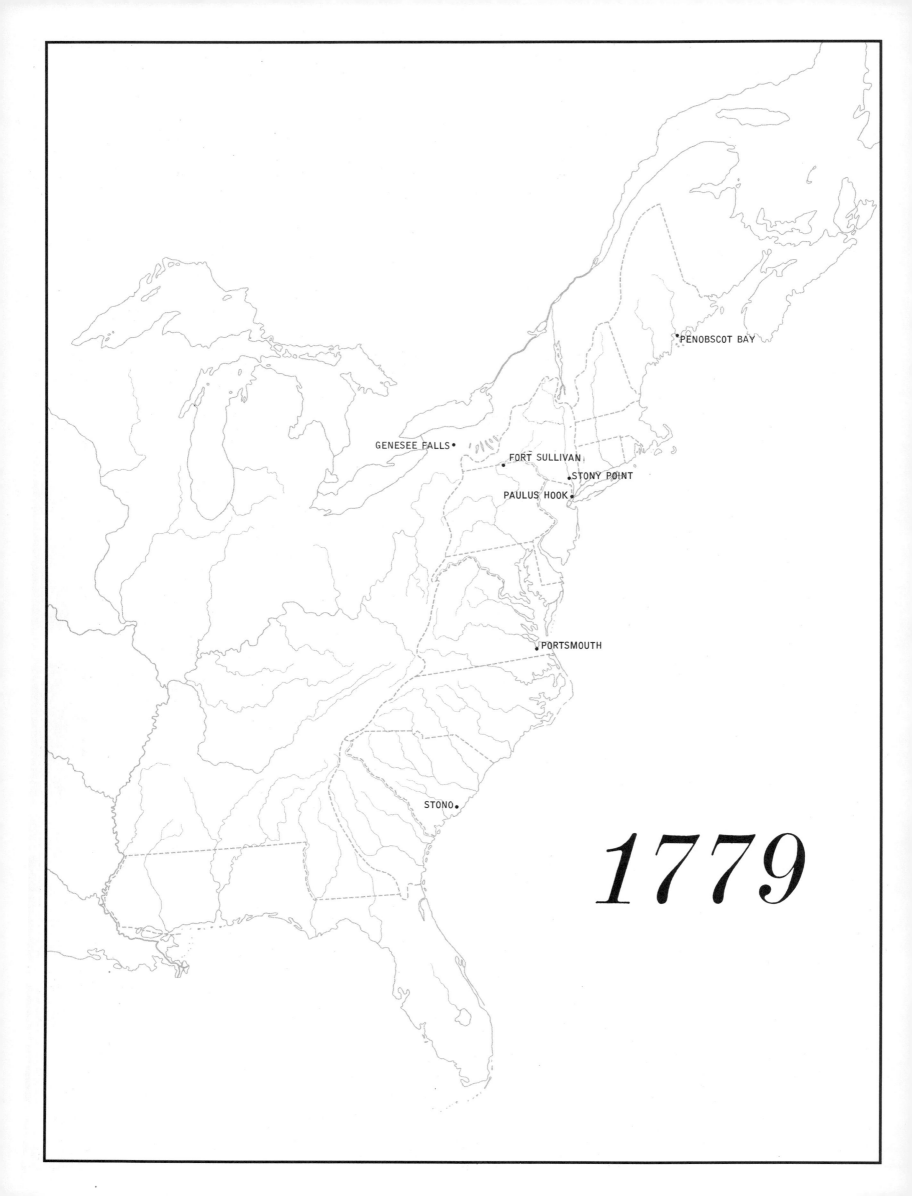

PENOBSCOT BAY

GENESEE FALLS

FORT SULLIVAN

STONY POINT

PAULUS HOOK

PORTSMOUTH

STONO

1779

In 1779 the stalemate of the previous year was repeated and the events which took place slipped into obscurity. Initiative lay with the British to expand their bases, but the delayed arrival of reinforcements precluded major operations until the Charleston expedition at the end of the year. Within the area of rebellion, British control was maintained at Savannah and New York harbor, while Newport was abandoned in December. The circumstances for both sides stood at the end of the year about where they had started at the beginning.

In the North, activity was limited to an uncoordinated American attack on a small British post in Penobscot Bay, an expedition against loyalists and British-allied Indians on the New York frontier, and raids along the Manhattan perimeter at Stony Point and Paulus Hook. In the South, the British threatened South Carolina, but were checked at Stono Ferry. Later, they successfully defended Savannah against a combined French-and-American assault.

Lack of supplies continued to be a serious problem for the British army. In New York City, Maj. Gen. Henry Clinton found food and forage so limited that in the first few months of the year he sent 2,500 men under Sir William Erskine to live off the crops of eastern Long Island. Erskine took with him all the cavalry and other army horses. The result was that his force used up the winter reserve and faced another shortage by spring. He was also hampered by rebel expeditions across the Sound to buy or destroy forage. In addition, American privateers captured two provision ships from England. Wood for fuel in New York also became scarce, and the farther woodcutters ranged, the more they were subject to capture.

General Washington also had problems in providing the necessary provisions for the American army. He had to disperse his cavalry mounts over five states in order to find sufficient forage. Although a broader area was available from which to procure food, inflation ruined the meager patriot purchasing power. Continental dollar bills, worth twenty-five cents at the beginning of the year, were only worth one cent by the end. Washington wrote that "a waggon load of money will scarcely purchase a waggon load of provisions." A captain could not buy a pair of shoes with a year's pay and junior officers ran so far in debt that several were resigning. It seemed that what the British could not accomplish by force, inflation might.

Despite these problems, the Continental navy emerged under Capt. John Paul Jones.

A war of stationary position required fortification, and it was the duty of the Corps of Engineers to provide these defenses for the British army. The size of the corps had been reduced by four from the previous year to a total of 18 officers on service in America and Canada. Yet the total available engineer talent was somewhat greater than this figure. The number of line officers that were commissioned as assistant engineers must have been almost equal in size at this point, and the engineers accompanying the German regiments may have supplied half again as many. But the level of training of assistant engineers was not always known and not all members of the Corps of Engineers were available for duty at any one time. Of 13 engineers on the establishment assigned to New York, only six were present on the return for 1779.

Engineer talent was eroded by members of the corps involved in seeking positions on the various headquarter staffs. Staff officers enjoyed preferential treatment in regard to duty assignments, meal arrangements, and proximity to the military power structure. It became fashionable and sometimes lucrative to obtain a coveted staff appointment. Aide-de-camps, deputy and assistant quartermasters, and deputy and assistant adjutants were the principal staff classifications that could be added to an officers commission. Eventually 8 out of the total of 36 members of the Corps of Engineers to serve in America acquired supplemental staff appointments. Commemorative maps of battles may have given a promising engineer the kind of recognition needed to obtain a staff position. This could account for the overrepresentation of this type of map. Since these maps were evaluated on their quality as drawings, it might also suggest why more useful surveys were not conducted. That is, the engineers with drawing skill were engaged in the practice of cartography to ensure their own advancement at the expense of maps which would have more value to the planning of military operations. Apparently, Capt. John Montresor was the only engineer who obtained a staff appointment and continued to draw maps. It may be concluded that while maps possibly aided engineers to obtain a staff position, the cartographic skills were unrelated to its retention, or to their new duties at headquarters.

Prevost in South Carolina

After the British capture of Savannah at the end of December, 1778, Maj. Gen. Augustine Prevost, who commanded the British forces in East Florida, assumed overall authority in the South in January, 1779. Hardly 20 miles up the Savannah River, Maj. Gen. Benjamin Lincoln had joined American forces under Maj. Gen. Robert Howe at Purysburg, South Carolina. Following the disastrous defeat at Savannah, Howe was relieved of his command and ordered to join Washington in the North. The Americans had fewer than 3,700 men, while the British had nearly 5,000.

In addition to disease and the decimating climate, the state of affairs in the Southern Department was deplorable. The relationship between the Continental Congress and the states was unclear, there was dissension among the officers, and the troops were undisciplined and unreliable.

Prevost sent Lt. Col. Archibald Campbell by ship to seize Augusta, which was quickly accomplished at the end of January. But when challenged by the Americans under Brig. Gen. John Ashe, Campbell abandoned Augusta and retreated downriver. Below Briar Creek, he halted after destroying the bridge there. When Ashe arrived he began to rebuild it while the British, in an unperceived movement, marched a column behind him. Ashe showed inconsistent leadership, and large numbers of his militia fled on attack. The Americans had been devastated. They suffered a severe defeat—150 killed, 27 officers and 200 militia captured, and more perished in the river—hardly one-third of those who had escaped rejoined Lincoln's army. The British lost only five killed and 11 wounded. Lower Georgia remained firmly in British hands.

Lincoln's forces were increased to 5,000 with the addition of 500 men from Orangeburgh and 700 from North Carolina. It was decided at a council of war to cut the enemy's supply lines, circumscribe their limits, and prevent their union with British-allied Indians. Lincoln took 4,000 men to Augusta and left only 1,000 at Purysburg under Brig. Gen. William Moultrie. Prevost decided to force Lincoln's withdrawal by invading South Carolina and threatening Charleston. To this end he started across the state with about 2,500 troops marching against Purysburg first. The map (overleaf) shows his route.

As he approached Purysburg (off the map), Moultrie began falling back toward Charleston. Prevost proceeded to Heyward's Landing on May 3, divided his forces at Pocotaligo Bridge the next day, reunited them at Fish Pond Bridge, and reached Ashley Ferry on May 10 (shown by the orange line on the map). Moultrie had retreated ahead of him, destroying bridges and trying to delay Prevost while his own force gradually diminished from desertion. He notified Lincoln of the British threat to Charleston. Finally, after numerous warnings, Lincoln turned back to protect the town just as Prevost crossed the Ashley River and approached Charleston from the north.

By May 9 Moultrie was in the city. He sent out Brig. Gen. Casimir Pulaski's legion of 125 men to offer a delaying action, but they were badly mauled on the afternoon of May 11. Prevost advanced to the city's defenses and waited. Although Moultrie was in command, the governor and council decided matters of "parlies and capitulation." The council and Gov. John Rutledge, believing Prevost had 7,000 or 8,000 men, and the Americans only about 2,000, advised Moultrie to negotiate. After several messages back and forth to Prevost, the governor and council offered terms whereby the state would remain neutral during the war and abide with the eventual winner of the conflict if the British would withdraw and recognize Charleston as a neutral port. Moultrie and several of his officers were dissatisfied over this offer. Prevost insisted that Moultrie's troops would have to surrender, but Moultrie refused. He was content to keep up an exchange of notes in order to gain time as Lincoln was expected at any moment, and additional militia had reported raising his garrison to about 2,500.

On May 12 Prevost learned of Lincoln's approach by the interception of a message to Moultrie. To avoid being crushed between the two American forces, he pulled out that night and recrossed the Ashley River. Why Prevost did not accept the governor's offer of capitulation is a matter for conjecture. The British retreated to Ashley Ferry, camped for two weeks opposite Charleston, and then turned southwest to Johns Island. Prevost stopped again at Stono Ferry and fortified the mainland side with three redoubts behind an abatis some 700 yards long. A bridge of boats led to it from the island. Lincoln moved a detachment down to Stono Ferry on May 31, while Pulaski reconnoitered the enemy position but did not attack.

The stalemate continued until June 16, when the British decamped to return to Savannah leaving 900 men under Lt. Col. John Maitland. Lincoln decided to advance, although his own forces were weakened by desertions and expiration of militia enlistments. On June 19 he ordered Moultrie to take all the troops he could spare from Charleston and cross to James Island so as to reinforce his own maneuver. Unfortunately, Moultrie's tardy procurement of boats meant that the troops did not move out until June 20. The failure of the subsequent effort resulted from this delay.

Meanwhile, Lincoln led his own troops—Continentals and some militia—to the fortification at Stono Ferry before daybreak on June 20. About 7:00 A.M., the attack began. Maitland did not hesitate to send two companies of the 71st Regiment to skirmish with the advancing Continentals. Although outnumbered, the British did not retreat until all of their officers were killed or wounded. The Americans then broke through the artillery fire; and the Hessian reserves gave way. Maitland rallied them, and the heavy firing was renewed. Disappointed that he did not receive the expected help from Moultrie and knowing that he could not destroy the enemy force, Lincoln ordered a retreat. Thereupon, Maitland counterattacked and forced Lincoln's troops out of the protective works. Pulaski's cavalry now entered the fight, but as they charged, the British closed their ranks to ward off the onslaught. It was the advance of a Virginia brigade that caused Maitland's troops to retreat; and Lincoln made good his disengagement and withdrawal.

Casualties were heavy on both sides in the approximately one-hour action. The British lost 26 killed and 103 wounded. Lincoln suffered 34 killed, 113 wounded, and 18 missing. If Moultrie had reinforced Lincoln's troops, there is little doubt that he would have been able to achieve a notable victory.

Maitland, however, now had time to carry off his wounded and depart on June 24. He rested on Edisto Island for a few days and then joined Prevost at Beaufort, Port Royal Island, on July 8. Here the latter had established a post, and Maitland was placed in command. Prevost took most of his army back to Savannah—just as the sickly season arrived. His troops had plundered the rich lowlands and attracted thousands of slaves to join them in vain expectation of freedom and care. Throughout this campaign Prevost had achieved very limited ends: he had thwarted Lincoln's occupation of Augusta, and by establishing a garrison at Beaufort gained a base for the future invasion of South Carolina.

The map of Prevost's march through South Carolina is probably the work of Lt. Alexander Sutherland, Corps of Engineers, who served with Prevost. It may have accompanied a report of the action sent to Sir Henry Clinton. Yet Prevost complained to Clinton that until adequate provisions were available, no British offensive in the South could be maintained. By October his garrison was besieged by French and American forces (see "Savannah").

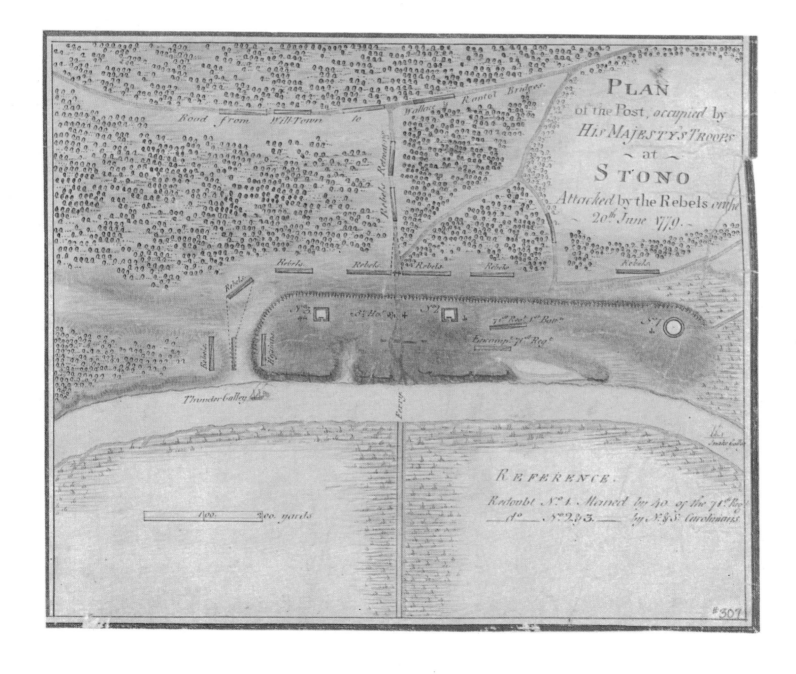

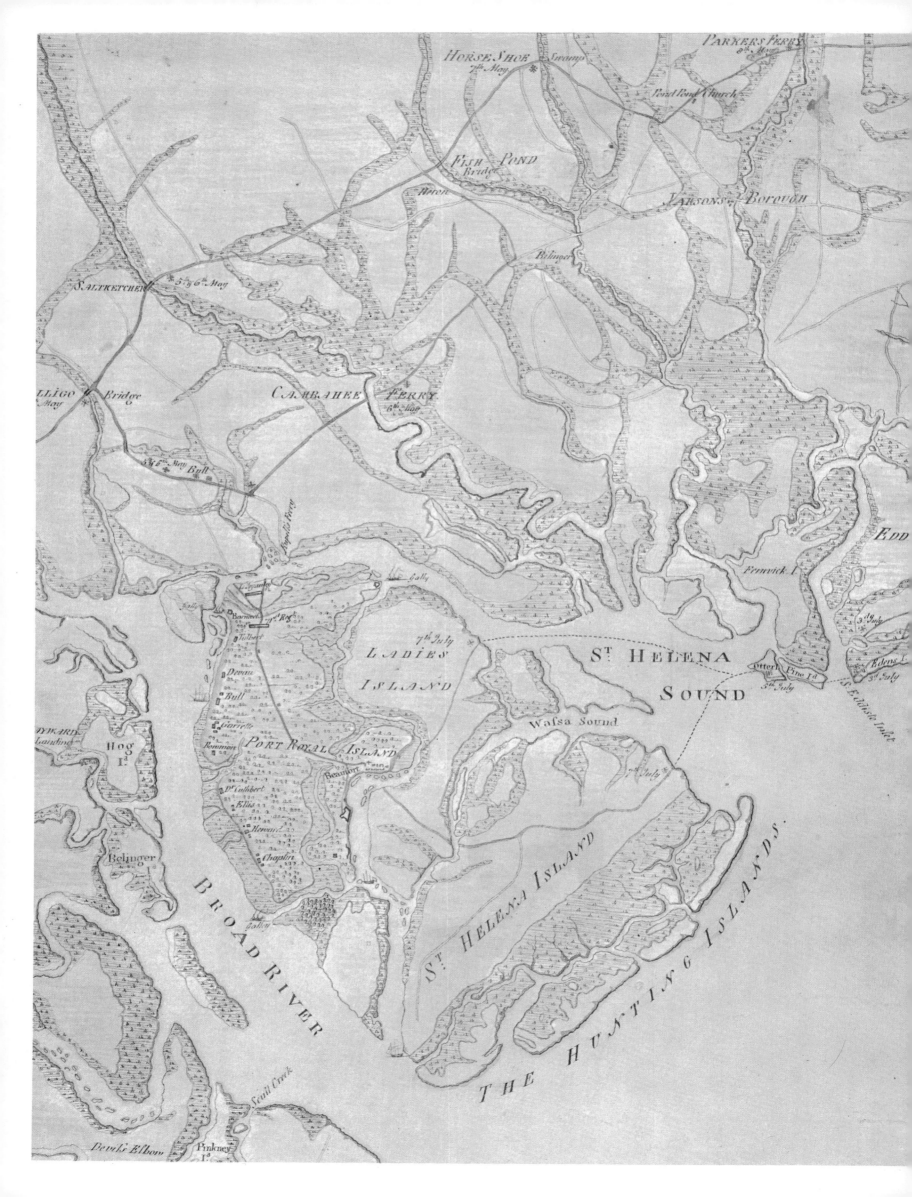

Penobscot Bay

On the northern fringe of the 13 colonies, a simple American expedition against a small outpost evolved into one of the most disastrous campaigns of the war.

In the summer of 1779 the British acted to extend their Nova Scotia establishment. A garrison of 3,500 men was assigned to outposts along this northern coast. In May, on orders from Sir Henry Clinton, the British sent Brig. Francis McLean with about 700 troops from the 74th and 82nd regiments at Halifax to Penobscot Bay on the end of a peninsula called Majabigwaduce (modern Castine, Maine). The troops were to construct a military base that would block patriot advances into Nova Scotia. It would also serve as headquarters for British marauding parties into New Hampshire and Massachusetts. Five warships and four transports carried the troops to the bay. Upon their arrival on June 13, they found the scattered settlers— many of them loyalists who had fled Massachusetts— "much inclined to be under the British government."

Massachusetts officials recognized the threat of the new outpost as soon as news of the British landing was received. The officials decided, without consulting the Continental Congress or the commander in chief, that the fort at Penobscot Bay should be eliminated. About 1,200 volunteers from several Massachusetts towns organized under the command of Brig. Gen. Solomon Lovell. The artillery unit was commanded by Lt. Col. Paul Revere. The naval force, consisting of three frigates and 37 other ships furnished by Massachusetts merchants, was commanded by Commodore Dudley Saltonstall. The expedition incorporated at least 2,000 men, including sailors, but the British reported the American strength at 3,300.

The British learned of the American plans through newly escaped prisoners from Boston who had been picked up by one of the British transports returning to Halifax. Messages regarding the American fleet were immediately sent to McLean at Fort George and Commodore George Collier in New York. By August 3 Collier had assembled seven warships to set sail for Maine.

The American fleet hove into sight on July 25 and proceeded to the west side of Majabigwaduce. Saltonstall reportedly favored a landing in force and general assault on the unfinished fort, but Lovell appeared cautious. He preferred trying occasional landing parties and using the ships' cannon to reduce the fort. Consequently, in late July a large landing force was dispatched, but was thrown back with heavy losses. The frigates engaged in a half-hearted cannonade of British ships but did very little damage. It was becoming apparent that neither Lovell nor Saltonstall displayed the organizational ability to coordinate an effective assault on the position.

The sparring continued for another two weeks. Saltonstall kept up intermittent cannonading, but was too far away from the fort to be effective. Lovell diverted his efforts by rounding up the loyalists in the vicinity whom he then put in irons aboard ship. He had issued a proclamation demanding that all patriots appear at his camp on Majabigwaduce with arms, or be considered traitors.

Additional problems plagued the Americans. Deserters reported to McLean that some of the American seamen threatened mutiny against Saltonstall because of his timidity. Finally on August 12 Saltonstall decided to attack the British warships but was deterred by the appearance of additional sails. Next morning, Saltonstall discovered that the new ships were British, and thus reembarked off Majabigwaduce and sailed north up the Penobscot River. The British set sail at the same time and "seeing them [the American ships] draw up in a regular line, imagined they meant to give us battle." Hence the engagement began.

About 2:00 P.M. three American ships separated from the fleet and attempted to run south along Long Island. Their escape route was cut off by two British vessels. Collier pursued Saltonstall up the Penobscot on August 13 and 14. Capt. Andrew Barkley, in a letter to Vice Adm. Marriot Arbuthnot, recalled about the American fleet, that "a most ignominious flight took place among them, their whole fleet flying in the outmost confusion."

Seven American ships were trapped in a small bay, and after landing the troops, were set on fire. The main fleet, still being pursued, began setting their sternmost vessels afire. That night the British ships anchored, and the American fleet moved farther up the river. On August 14, the patriots, seeing that they could not escape the British, set fire to their remaining vessels. Barkley wrote, "no vessel of any kind of their whole armament escap'd (not even a whale boat).... Their army.... are now exploring their way thro' the woods and wilderness, where most likely many of them will perish for want of food, and thro' fatigue before they reach Boston."

The British admitted to 70 killed, wounded, and missing, and estimated that the Americans lost 474 killed, wounded, and captured. The latter figure may be high.

The result at Penobscot Bay caused bitter enemies in Boston. The Massachusetts Board of War totaled the cost of the expedition at £1,139,175. Committees of investigation were formed. Saltonstall was court-martialed and dismissed from the navy in October. He then began privateering, regained his reputation as a bold fighter, and became wealthy. Even the diligent Revere was accused of some trivial dereliction. It took him five years to clear his name. Since a Continental navy officer was made the scapegoat, Massachusetts importuned the Continental Congress for reimbursement of the expedition's cost. The state eventually recovered two million dollars.

The American expedition on Penobscot Bay was so disastrous and "the relief of the siege was so successful" that no further attacks were made on the British in Castine throughout the Revolutionary War. Fort George was considered of only peripheral importance to both the Americans and the British. Washington knew that ultimately the diplomats would determine the boundary lines of the new nation. And for the British, the fort only provided access to the tall pines needed by the navy shipyards.

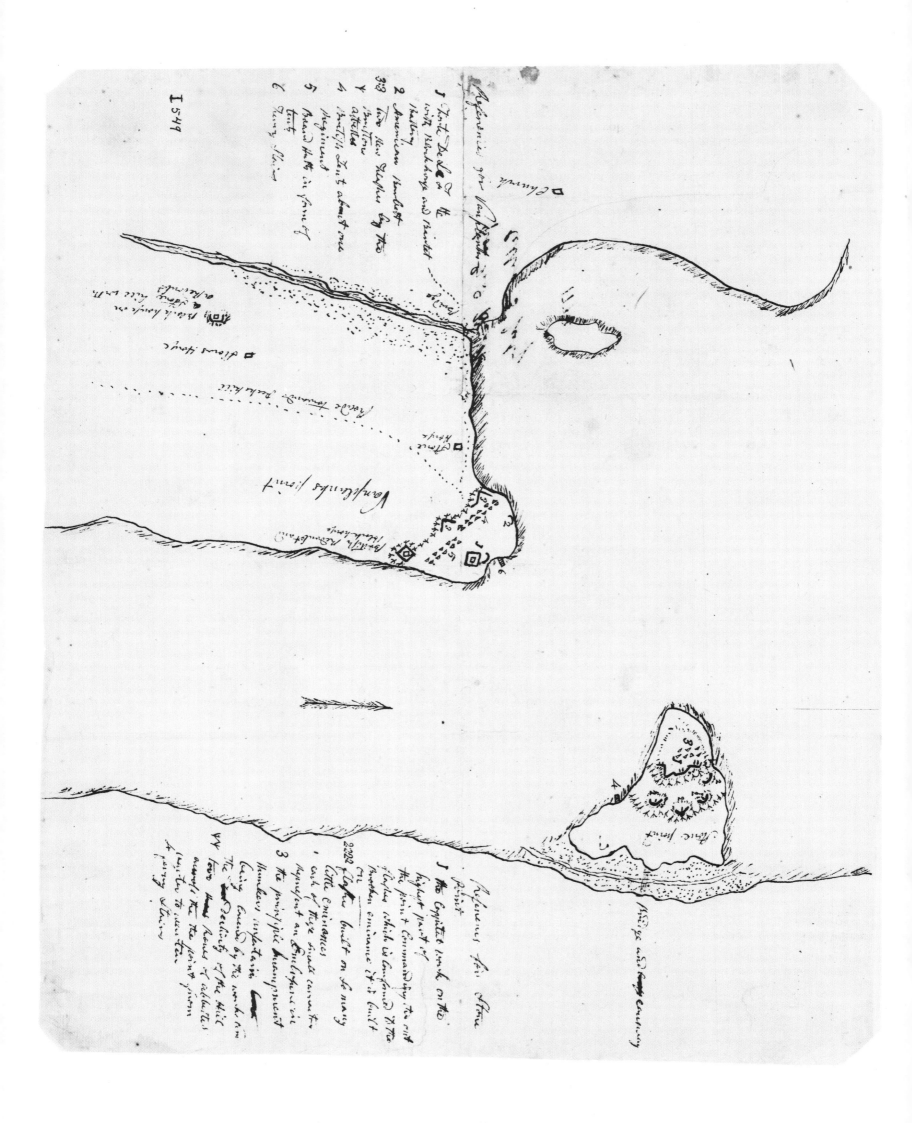

The two maps are among four made by Lt. George W. D. Jones, assistant engineer. He belonged to the 7th Regiment stationed in New York and undoubtedly arrived with Collier's reinforcement. He made the plan below in 1780, after the fort was finished. It shows Fort George to be an orthodox wooden rectangle with a bastion jutting out of each corner. The "rebel" batteries west of the fort, to the north, and one to the east are shown on the map overleaf. The plan was drawn 520 yards to the inch, and both map and plan were forwarded to Sir Henry Clinton.

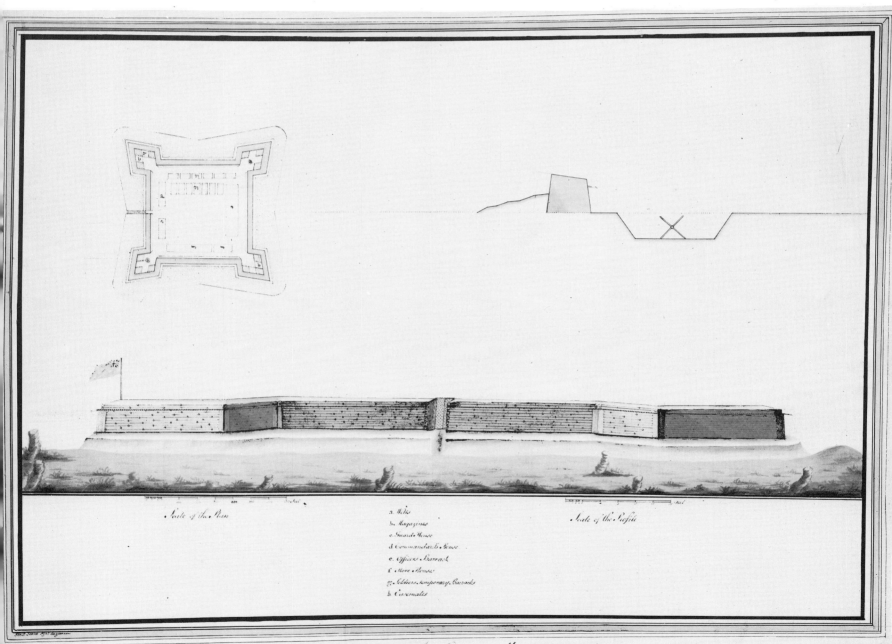

A Plan, Profile and Front View of Fort George Majabigwaduce

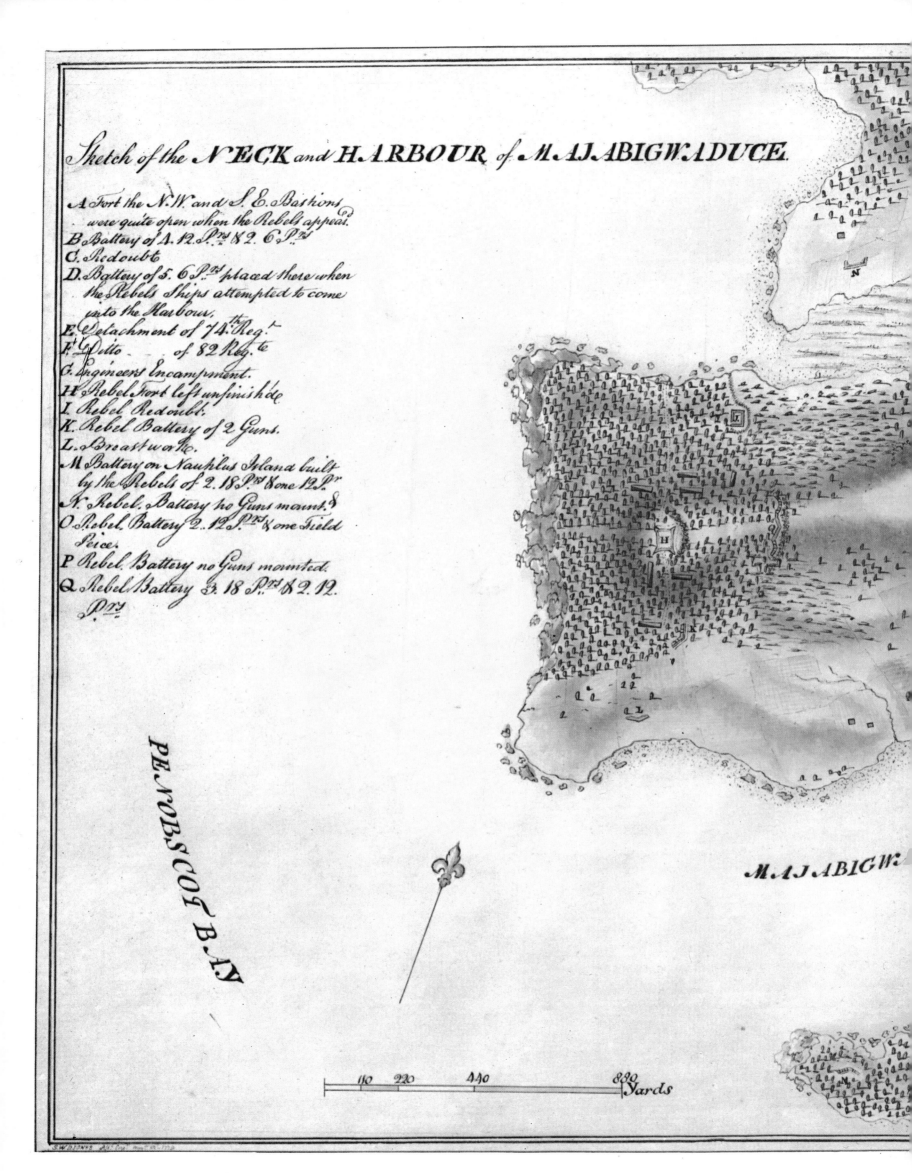

Sketch of the NECK and HARBOUR of MAJABIGWADUCE.

A Fort the N.W. and S.E. Bastions
   were quite open when the Rebels appear.d

B Battery of 4. 12 P.rs & 2. 6 P.rs

C Redoubt

D Battery of 5. 6 P.rs placed there when
   the Rebels Ships attempted to come
   into the Harbour.

E Detachment of 74.th Reg.t

F Ditto   of 82 Reg.te

G Engineers Encampment.

H Rebel Fort left unfinish'd.

I Rebel Redoubt.

K Rebel Battery of 2 Guns.

L Breastwork.

M Battery on Nautilus Island built
   by the Rebels of 2. 18 P.rs & one 12 P.r

N Rebel Battery no Guns mount.d

O Rebel Battery 2. 12 P.rs & one Field
   Peice.

P Rebel Battery no Guns mounted.

Q Rebel Battery 3. 18 P.rs & 2. 12
   P.rs

PENOBSCOT BAY

MAJABIGW:

110   220   440   880 Yards

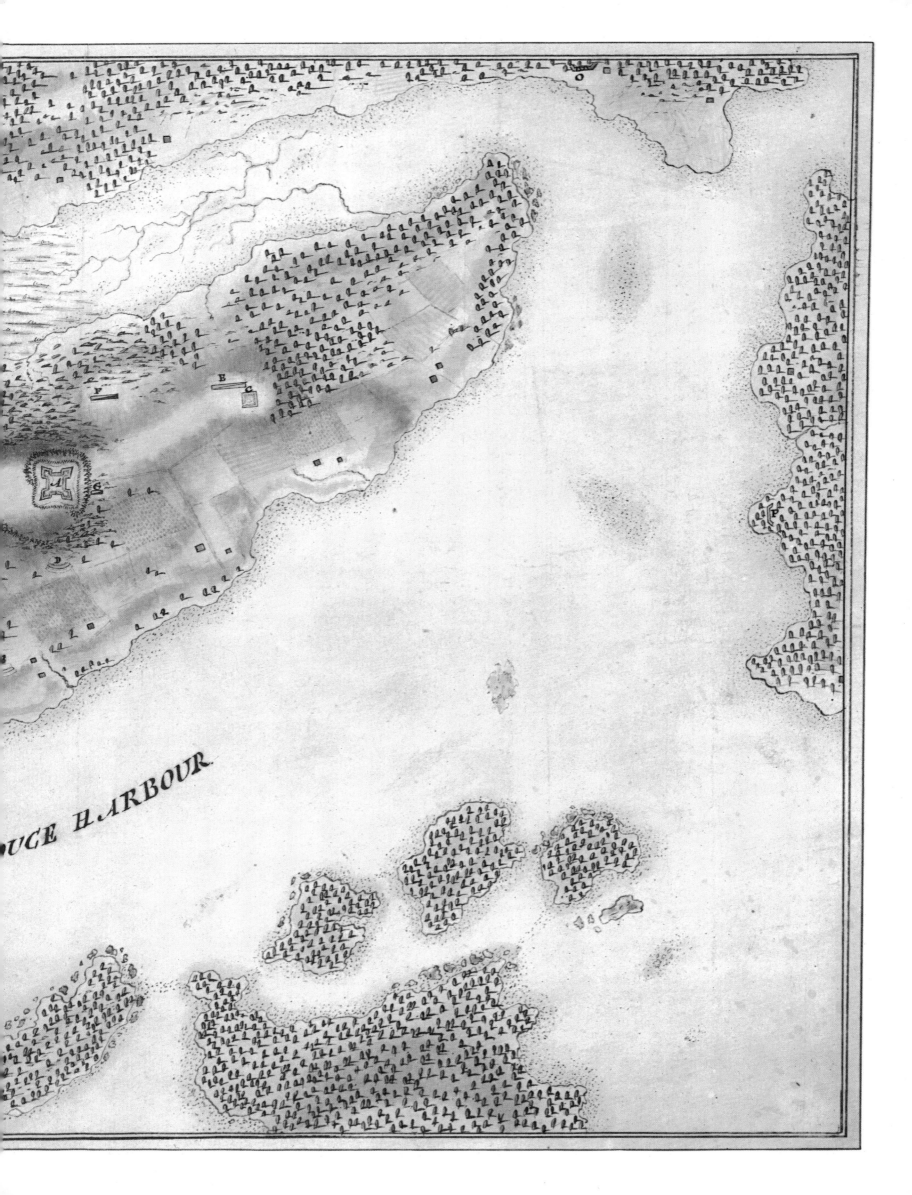

DUCE HARBOUR.

Paulus Hook

Paulus (or Powles) Hook was a sandy peninsula at the end of a salt marsh. It extended into the Hudson River opposite New York City and is now part of Jersey City. The British had occupied it since 1776, and if it was not much protection to the city, it at least served as headquarters for foraging expeditions into northern New Jersey. On July 14, 1778, Capt. John Montresor noted in his diary, "I detached 3 established engineers to strengthen the Paulus Hook by cutting a fosse across the neck." This ditch (or moat) through the marsh filled with water at high tide and made the point a small island. It was reached by a bridge at the end of a single road from Bergen. The British had erected two redoubts holding six and four cannon, three blockhouses, some breastworks on the harbor side, and three barracks. The garrison of 200 to 300, commanded by Maj. William Sutherland, felt quite safe; the force was composed of part of the 64th Regiment, some New Jersey loyalists, and a few invalids.

In August, 1779, a month after Brig. Gen. Anthony Wayne's dramatic success at Stony Point, Washington was searching for another outpost which might be taken without a major battle. Isolated Paulus Hook suggested itself. Maj. Henry Lee reconnoitered the area, and Washington decided there were too many risks involved for an attack. But Lee was not satisfied that this was the case; he finally prodded Washington into giving qualified approval for a surprise attempt. Lee's explicit orders were not to occupy the Hook, but to make a quick raid on the garrison.

Lee was permitted to take a force of less than 400, made up of 200 Virginians, two Maryland companies, and Capt. Allen McLane's troop of 100 dismounted Delaware dragoons. (Lee's own "Light Horse" legion had not yet taken shape.) On the morning of August 18 Lee started south from Paramus with the Maryland companies and several wagons to give the appearance of a foraging expedition. He collected the rest of his troops at New Bridge, about four miles farther, across the Hackensack River. The expedition, which was wholly dependent on precise timing, now became burdened with troubles. Lee's guide, whether from ignorance or treachery, misled the column around an enemy outpost, losing some of the men and prolonging the march by three hours. Then Maj. Jonathan Clark began a quarrel with the 23-year-old Lee over his command since Clark's commission was dated earlier than Lee's. Soon thereafter, nearly 100 of the Virginians disappeared from the expedition (either lost or deserted). Clark, however, remained with the others from his state. Lee had expected to reach the Hook shortly after midnight, before the tide rose. Yet it was 4:00 A.M. on August 19 when his tired men arrived at the bridge that led onto the point.

Lt. Michael Rudolph of Maryland reported that the water in the ditch was deep, but could be waded. He was to lead one small advance party, and Lt. Archibald McAllister, also from Maryland, commanded another. McLane's troop followed Rudolph, and Clark's Virginians were behind McAllister. Capt. Levin Handy brought up a reserve of the remaining Marylanders. The men were warned to be perfectly quiet and to rely on their bayonets. But the detachments of the two lieutenants splashed across the ditch and aroused the British sentinels. As the general alarm sounded, Clark's men swept into the stronghold and quickly seized a blockhouse. In the darkness they bayoneted any British soldier who did not promptly raise his hands in surrender. McLane's troops overran a second blockhouse, followed by Handy with his reserves.

The enemy garrison was manned almost completely by regulars at this time. Two days earlier, Lt. Col. Abram van Buskirk had taken out 150 loyalists on a foraging expedition, and they were replaced by some Hessians and a light infantry company. On this night Capt. Heinrich von Schaller held the round redoubt with a few dozen Hessians, Sutherland along with them. The Americans now discovered that their powder was wet from wading the ditch, and they could not break into the redoubt with its six cannon. Alarm guns began sounding across the river in New York City. With the surprise ended, Lee was in a dangerous position. Dawn was breaking, the six cannon would soon rake the open ground around the redoubt, and Buskirk could be returning. Lee resisted burning the barracks when he learned that women, children, and wounded were housed therein. He rounded up his prisoners and ordered a fast withdrawal. The battle had lasted barely one-half hour.

The expedition retreated back to Bergen, where Lee had ordered boats to carry him to the west shore of the Hackensack. Capt. Henry Peyton had gathered up the boats, but when Lee failed to appear at the appointed hour, Peyton took the boats around into the Passaic River to Newark. Lee had no choice but to march his exhausted men straight north back to New Bridge and then to Paramus. Five miles along the road they met Capt. Thomas Catlett with 50 Virginians, probably some of those who had left the expedition the previous afternoon. Since their powder was dry, Lee designated Catlett's men the rear guard. Opposite Fort Lee a relief column met the expedition. Three miles farther north at Liberty Pole Tavern (now Englewood), Buskirk's loyalists caught up with Lee and attacked but were driven off after a brief skirmish. By 1:00 P.M. the Americans had reached safety and rest at New Bridge.

Lee's men had killed and wounded ("put to the bayonet") about 50 of the enemy. They took 158 prisoners. The Americans lost only four killed, three wounded, and ten captured, some by Buskirk.

Lee's assault had avenged the Americans in some measure for the British raids along the New England coast. Despite Lee's minimal mistakes—keeping his column open, issuing insufficient rations, failing to retain dry ammunition and to secure the boats for his retreat—he and his troops had acted courageously and provided a lift for American morale. The enterprise did little but reduce the garrison and lacked the finality of Stony

Point, yet it was a commendable undertaking. Congress ordered a gold medal struck to commemorate Lee's exploit (it matched the medal presented to Wayne). Still, disgruntled Virginia officers resented such a command being assigned to a young new major. They demanded Lee's court-martial—for assuming command over his superiors, even though he did so on Washington's orders! He was acquitted with high praise by the court.

Sutherland fared less well. The Hook's natural barrier had caused him to neglect adequate security, and he was found guilty of misconduct by a British court of inquiry. However, he was subsequently acquitted by a court-martial. When Sir Henry Clinton learned about the attack on Paulus Hook, following on the heels of the loss at Stony Point, one of his officers remarked, "I am afraid his temper from these two unlucky blows of fortune became much soured."

The map was made in 1778, probably by one of Montresor's three engineers. The two redoubts are shown, and the artillery of one is marked. Apparently there was also a magazine. Lee, in his report to Washington, claimed he lacked time to find the key to it before his hasty retreat. There is no magazine labeled on the map, although it may have been built in the year between this sketch and the raid. Later revolutionary maps of Paulus Hook show that additional works were built by the British.

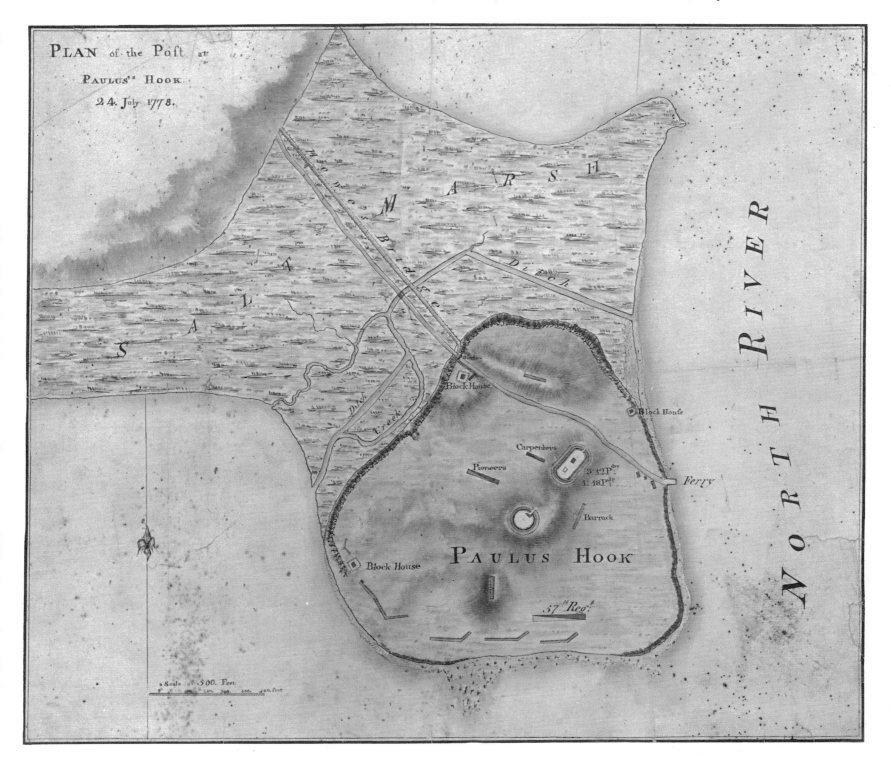

Sullivan's Expedition

The coming of war to the frontier repeated the grim pattern of raid and reprisal that had been enacted since colonial times. In New York and Pennsylvania, white civilization snaked up the Mohawk and Susquehanna river valleys and settled among the Indian societies in uneasy proximity. Open war ignited the submerged struggle between cultures. Borderland loyalists prevailed on the British to reactivate the historic alliance with the Iroquois. In all, perhaps 1,600 of these warriors became participants. In July and November, 1778, loyalists and Iroquois launched what became known as "massacres" in Wyoming Valley, Pennsylvania, and Cherry Valley, New York. At least 265 patriots were killed, and many farms and settlements ruined.

That winter, frontier Americans increasingly demanded retribution. The New York Assembly voted to recruit 1,000 men for border defense. Washington laid before Congress a plan to invade the Indian country, lay waste to their towns, and take hostages to bargain for future good behavior. The first move was to be made by Brig. Gen. James Clinton. While he was raising troops to join the main expedition under Maj. Gen. John Sullivan, he sent Col. Goose Van Schaick to the principal village of the Onandagas, at modern Syracuse. This expedition, in April, 1779, burned the town and returned without losing a man.

Washington's plan called for a pincer operation. In March he ordered Col. Daniel Brodhead at Pittsburgh to drive northward up the Allegheny River with 600 men and head for the Genessee River in western New York to join Sullivan's column, the other jaw of the pincer. Together they would advance against Fort Niagara. Sullivan mobilized his troops at Easton, Pennsylvania, in May. He was given the brigades of Brig. Gens. William Maxwell, Enoch Poor, and Edward Hand, along with Col. Thomas Proctor's artillery. He had to procure boats, horses, cattle, and supplies. In the middle of June he marched over a newly cut road to Wyoming, on the Susquehanna. His force was imposing: 2,300 men, 1,200 pack horses, 700 beef cattle, and 120 boats.

Sullivan finally got under way July 31 and moved up the river, reaching Tioga (Athens, Pa.) 11 days later. There a stronghold, named Fort Sullivan, was built to contain supplies and a rear guard. Twelve miles west, up the Chemung River, was an Indian village of that name which the frightened inhabitants were preparing to abandon. Hand was ordered to make a night march against them, but he found the town deserted. He pushed on and met a party of warriors who gave battle. The Americans lost six killed and seven wounded before the skirmish ended. They burned the huts and destroyed the corn before returning to Tioga.

Poor's brigade was ordered eastward up the Susquehanna branch to meet Clinton's brigade coming down from Otsego Lake. Sullivan's main body followed more slowly. To ensure the passage of his 1,000 men in 200 boats down the sometimes shallow river, Clinton dammed the stream as it issued from the lake. Then he broke the dam and floated down on the flood, joining Sullivan near modern Binghamton on August 19.

The enlarged expedition returned to the Chemung River. On August 29 it approached the Seneca village of Newtown. Here the loyalists and Indians, numbering about 1,100 under Capts. John and Walter Butler and the Mohawk chief, Joseph Brant, had determined to make a stand. They had barricaded the trail and spread themselves on either side of it for one-half mile. Sullivan distributed his superior force even wider. Skirmishing commenced while Poor's brigade filed off to the left. Proctor brought up his cannon and fired on the breastwork. Poor's troops climbed a hill and opened fire on the enemy's flank. The stubborn engagement lasted six hours before the Indians broke up in flight. Enemy losses could not be learned, as the Indians carried off most of their casualties. Sullivan suffered only 4 killed and 35 wounded.

On August 31 the expedition moved forward to a recently deserted Indian village at the site of modern Elmira and then turned north. After burning Catherine's Town, they passed up the east shore of Seneca Lake, scorching more fields and villages as they went, including the Seneca capital of Kanadeaseaga (Geneva). When the army reached Hanneyaye at the foot of Honeoye Lake (not named on the map, but lying west of "Long Lake," which is Canandaigua Lake), it turned one of the houses into a fort and deposited most of its provisions and ammunition under guard.

The main body then made a loop south and northwest to another Seneca stronghold on the Genessee River, near modern Cuylerville. Sullivan sent out a reconnoitering party of 24 Pennsylvania riflemen under Lt. Thomas Boyd. They were discovered and surrounded by Indians and loyalists. A few escaped, and the rest, except two, were killed. That night Boyd and an Indian guide were slowly butchered. The advancing column found their mutilated bodies and in revenge burned the 130 dwellings and extensive fields. The Americans learned that John Butler and Brant had been in command and now had fled to Fort Niagara, 80 miles farther west.

Brodhead was nowhere in sight. He had cut a similar swath of destruction up the Allegheny Valley during August, but stopped just across the New York border. He had taken only a month's provisions, and his men badly needed shoes. Turning back on a slightly different route, he destroyed more Indian villages and reached Fort Pitt on September 14, without a single casualty.

Sullivan did not pursue the enemy farther. He turned back east, setting fire to more cornfields en route. When he came to the foot of Seneca Lake, he sent out three detachments to destroy all settlements. Some 40 Indian towns and hundreds of acres of corn and orchards had been devastated.

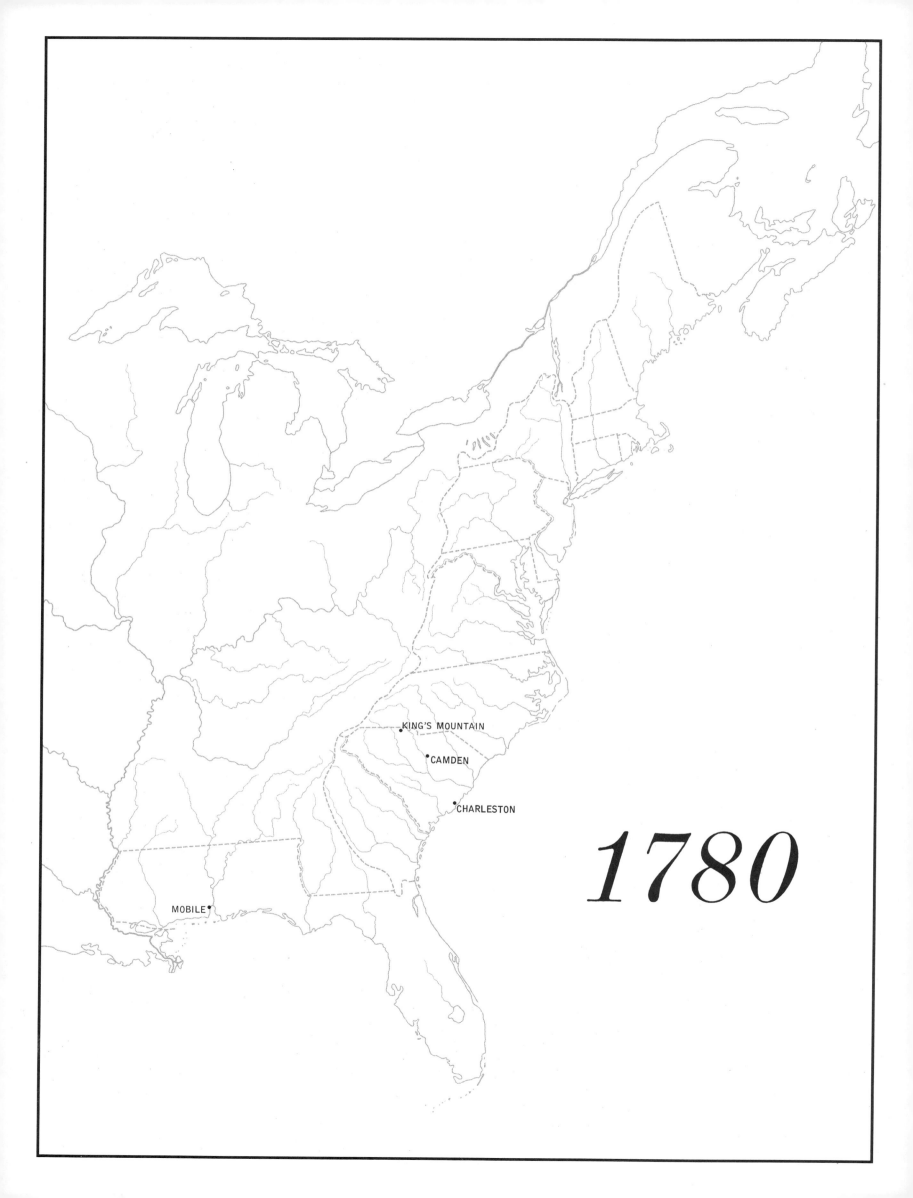

KING'S MOUNTAIN

CAMDEN

CHARLESTON

1780

MOBILE

For the British command, the new year opened the prospect of establishing another base of operations in America. Savannah was already under firm control and an expedition had been launched on Charleston. These ports were to form the fulcrum for a southern strategy. From there it would be possible to garrison South Carolina and work into North Carolina and Virginia. An occupied South would segment the Revolution and Washington's army could then be drawn into a pitched battle and defeated. All the disappointments that had gone before might suddenly be redeemed.

The plan had much to recommend it. Loyalist sentiment was particularly strong in the South and this element could provide and provision troops. Tactically, Charleston could be enveloped in a textbook land and sea maneuver. Patriot morale in the South was known to be low since the defeat of American forces at Savannah in 1779.

The first phase was accomplished on May 12, 1780. Charleston was the greatest victory of the war for the British—5,500 men were captured, along with a vast supply of munitions and stores. But this was to be only a beginning. The plan unfolded with the regular army marching north and leaving garrisons defended by regulars and loyalist units in their wake. Lord Cornwallis was assigned to spearhead this operation. Lt. Col. Banastre Tarleton caught up to a regiment of Virginia Continentals on May 29 after a punishing ride of 105 miles in 54 hours. At Waxhaws, S.C., his mixed force of dragoons and loyalists killed 113 and captured 203 Americans in a crushing frontal assault, while losing only 19 of his own men. Important actions involving loyalists that summer took place at Williamson's plantation, Rocky Mount, and Hanging Rock. An American army under Maj. Gen. Horatio Gates was demolished at Camden on August 16 to end temporarily organized patriot resistance in the South.

The creation of a self-sufficient base of operations in the South depended on logistical considerations. The presence of the French fleet in American waters discouraged British reliance on resupplying by sea. To sustain the army of 8,500 men required effective innovation; one result was the creation of a Commissary of Sequestered Estates. This department functioned as a private business, and at its peak managed over 100 plantations and the work of 4,000 slaves. It was possibly the most imaginative attempt of the war to coordinate agricultural resources with military needs. Yet by the summer of 1781 its effectiveness had been reduced to a few plantations in the vicinity of Charleston with only enough output to feed its slaves.

The cause of the British demise in South Carolina was the result of effective partisan activities. Francis Marion, Thomas Sumter, William Davie, and William Lee Davidson among others organized successful irregular forces for the American cause. Their continuous harassment kept the British army on the defensive in scattered garrisons and eroded its source of supply. These raids made regular transport unpredictable, and as on Long Island, prevented the orderly development of the territory. The partisan bands represented the only defenders of the American cause in the South until Nathanael Greene was appointed commander of the Continentals in October.

British occupation of the South was also contested by patriots on the frontier. There was considerable resentment over the Indian alliance, coupled with traditional backwoods resistance to authority. On October 7, a force of the "over mountain men" surrounded and cut down a force of 900 loyalists under Maj. Patrick Ferguson at Kings Mountain, S.C. The American leaders lost control of the situation, and militia Col. William Campbell cried out, "For God's sake, quit! It's murder to shoot anymore." Ferguson was found dead with seven bullet wounds.

The British control of the South was not accompanied by any systematic effort at surveying. The problem was not a shortage of personnel because at least six members of the Corps of Engineers were on duty in South Carolina throughout 1780, each of whom could draw maps. Survey teams could have been organized from among the troops.

In the absence of military surveys, British officers were forced to rely on available printed maps; notably the 1773 James Cook map of South Carolina and the 1770 John Collet survey of North Carolina. Sir Henry Clinton possessed a copy of both. Prewar southern governors had encouraged colonial surveys, while the record of the northern governors was not nearly as consistent. Yet the use of these maps for military maneuver was hindered by their inaccuracy. A computer analysis of the placement of 20 settlements on the Cook map of South Carolina reveals considerable distortion. The position of settlements in relation to their nearest neighbor represents an average dislocation of 6.9 miles and 15 degrees. The first figure invites comparison with the map of New Jersey on the front endpaper which registers an inaccuracy of 3.25 miles— less than one-half of that for South Carolina. In terms of military operations, an additional march of seven miles beyond a projected destination would disrupt orderly maneuver of troop detachment and supply.

The documentary evidence supports the statistics. During the occupation of South Carolina, Lord Francis Rawdon complained to Tarleton in a letter of October 23, 1780, that he was forced to rely on other methods of reconnaissance in that, "all the maps of the country which I have are so very inaccurate." He added that it was difficult for him to estimate distances because, "I speak from maps, in which I suspect the relative positions to be ill laid down."

Partisan raids by American forces depended on superior reconnaissance, but they also relied on the topographic confusion of the enemy. In this sense, the absence of accurate maps handicapped the British army and contributed to their failure in the South.

Mobile

Isolated at the far extremity of the 3,000-mile colonial coastline was the province of West Florida. The British had taken possession in 1763. Mobile and the territory west to the Mississippi River were ceded that year from the French. Its military advantage was viewed as the protection against foreign influence over the powerful southern Indian tribes and the prospect of opening the Mississippi to British commerce.

The prospect proved illusory. British navigation on the river had to bypass Spanish-held New Orleans. A number of schemes were attempted to dredge tributaries farther north leading directly to the Gulf of Mexico. All were unworkable. But settlement was encouraged and garrisons were established near present-day Baton Rouge and Natchez. By 1770 the British population of the colony numbered about 2,500. It was to triple over the next nine years principally from the influx of loyalists to farms along the Mississippi.

The outpost at Mobile exemplified life on the tropical frontier. It was a village of about 350 inhabitants when the British first took control. The fetid, miasmal climate and the brackish well water decimated successive regiments sent there. The garrison was reduced to a small detachment for several years until war reached the fringes of empire. Tedium and monotony of garrison life in the colonial backwater was interrupted by the British fantasy of seizing New Orleans—120 miles from Mobile.

By the time war had spilled into the Caribbean at the end of 1778, Sir Henry Clinton committed over 1,000 additional troops to West Florida. This action removed them from effective use with the main army and sentenced them to the fate of garrison soldiers in the tropics. Within six weeks the crack grenadier company of the Waldeck Regiment alone saw 15 die from disease and another 18 desert. In September, 1779, 70 soldiers were sick at Mobile, and desertions of up to seven men at a time were frequent, all of whom "ran the most hazardous risks in attempting their escape."

Relations between Spain and Britain in these latitudes had never been friendly. The Spanish governor of Louisiana, Col. Bernardo de Gálvez, had continued a policy of financial aid to the rebels after his appointment in 1777. He sent money, powder, and supplies to Col. George Rogers Clark in Illinois and provided services for Capt. James Willing's raid on Natchez in 1778. When Gálvez was notified that a formal declaration of war had been signed between England and Spain in June, 1779, he struck before the British learned of it. By estimates of the defenders, a mixed force of 2,000 veterans, Mexican recruits, blacks (200 of whom were armed), Indians, and militiamen of every class and color fell on the lower Mississippi settlements. They quickly captured the frail British forts under Lt. Col. Alexander Dickson in September and imprisoned a total of 450 men.

Gálvez was able to regroup at New Orleans before setting off to conquer Mobile with a smaller force of 754 in 12 ships. After a difficult voyage of almost a month, he entered Mobile Bay on February 10, 1780, where one-half of the fleet promptly ran aground on the treacherous sand bar at the mouth of the harbor. A reinforcement of five ships carrying 1,412 troops from Havana arrived, and on February 26, Gálvez began formal siege operations at 2,000 yards from Fort Charlotte.

The British force of about 300 men was commanded by Capt. Elias Durnford, Corps of Engineers, and lieutenant governor of the colony. He was known as "the Black Prince" from his years in the Florida sun. Legend records that unarmed, he once stared down a tiger. It was unusual for a member of the Corps of Engineers, whose unit was administered separately from the regular army under the Board of Ordnance, to assume command of garrison troops. However, in a letter dated December 15, 1779, Durnford insisted that his seniority as an officer gave him that right and he expected, "the command will belong to me when present." His forcefulness, and possibly his logic, won the argument.

The siege of Mobile was conducted with considerable formality. On March 1, Gálvez sent an officer, Francisco Bouligny, to ask for the surrender of the fort. Durnford knew Bouligny and invited him to dine under a flag of truce. After a pleasant visit, the defending commander politely declined to give up. A few days later, Durnford sent a dozen bottles of wine, 12 loaves of bread, and 12 chickens through the lines for the prisoners that the Spanish had seized. Gálvez responded to this gesture with two cases of wine, a crate of oranges, some tea biscuits and corn cakes, and a box of Havana cigars, and with assurances that all British prisoners he held were being well treated. Meanwhile, a relief column under Maj. Gen. John Campbell had started by land from Pensacola—a distance of 100 miles. On March 12, they camped in the Tensaw region, 30 miles around the bay from Mobile, and heard the sound of gunfire across the water gradually fade away.

On that day Gálvez had mounted nine cannon on his forward battery and opened fire. Fort Charlotte sustained considerable damage, and at sunset the British surrendered. Gálvez reported the capture of 307: 13 officers, 113 soldiers, 56 sailors, 70 hunters and habitants, and 55 armed blacks.

Campbell hurried back to Pensacola. Twenty-nine Spanish sails appeared off the harbor on March 29 but did not attack. Two weeks later Pensacola was relieved by 11 vessels with supplies and reinforcements. For the moment, the remnant of British authority in West Florida was safe. Yet Clinton regarded the outpost as "beyond the reach of timely assistance from me," and the aggressive Gálvez at Mobile posed an ever-present threat.

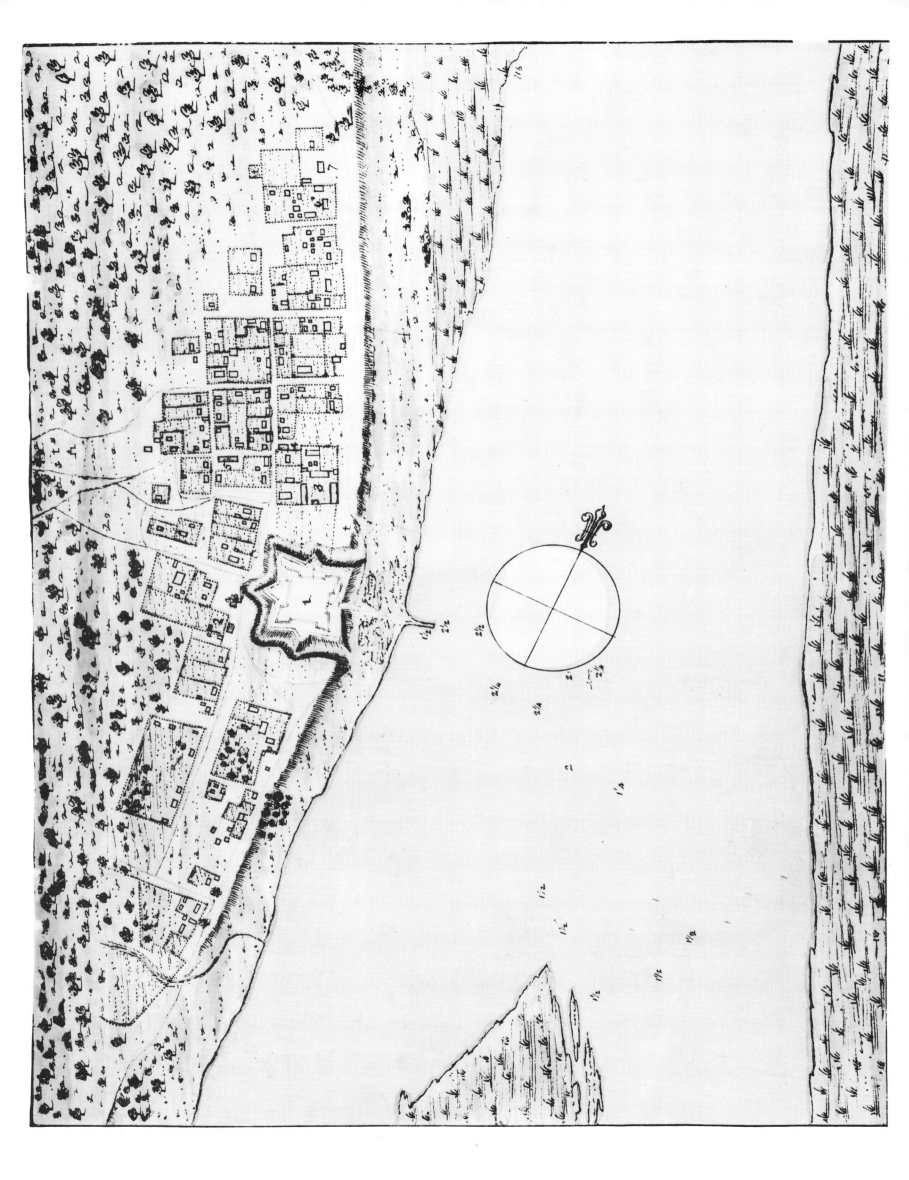

Charleston

Since the British defeat near Charleston in 1776, numerous proposals had been put forth for another attempt. Charleston was an important source of supplies and revenue. Its capture would provide an excellent base from which to launch military operations. Loyalists were plentiful in the South, and their spokesmen urged a British invasion. The British colonial secretary, Lord George Germain, recommended to Sir Henry Clinton in 1779 that he add South Carolina to the British control of Georgia. Clinton, for his part, had already decided to end the year with an attack on South Carolina.

Yet Clinton foresaw difficulties. A large force would have to be left in New York to oppose Washington. He had doubts about his ability to obtain provisions in the South, and about the safety of his line of communications to New York. Also, to avoid repeating the disaster of 1776, Clinton needed the cooperation of the Royal Navy but did not hold a high opinion of its new commander, Vice Adm. Marriot Arbuthnot.

It was December 26 before Arbuthnot set sail. He commanded 5,500 sailors and marines on 10 warships, escorting 90 transports filled with about 8,000 troops under Clinton, with 400 horses, numerous cannon, and other equipment. The winter voyage was a five-week ordeal of stormy weather before the expedition reached the Savannah River. Nearly all the cavalry mounts and much of the artillery were lost. One troop transport lost its masts and was blown across the Atlantic to Ireland.

After reprovisioning at Savannah, on February 11 the troops disembarked on Simmons Island, southwest of Charleston. Clinton began the slow and cautious deployment that was to take the army another one and one-half months to reach the town (see map on pages 84-85). Clinton was at odds with Arbuthnot and later quarreled with his second in command, Lord Charles Cornwallis, which cost him their full cooperation.

The defenses of Charleston were in the hands of Maj. Gen. Benjamin Lincoln. His force numbered about 1,600 Continentals and 2,000 militia from North and South Carolina. Attempts to raise more troops in South Carolina were unsuccessful. Lincoln even tried to recruit Spanish forces in Havana. He had described the town as defenseless in November, and the attack by Maj. Gen. Augustine Prevost earlier that year had demonstrated the need for both land and sea defenses. On the land side of the town, the Americans had a ditch dug and filled with water. Behind this was constructed a line of breastworks which masked 66 cannon and additional mortars. Ships were sunk in the Cooper River to prevent the enemy from approaching by sea. A smallpox epidemic disrupted construction, and the defenses stood incomplete when the British arrived. Lincoln did not feel he could evacuate the town while civilian authorities in Charleston insisted he should hold it.

The lost ordnance delayed the British advance. Not until March 28 did the army arrive on the Ashley River.

That night a fleet of small boats moved up the river past the ferry to where Cornwallis's troops waited. He crossed the river and moved back toward the town virtually unopposed. Lincoln, who had expected Cornwallis to cross at the ferry, had been outmaneuvered.

The British moved to within 800 yards of the city and began trenching operations. Earlier, Arbuthnot had crossed the bar with several ships. A combination of tides, winds, and low water had made it impossible for the few American ships to oppose him. On April 8 the British sailed past the fire of Fort Moultrie. The town was now confronted on three sides. On land the British employed typical siege tactics of that time. This consisted of the construction of "parallels" or trenches to provide shelter for the troops and artillery. Each successive parallel was constructed at an angle to the defenses until the guns could breach the walls of the town. When the first parallel was completed on April 10, the British commanders called for Lincoln to surrender. He refused, and work began on the second parallel.

Clinton also dispatched Lt. Cols. James Webster and Banastre Tarleton on a great circle march to cut off Lincoln's supply line at Monck's Corner. They surprised and scattered an American detachment. Then Webster's force crossed to the east bank of the Cooper River and further tightened the British hold on the town. Lincoln could see the inevitable. Gov. John Rutledge had already slipped away and other civilians threatened to aid the British if the army attempted to leave. On April 21, Lincoln proposed to surrender the town if he could remove his army. Clinton refused, and three days later Cornwallis crossed the Cooper River with reinforcements.

Lincoln ordered a sortie that cost the British some casualties but did not dislodge them. The British trenches were coming closer and they had begun to drain the defensive ditch. On May 8 Clinton sent in another demand for unconditional surrender. When negotiations broke off the British fired hot shot into Charleston. This, plus the continuing depletion of the town's food supply, led to petitions for Lincoln to accept the best terms available. On May 12 the American army formally surrendered. The militia were allowed to go home on parole but the Continentals were taken prisoners. Clinton's plan to use the captured American weapons to arm loyalists was hampered by the explosion of a powder magazine.

The British counted nearly 5,500 Americans captured, which included many inactive town residents nominally enrolled in the militia. Even so, it was numerically the largest American defeat of the war. In June, Clinton took one-third of his force back to New York and left Cornwallis with 9,000 men to extend British control.

On the map opposite, the road down the center of the Charleston peninsula is the route followed by the British. The Ashley River is on the west, and sunken American ships block the Cooper River on the east.

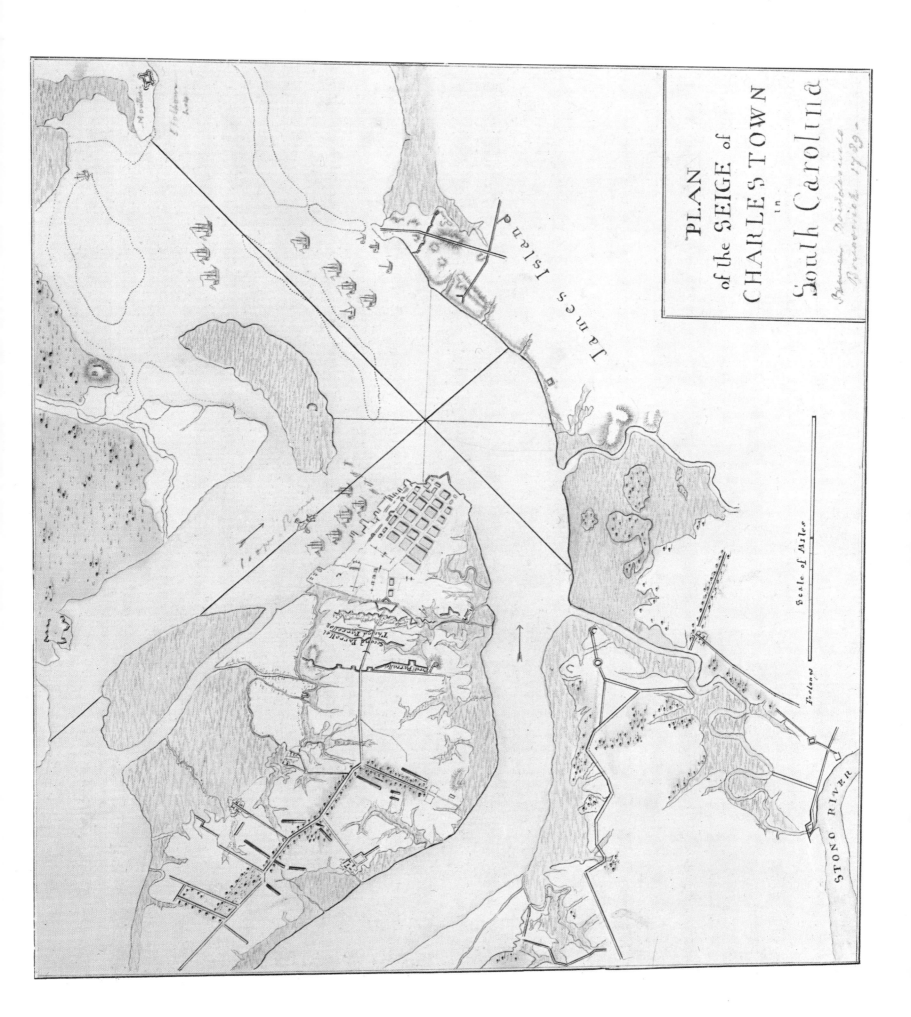

PLAN
of the SEIGE of
CHARLES TOWN
in
South Carolina

James Island

STONO RIVER

Scale of Miles

Camden

Upon learning of Maj. Gen. Benjamin Lincoln's surrender at Charleston, the Continental Congress appointed Maj. Gen. Horatio Gates to command the Southern Department. Secluded on his Virginia farm, Gates commented on the prospects of his new command: "an army without strength—a military chest without money, a department apparently deficient in public spirit, and a climate that encreases despondency."

To retrieve the patriot cause in South Carolina, Gates decided to advance on the British supply depot at Camden. Instead of a circuitous route with more plentiful forage, he elected an approach through barren and hostile territory. On July 27 the remnant American southern army of about 900 Maryland and Delaware Continentals marched south from Hollinsworth Farm, N.C., and was joined en route by 2,100 North Carolina and Virginia militiamen. All units were desperately short of provisions to the extent that the men were issued molasses in place of rum, and the officers used hair powder to thicken their soup. This purgative diet was predictably disastrous.

Gates's reputation, gained at Saratoga, was based on his careful attention to supplies, effective use of militia, and prudent commitment of troops to battle. Curiously, his actions in this campaign were directly opposite to these circumspect qualities. During a night march beginning 13 miles north of the objective at Camden, his army unexpectedly blundered into advance units of British cavalry.

Unknown to Gates, the British commander at Camden, Francis Hastings Rawdon, had been reinforced by 900 light infantry under Maj. Gen. Charles Cornwallis, which brought troop strength to 2,200. Alarmed by reports of American intentions, the royal army was moving north on the evening of August 15 to intercept Gates. A brief firefight ensued as the two forces met and then deployed on parallel lines in darkness to await dawn. Upon taking a captive, Gates learned the actual strength of his opponents and quickly called a council of war. Although no battle plan had been prepared for this type of surprise, there was little choice for the Americans. Militia Maj. Gen. Edward Stevens summed it up when he asked, "Is it not too late *now* to do anything but fight?"

The prospective battlefield was no more than a clearing in the dense woods. Thomas Barretté, a British lieutenant in the 23rd Regiment, depicted the arrangement of troops on the morning of August 16. The Americans held a slight uphill advantage with an open field behind in which to fall back and regroup if necessary. For the British, a stream behind their lines and swamps on either side would block a hasty retreat. Barretté's map erred only in estimating the strength and dispersal of American troops. The combined forces numbered less than half the cartographer's estimate of 7,000, and the Continentals were clustered on the right with the militia on the left. By chance, Cornwallis put his regulars opposite the American militia, and his loyalist militia opposite the Continentals. The lines were drawn.

At dawn the British force advanced. The morning haze and smoke which hung over the battlefield at first obscured a full view of their approach. The American militia was no match for the British light infantry and 23rd Regiment under Brig. James Webster. After firing a single volley, the militia was routed by a bayonet charge. The disciplined British line "firing and huzzaing" proved too much for the erstwhile civilians. One participant observed that they fled "like a Torrent and bore all before them." In trying to rally these troops, Gates was caught up in the human tide and swept off the field.

Only the Delaware and Maryland Continentals held their ground on the other side. Their leader, self-styled "Baron" Johann de Kalb, a giant in stature and spirit, was seen in many places exhorting the troops and fighting hand-to-hand. They exchanged volley for volley with the opposing loyalists under Rawdon until the latter were stopped and then driven back. Unknown to Kalb, the American militia had been eliminated. Cornwallis, sensing that the left flank of the Continentals was unprotected, ordered up Lt. Col. Banastre Tarleton's cavalry. Kalb fell dead with 11 wounds in that charge. Heroically, the Continentals advanced once again before they broke. Then it was over.

The battle had lasted less than an hour. The American survivors faded into the swamp or wilderness, and left behind about 250 killed and 800 prisoners, including the wounded. The loss included 70 officers, 8 cannon, and a roadway strewn with wagons, stores, and baggage.

The British counted 68 of their own men killed and 245 wounded. Cornwallis ordered Tarleton's cavalry to chase the stragglers. The 26-year-old officer carried out the command with the alacrity that earned him the name "Bloody Tarleton." Two days later, with 160 cavalry and light infantry, he scattered a force of 800 partisans under Brig. Gen. Thomas Sumter.

This combined disaster temporarily ended organized American resistance in the South. Ten days later only 700 men reassembled 180 miles north of the battle, at Hillsborough, N.C. Gates was condemned by everyone but the surviving soldiers. Congress stripped him of command, leaving the choice of a successor to Washington.

Yet British success was not secure from guerrilla harassment or sickness. Determined to carry the war into North Carolina, Cornwallis ventured into territory patroled by American partisans. On September 22, British headquarters was established at Charlotte, N.C.; but the lower counties proved infertile soil in which to plant the royal flag. Tarleton found the area "more hostile to England than any in America." It became evident that Cornwallis had overestimated loyalist support when foraging parties were attacked and collaborators demanded the king's protection. Communications between Camden and Charleston were endangered. Malaria and yellow fever reduced the ranks. The fruits of British victory in the South could not be harvested.

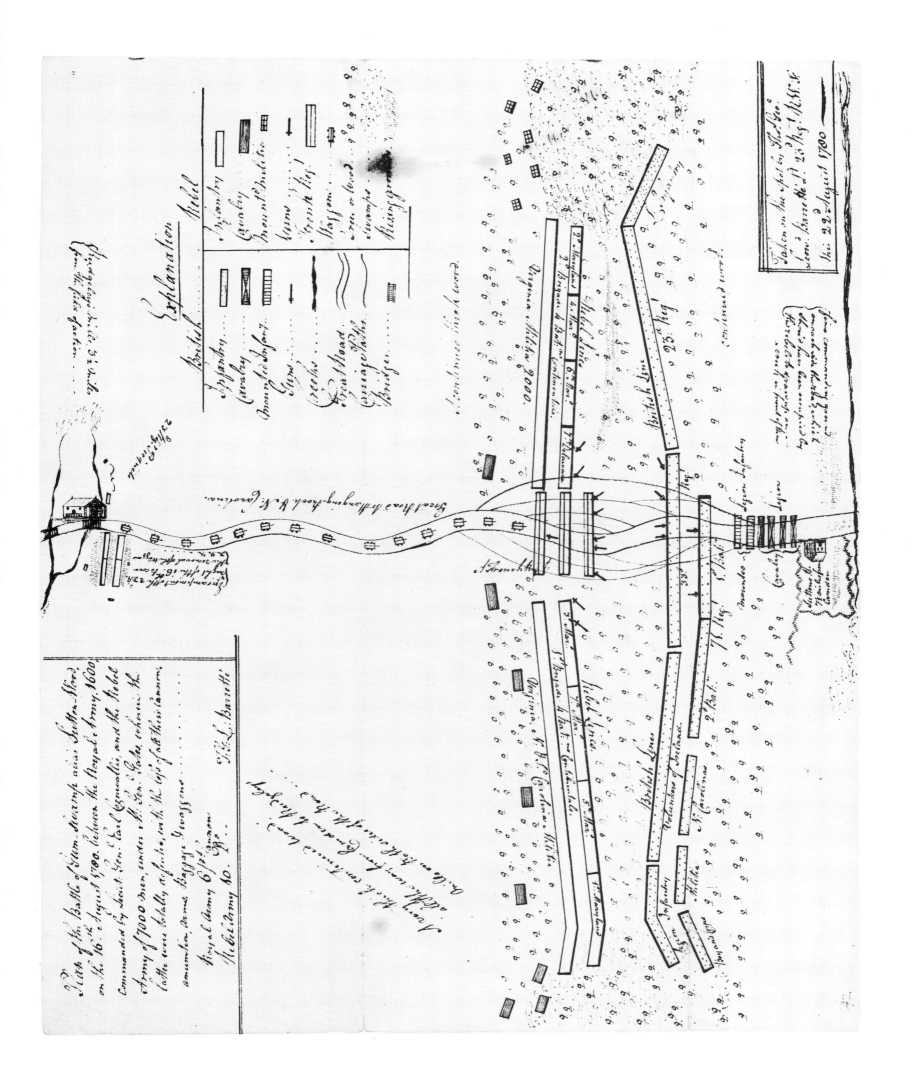

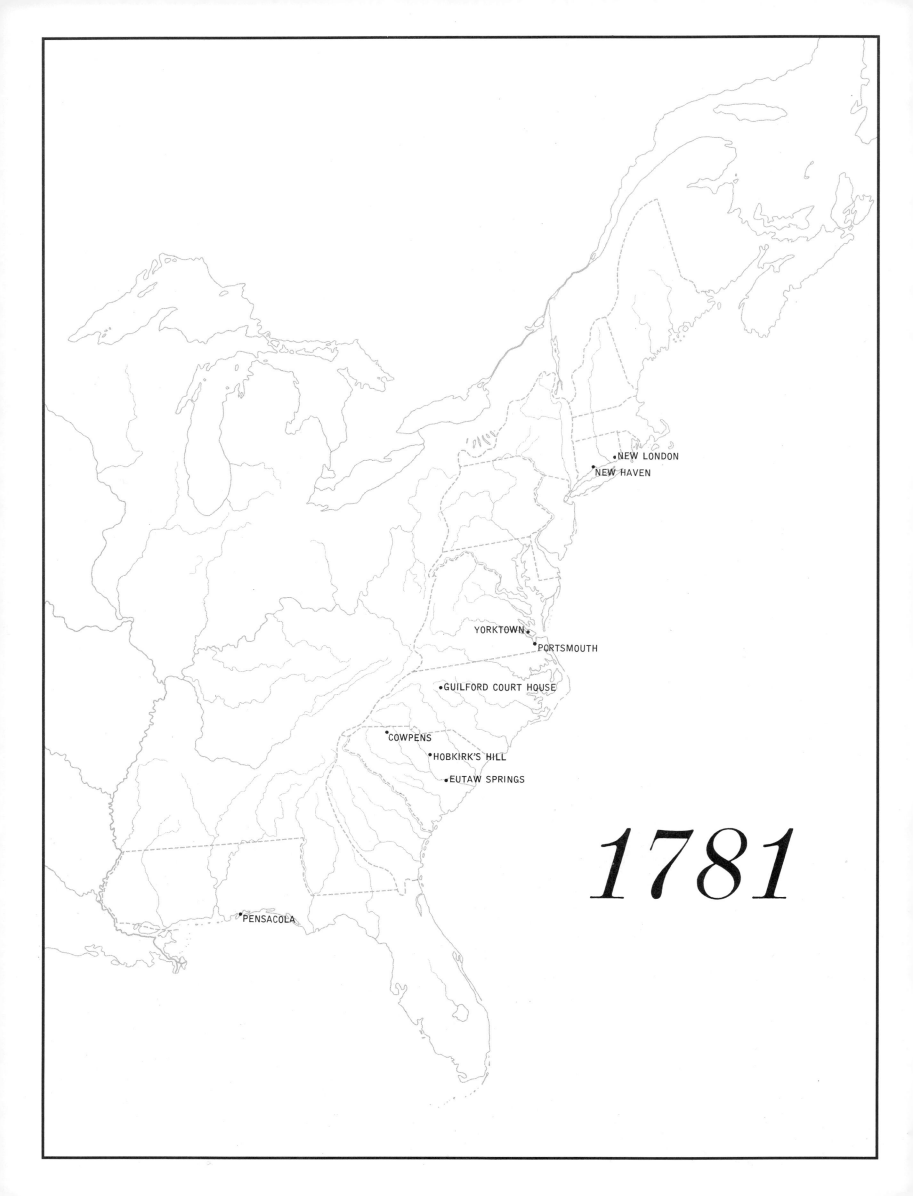

•NEW LONDON
•NEW HAVEN

YORKTOWN•
•PORTSMOUTH

•GUILFORD COURT HOUSE

•COWPENS

•HOBKIRK'S HILL

•EUTAW SPRINGS

1781

•PENSACOLA

The year that was to end so gloriously for the United States began inauspiciously and even dangerously. In January Brig. Gen. Anthony Wayne was forced to suppress a mutiny by the Pennsylvania regulars. Meanwhile, congressional war financing had collapsed and American commanders were sometimes reduced to borrowing funds from merchants and French officers. The alliance with France proved not the panacea expected. And the war now included an active southern theater with the British firmly entrenched in the most important southern cities.

In the South Maj. Gen. Nathanael Greene faced superior British forces under Lord Cornwallis. The revitalized American army initiated the campaign with a solid victory at Cowpens on January 17. In February, Greene began the series of actions that was to gain back the whole South. Cornwallis's proposals for offensive action had been favorably received in London by colonial secretary Lord George Germain, and Cornwallis began to operate a virtually independent command. Ignoring Sir Henry Clinton's defensive entreaties, Cornwallis began to chase Greene across the South. By calculated retreats and cautious troop commitments, Greene pulled Cornwallis into North Carolina. In his pursuit the British commander overextended himself and soon lost contact with his South Carolina bases. After the action at Guilford Court House on March 15, Cornwallis withdrew to Wilmington and started on his fateful move northward into Virginia.

Cornwallis reached Virginia in May. A British expedition under Maj. Gens. Benedict Arnold and William Phillips had been raiding the countryside since January. Washington was forced to dispatch the Marquis de Lafayette with some Continentals to bolster the Virginia militia. Lafayette shadowed the British until reinforced by Wayne in May. The two American commanders were then buffeted across the state by Cornwallis before the latter took up defensive positions at Yorktown.

In the North Washington met with the Comte de Rochambeau at Wethersfield, Conn., on May 22 to formulate plans for combined French-American operations. Washington envisioned a diversionary attack on New York City to draw off British troops from Virginia and the Carolinas. Word that Cornwallis had arrived in Virginia added urgency to the planning. Although their strategy was somewhat compromised when Clinton received word of the New York plan, the French and American forces joined together July 6 and spent the month pressuring the outer defenses of New York. On August 14 Washington received word that the long-awaited French fleet under Adm. de Grasse planned to head for the Chesapeake. Washington then made the risky decision to leave New York, divide his army, and move on Cornwallis in Virginia. The allied army was in Philadelphia before Clinton became aware of their true destination.

Clinton had been assured that de Grasse's fleet would be followed closely by the British navy and was unworried.

He dispatched Arnold on a diversionary raid to New London on September 6, unaware that a naval battle off Chesapeake Cape would trap Cornwallis at Yorktown. With access to the sea blocked, Cornwallis surrendered his army on October 19. This ended British attempts to occupy territory beyond the four ports which they already possessed. Another campaign was never mounted.

Inadequate reconnaissance was a factor in the British loss at Yorktown. Cornwallis's engineer claimed not to have been familiar with the site of the defensive fortifications. Because maps were only one source of local information, spies, scouting parties, deserters, and guides were assigned to gather reconnaissance. Loyalists were a particularly valuable source. Lt. Col. John Graves Simcoe of the Queen's Rangers took advantage of the local knowledge possessed by his troops. He made a list of the areas in which each of his men originated. These records had been used when Clinton asked Simcoe to provide guides for the withdrawal of the army from Philadelphia. It is significant that while several maps of the route were available, Clinton chose to rely on a guide.

The Corps of Guides and Pioneers was formed in late 1776. It maintained an average strength of 250 throughout the war. Pioneers were employed to fell trees, repair roads, and mend bridges. In the South, a unit of black troops was incorporated into the organization. The Guides performed a reconnaissance function and were used as escorts to the main army as well as assignment to accompany detachments in various locations throughout America. At least three officers in this corps had cartographic training. Pierre Nicole and Charles Blaskowitz were of Swiss and Prussian origin respectively and had previously served as draftsmen to the British army before receiving officer commissions. In 1778, Blaskowitz was prohibited from filling vacancies in his company in order to devote more time to making maps. George Taylor arrived from Scotland in 1781 to make large-scale topographic surveys of the British base at New York (see map on pages 128-29).

Apparently, no effort was made to coordinate the cartographic effort of the Guides with the work of the Corps of Engineers. It is not known if the officers in the Guides had access to the drawing room in New York. Their foreign origin and commissions in a unit designed to reward the "most needy" may have segregated them from frequent contact with socially conscious engineer officers. Their situation is an example of the pervasive overlapping of responsibility as it was the official duty of the engineer department to provide maps to the army. But the absence of drawing and surveying skills among many engineers and their preoccupation with fortification limited their ability to provide maps. The Guides came to assume an important role in providing military reconnaissance. They served as a source of topographic information in both an oral and cartographic tradition.

Guilford Court House

The battle at Guilford Court House marked the end of a long duel between Maj. Gen. Nathanael Greene and Maj. Gen. Charles Cornwallis in the Carolinas. After the disastrous defeat of the British at Cowpens, S.C., on January 17, 1781, Cornwallis decided to pursue the rebels.

Believing that in order to catch the Americans his whole army would have to become a fast-moving unit, Cornwallis set the example by tossing on the ground his own personal baggage and comforts, "an action which was followed by every officer . . . without a single murmur." Although the officers did not complain, the men suffered a greater loss, that of their rum. Without the comforts of the rum, the number of desertions increased. "In this situation," an officer wrote, "it was resolved to follow Greene's army to the end of the world."

Cornwallis pushed on, hoping to force Greene into action before the latter could be reinforced from Virginia. After Greene crossed into southern Virginia, Cornwallis turned back on February 17, in hopes of receiving support from the loyalists and supplies for his soldiers. The British were so desperate for food that "sometimes we had turnips . . . when we came to a turnip field; or at a field of corn, we converted our canteens into rasps and ground our Indian corn for bread; when we could get no corn, we were compelled to eat liver as a substitute for bread." Greene promptly followed him into North Carolina. For another three weeks he teased and harried the Englishman while avoiding a general engagement until he had additional brigades. Finally on March 14, Greene decided to make a stand at Guilford Court House. He outnumbered Cornwallis's force by two to one.

Although Greene had chosen the place and time for battle, he waited that night in hope that neither of two things would occur—rain and a night attack. Rain would make American muskets useless and give the advantage to the British bayonets; and a night attack would make his militia and inexperienced regulars uneasy. The weather, however, remained fair, and Cornwallis had just confirmed reports concerning Greene's position that night, and so prepared for battle the next day.

The countryside around Guilford Court House offered many advantages for the defenders. The dense wood provided protection to the American flank and made artillery ineffective. The Americans held a tremendous advantage. Having chosen his ground on a slope between the court house and a rivulet south of it, Greene drew up his army in three parallel lines. Perhaps Greene's lines were too far apart; certainly he had no reserves, and from his position at the rear he could not see the front.

On March 15, Cornwallis marched his men northward to Guilford. At 1:30 P.M. he signaled to advance on the American first line. When the British were within 150 yards, the patriots opened fire upon command. William Montgomery, who was present at the first volley, reported that "the part of the British line at which they aimed looked like the scattering stalks in a wheat field, when the harvest man has passed over it with his cradle." The British troops regrouped and continued to advance, yelling and charging straight at the first line with their bayonets fixed. Many of the militia—mainly inexperienced—fled upon the sight of the bayonets, and soon the redcoats forced the American left to withdraw to the woods. The British charged once more, and the whole front line fell back.

The fighting moved from the cleared fields into the dense woods where the second line was positioned. Slowly, with assistance from the cavalry, the British forced the second line to retreat.

Greene had placed his most experienced men in the third line with two six-pound cannon positioned in the center. His line was in a command position atop a hill with a brook below which the British would have to cross under fire. The American commander was confident of a victory.

The British light infantry charged, but were forced to retreat and await reinforcements. The American cavalry held back the advance and soon forced them to fall back. Cornwallis, fearing a general retreat, ordered two three-pound cannon to fire "into the midst of human melange" killing friend and foe alike. When the smoke cleared, more British troops charged and "the enemy were soon put to flight."

Greene withdrew to Reedy Fork, three miles from Guilford, waited for some stragglers, and then marched all night to his former camp, 15 miles from the battlefield. He listed 78 killed and 183 wounded. One thousand of the North Carolina militia and others were missing. Cornwallis suffered 143 killed and 389 wounded. Apparently no prisoners were taken on either side, although Cornwallis reported that he had captured a few.

Staggered from fatigue and hunger—as they had not eaten anything in 24 hours—Cornwallis's men camped on the battlefield for three nights in a pouring rain. On March 18, leaving behind 70 of his wounded, he withdrew 175 miles to Wilmington, N.C., where he could obtain supplies by sea. Meanwhile, Greene crossed North Carolina and invaded South Carolina.

Thus ended Cornwallis's campaign to clear the Carolinas. Long afterward, Sir Henry Clinton summed up the effort: "After forcing the passage of several great rivers, fighting a bloody battle, and running 820 miles over almost every part of the invaded provinces at the expense of above 3,000 men, he accomplished no other purpose but the having exposed, by an unnecessary retreat to Wilmington, the two valuable colonies behind him to be overrun and conquered by that very army which he boasts to have completely routed but a week or two before."

The map of the action was made in the days that followed the battle and was sent to Clinton. It shows the first, second, and third positions of the two armies; red indicates the British, and yellow marks the position of the Americans.

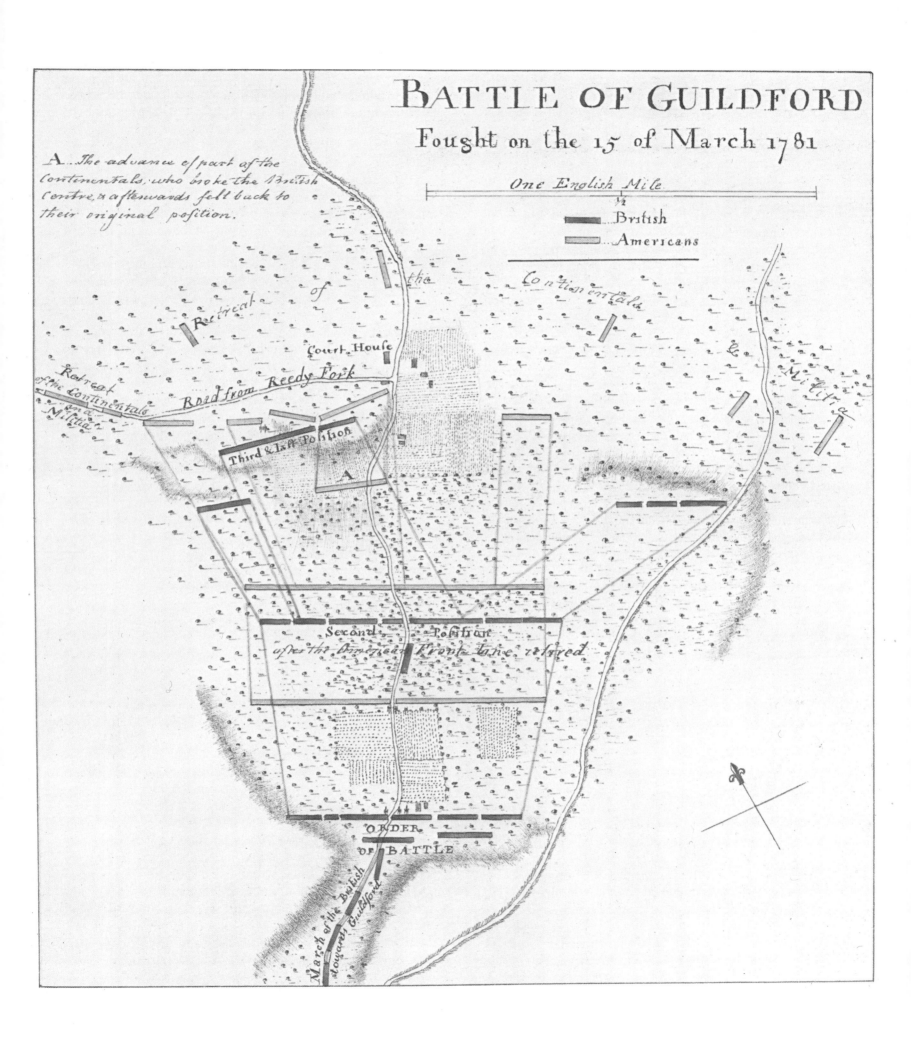

BATTLE OF GUILDFORD
Fought on the 15 of March 1781

A. The advance of part of the
Continentals, who broke the British
Centre, & afterwards fell back to
their original position.

One English Mile

British
Americans

Retreat of the
Continentals

Court House

Retreat of the Continentals and Militia

Road from Reedy Fork

Third & left Position

A

Militia

Second Position

after the American Front line, retired

ORDER
OF BATTLE

March of the British towards Guildford

Hobkirk's Hill

Three weeks after the battle at Guilford Court House, Maj. Gen. Nathanael Greene started his reduced force of 1,500 men marching southward across North Carolina. His aim was to surprise Lord Francis Rawdon at Camden, S.C., just south of where the disastrous defeat of Gen. Horatio Gates had taken place the previous August. After the capture of Charleston, Rawdon, a 26-year-old lieutenant colonel who had distinguished himself in America, remained in South Carolina under Maj. Gen. Charles Cornwallis. Rawdon depleted his force by sending 500 men under Lt. Col. John Watson on a raid eastward to find and destroy Brig. Gen. Francis Marion's partisans. However, "by arming our musicians, our drummers, and in short everything that could carry a firelock, I [Rawdon] mustered above 900 for the field."

Greene ordered Marion and Lt. Col. Henry Lee's legion to attack Fort Watson, about 27 miles south of Camden. Fort Watson was a stockaded fort built atop an old Indian mound. The Americans had no cannon, so the fort seemed inaccessible. Col. Hezekiah Maham of South Carolina had an ingenious idea. He took some men into the pine woods and for five days cut and notched log timbers. On the night of April 22, they dragged out the timbers and fitted them together into a tower with a platform on top protected by log siding. When dawn broke, a company of riflemen started to fire *down* on the startled British. The fort was forced to surrender. Lee and Marion then pursued Watson in order to prevent his return to Camden.

Meanwhile, after a march of 140 miles, Greene reached Hobkirk's Hill on the north edge of Camden on April 19. He awaited reinforcements from Brig. Gen. Thomas Sumter, but none arrived. "A comfortable supply of provisions" was brought to camp on April 25, and the patriots took advantage of the short-lived peace. Soon, the sound of musket fire was heard coming from the plain below the southeast side of the hill.

With his mixed force of 900, Rawdon attacked the picket guard and light infantry under Capt. Robert Kirkwood. Learning military tactics from the American general Daniel Morgan, he ordered his marksmen to concentrate on American officers. The guard, however, delayed the advancing British long enough for the troops on the hill to form their defense. Observing that the enemy line was not as extensive as his, Greene decided not to await Rawdon's assault but to take the initiative. He ordered an attack.

The Virginia and Maryland regiments advanced while two other regiments enveloped Rawdon's narrow front. Rawdon, realizing the error in his formation, quickly reinforced his front line. It was held in check by the oncoming Americans until "extremely improper and unmilitary" orders given by Col. John Gunby caused confusion among the troops. Gunby's regiment started to falter and instead of rallying his men, he ordered his whole regiment to halt and regroup in the rear. Rawdon quickly ordered a bayonet charge and routed the regiment. Disorder spread. Other regiments then panicked and broke lines.

At the same time, Lt. Col. William Washington's cavalry was ordered to attack the British rear. Because of the dense woods, the cavalry circled so far around the ongoing engagement that it emerged far behind the enemy's line. Instead of striking the fighting men, Washington began to capture all the noncombatants and stragglers he could find. He took 200 prisoners. But when he heard of the American retreat, he was too encumbered with captives to finish the plan. Leaving most of the prisoners behind, he headed back to the hill. There was nothing Greene could do except withdraw. Lee said that Greene, "finding every effort to reinstate the battle illusory, conscious that his reserve was not calculated to face the veteran foe, wisely determined to diminish the ills of the sad and unaccountable reverse by retiring from the field."

Once Greene retreated, the outnumbered Rawdon returned to the defenses of Camden. He suffered 258 casualties, 38 of them killed. He had made an admirable show against a superior force, but the victory gained no advantage. Camden became only an outpost after the loss of Fort Watson and the decision of Cornwallis to march into Virginia. Consequently, on May 10 Rawdon retreated to Monck's Corner, 12 miles north of Charleston. Before leaving Camden, he destroyed everything he could not take with him. He carried off 400 or 500 blacks, and "all of the most obnoxious loyalists."

Greene reported only 18 killed, 108 wounded, and 138 missing, some of them probably prisoners, the others deserters. All of the American wounded were taken back to the main force, for the recovery of these men was consoling to the others. He was greatly disappointed and blamed Gunby for the loss. In a letter to Joseph Reed he wrote, "We should have had Lord Rawdon and his whole command prisoners in three minutes, if Colonel Gunby had not ordered his regiment to retire...I was almost frantic with vexation at the disappointment." It was an engagement which the Americans should have won. However, the abandonment of Camden achieved Greene's objective and softened his defeat.

No manuscript map of this battle is known. However, Capt. Charles Vallancey, a participant with the Volunteers of Ireland, made a drawing which was published in London in 1783 and is reproduced here. It shows Rawdon's approach to the hill from the southeast and his extended front line. The American line is shown with Kirkwood out in front and the North Carolina militia in reserve behind. Washington's dragoons are not shown; perhaps they were on their sweep south of "Log Town."

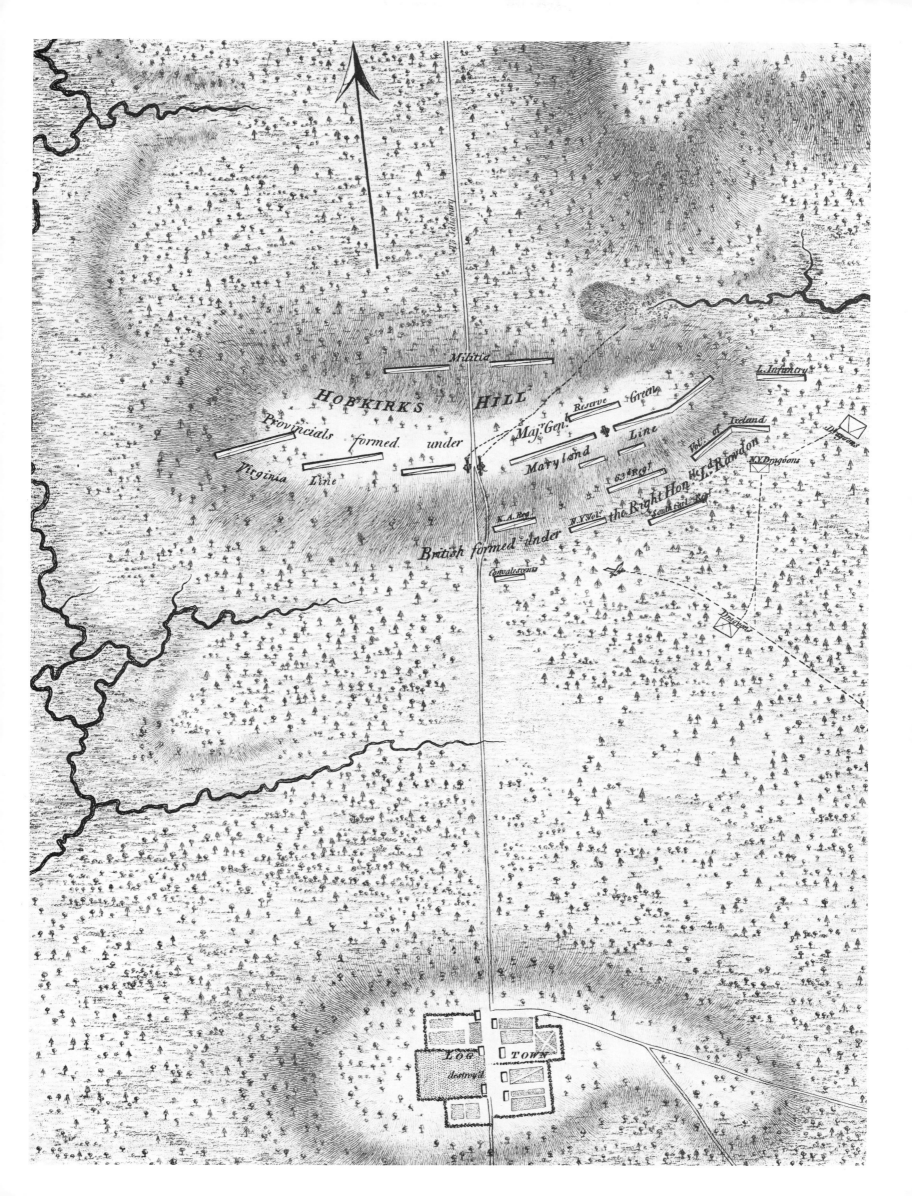

Militia

HOB'KIRK'S HILL

L. Infantry

Provincials formed under

Reserve   Green

Majr Genl

Virginia   Line

Maryland   Line

Voll of Ireland

N.Y.Dragoons

Dragoons

K.A.Reg.

63 Regt

British formed under   W.Y.Vol. the Right Hon ble L.d Rawdon   South Cart. Reg.

Convalescents

Dragoons

LOG   TOWN

destroyd

New Haven

The 1781 raid on New Haven was an example of the frequent conflict between British and American raiding parties back and forth across Long Island Sound. This continuous warfare pitted patriots from Connecticut against loyalists on British-held Long Island. The raids were small in scale, but the hard fighting and bitter feeling represented a microcosm of the larger war. Homes were burned and property was confiscated in retaliation for real or imagined collaboration with the enemy. Baroness Frederika von Riedesel, whose house on Long Island overlooked the lights of New York City in 1781, lived in nightly fear of being kidnapped by the raiders. Lt. Col. John Graves Simcoe, a specialist in irregular warfare and commander of the Queen's Rangers, calculated that Long Island had many favorable landing places opposite the New England shore. The Sound was a barrier of not more than twelve miles and sometimes only seven or eight. "The enemy could raise any number of men for such an expedition . . . there were whale-boats sufficient to carry two-thousand men, who, in three hours might attack. . . ."

Each raid left grudges to settle and rekindled local conflicts between patriots and loyalists. Citizens who wished to remain neutral found the task impossible; silence merely attracted suspicion from both sides. While estimates are deceptive conjectures, perhaps one-fifth of all American colonists could be classified as loyalists. Their relationship to British culture remained organic rather than attached to specific policies or leaders and this circumstance made it difficult to organize politically. Not until May, 1780, did William Franklin (son of Benjamin and former royal governor of New Jersey) receive permission from reluctant authorities to form the Board of Associated Loyalists—a unit designed to coordinate political authority with military action.

British strategists took loyalist support into account when planning campaigns in America and frequently overestimated its influence. After 1776 a calculated effort was made to enlist loyalists in provincial corps—at first only as menial guards and drivers. But by the end of the war at least 19,000 native Americans had served in over 40 provincial units, while the number of others who joined militia, regulars, irregulars, Royal Navy, privateers, and the civil departments of the army has never been computed but may approach 50,000. Recruitment was generally effective when coordinated with the movement of the regular British army and correspondingly diminished whenever the army was withdrawn—except along the western and northern frontiers where loyalists remained active throughout the war. In western New York, for example, several units were raised and maintained with Indian and Canadian assistance; among them John and Walter Butler's provincial ranger regiment (see "Sullivan's Expedition").

Raids involving contingents of loyalists assumed a growing importance. In the North, Brig. William Tryon was a tireless proponent of loyalist operations against the Connecticut shore and managed to see that propaganda was distributed behind enemy lines. While one wit remarked that his "sermons" provided the rebels with material to "light their tobacco pipes," there is evidence that Tryon's efforts had an unsettling effect at a time of colossal inflation, food shortages, and general war weariness. To take advantage of this situation, Tryon also helped organize and conduct the raid on Connecticut in July, 1779, which destroyed Norwalk, burned Fairfield, and plundered New Haven. The raid reflected the deeper anger and disillusion of the loyalists with the unimaginative British conduct of the war. For three years men like Tryon had waited for the king's troops to put down the rebellion, and by 1779 they seemed further from that end than they had been in 1776. If the war was ever to be won, they reasoned, it would have to be won by loyalists themselves fighting a new and less conventional kind of war. Tryon's raid, largely loyalist in composition, demonstrated the possibilities of these tactics. When Tryon left America in September, 1780, others continued to advocate the policies he had begun.

The board was empowered to conduct military operations with its own officers—a significant advantage to the loyalists over earlier arrangements which had seen their own interests sublimated to those of the regulars. An example of how the board worked may be seen in the 1781 raid on New Haven, which made use of Capt. Nathan Hubbel's armed boat company based at Lloyd's Neck.

Reconnaissance of the coastline across Long Island Sound was good. Some of the men in Hubbel's company were loyalists who had fled Connecticut and possessed local knowledge. Several maps of the area were in existence and Sir Henry Clinton possessed seven manuscript maps of sections of the coast. Maj. Patrick Ferguson had submitted a particularly detailed description and sketch of the area raided in 1779.

At sunset on April 18, 1781, Hubbel's raiders pushed out into Long Island Sound toward New Haven in eight whaleboats. Near Newfield Harbor they spotted a rebel schooner and had hopes of taking a prize. But upon pursuit, the ship slipped out of range. Hubbel landed one-quarter mile from the New Haven fort. The raiders passed by the first defenses before a sentry challenged them. He was quickly subdued and the barracks were surrounded and entered. One patriot attempted to resist but was killed. The remaining eleven defenders were captured without a fight. "We took and brought off the colours, effectively destroyed two double French nine pounders,—burned the barrack cut to peices [sic] the flagstaff—took eighteen stand of militia small arms, and having effected the business returned without any loss to Lloyd's Neck—the platforms and everything in the fort which could be destroyed by fire were burned." The crude sketch is one of the few surviving maps to document these frequent raids.

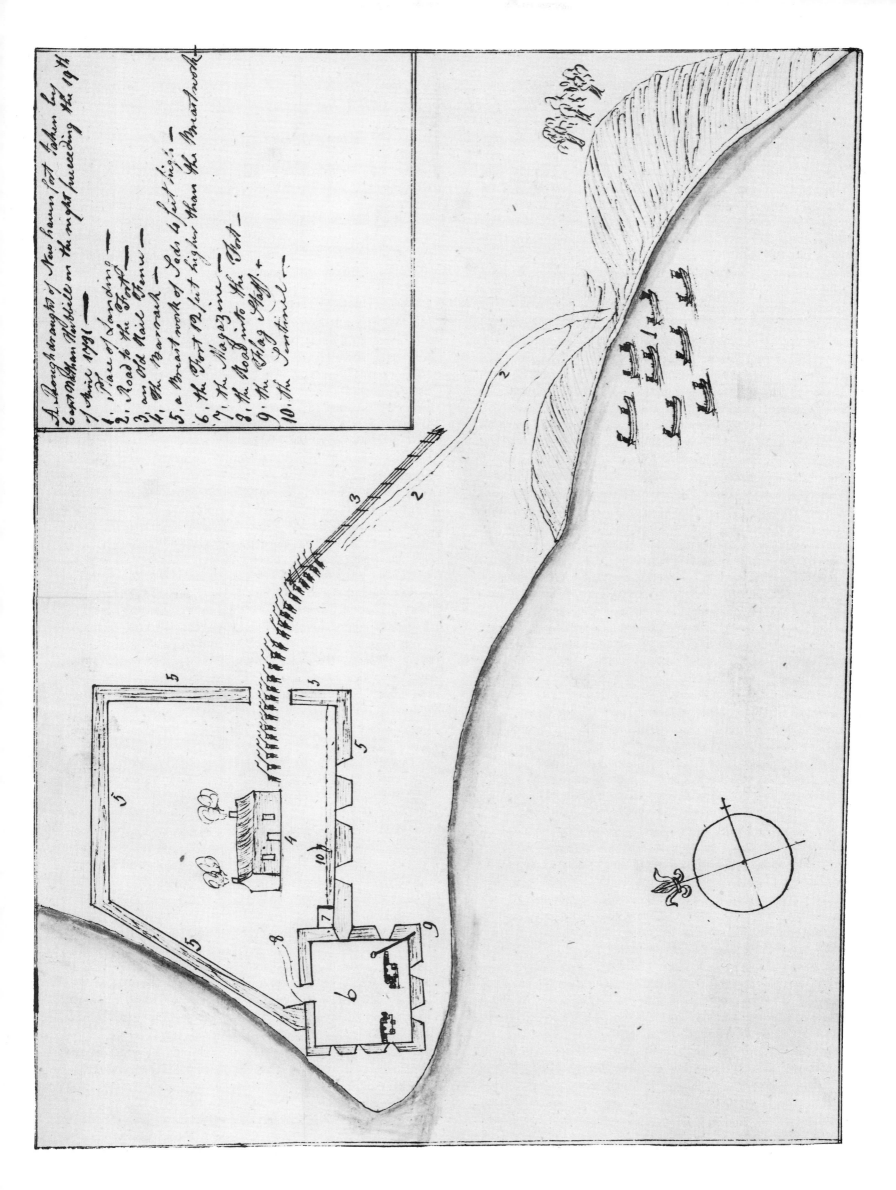

A Rough draught of New haven fort taken by
Capt Maltham Hubbell on the night preceeding the 19th
of April 1781

1. Place of Landing
2. Road to the Fort
3. an Old Nail Fence
4. the Barrack
5. a Breast work of Sods 10 feet high
6. the Fort 12 feet higher than the Breastwork
7. the Magazine
8. the Road into the Fort
9. the Flag Staff
10. the Sentinel

Virginia Strategy

After the burning of Norfolk on January 1, 1776, and the expulsion of Gov. John Murray, Lord Dunmore, Virginia escaped direct battle action for the next three years. The state's role became that of purveyor of troops and provisions to the American cause, increasingly after 1779. From Hampton Roads on the Chesapeake Bay, boatloads of tobacco were shipped to the West Indies and exchanged for French munitions and stores. Virginia's tobacco economy suddenly provided the basis for much of America's foreign credit; in 1775 the same economy had driven up a debt of £2,000,000 to British creditors.

But in the back country of Virginia, support for the Revolution steadily eroded. The prolongation of the war, heavy taxes, and frequent militia drafts caused civil strife. While malcontent citizens were not transformed into loyalists, they nevertheless pursued a general policy of lawlessness. In 1780 Gov. Thomas Jefferson ordered mounted state infantry to patrol the frontier and to bring "those paracides" to trial. Yet his leadership in this objective became diverted toward the immediate problem of the extension of war into Virginia. The British invasion assumed first priority and backwater discontent was left simmering.

The British command had long-standing hopes to exploit the Chesapeake region (see "Chesapeake Bay"). Sir Henry Clinton had even considered the establishment of a naval post there. From that base rebel supply lines could be cut, stores and provisions could be gathered, and an asylum for the loyalists would be created. Some officers thought that the attempt to segment the colonies along the Hudson River in 1777 could be repeated farther south on the James River. But Clinton shrewdly perceived that a new base in Virginia would have to be supplied by sea, and thus would be exposed to envelopment by the superior French fleet. Moreover, experience had taught him to distrust exaggerated reports of loyalist support. The more reasonable strategy after Charleston was seized in 1780 was to encourage Lord Charles Cornwallis to secure an ever-widening territorial enclave. Cornwallis was to occupy South Carolina and continue north in successive stages until all of the southern states were under firm control. That was the plan. Reality was different.

Cornwallis encountered stiffening resistance from the American army and partisan marauders. North Carolina failed to provide the anticipated support for the British cause. In order to achieve Cornwallis's designs for territorial expansion, Clinton was forced to plan supportive raids. The plot to capture West Point failed in a cloud of treachery and the death of Clinton's beloved aide-de-camp, Maj. John André. A raid to Virginia was scheduled, and the prize of the West Point fiasco, Benedict Arnold, was given command. Arnold left New York with nearly 1,700 men in December, 1780. His force sailed up the James River and occupied Richmond on January 5, where tobacco stores and public buildings were burned. The British troops then withdrew downriver to the Westover plantation. Three days later, the loyalist contingent of Queen's Rangers under Lt. Col. John Graves Simcoe broke up rebel militia units at Charles City Court House in a night raid. All British forces eventually converged at Portsmouth.

Back on the Hudson, Washington prepared to aid the Virginia militia by dispatching the Marquis de Lafayette and 1,200 Continentals with instructions to coordinate plans with the French fleet and to capture and hang Arnold. After he began the march south, three French ships escaped the British blockade in a storm at Newport and reached the Chesapeake in early February. But Arnold had safeguarded his own little fleet by moving it up the Elizabeth River behind Portsmouth, out of reach of the large French vessels. They headed back to Rhode Island, having accomplished nothing except delay. When the full French fleet was ready to sail a month later, it was destined for yet a worse fate than the original expedition. A British fleet under Adm. Marriot Arbuthnot intercepted the French outside Chesapeake Bay on March 16. An hour-long battle caused sufficient damage to both squadrons that the French returned to Newport and Arbuthnot limped into the bay to meet Arnold. On March 26, Arnold was reinforced by 2,575 troops under Maj. Gen. William Phillips who assumed command.

Despite the failure of the French fleet to rendezvous, Lafayette proceeded to Virginia, there to await reinforcements from Pennsylvania under Brig. Gen. Anthony Wayne. In the meantime, Phillips raided the interior. The British seized Petersburg on April 25 and laid waste to more tobacco, ships, warehouses, and mills. Five days and several forays later, Phillips arrived opposite Richmond on the James River. But Lafayette had entered the town the night before. Phillips withdrew to Jamestown, where he learned on May 7 that Cornwallis would join him at Petersburg.

In New York Clinton was shattered by the news of Cornwallis's move to Virginia, a complete subversion of the projected strategy. Unfortunately Clinton had been at odds for some time not only with Cornwallis, but with the ministry in London and the naval commanders in America. His sensitive disposition had reduced his effectiveness. He especially failed to communicate his intentions clearly to Cornwallis, and the willful, ambitious second in command had thus been able to establish a virtually independent command in the South.

But Cornwallis's own strategy for Virginia remained ill-defined. He had extended his forces north from South Carolina in the belief that pacification efforts there would require the subjugation of North Carolina and Virginia as well. He was determined to make Virginia the seat of war in the colonies and hoped to induce Clinton to abandon New York in favor of British concentration in the Chesapeake. From the Carolinas he had written Phillips, "I am quite tired of marching about the country in quest of adventure." Yet it is difficult to justify his movements in Virginia as anything but more of the same, with even fewer results.

When Cornwallis arrived at Petersburg on May 20

with his 1,600 men, he learned that Phillips had died of typhoid fever a week earlier. Cornwallis now had 5,800 troops at his disposal, a number soon swelled by 1,200 reinforcements sent by Clinton to strengthen Phillips. At Clinton's request, Arnold returned to New York with a few hundred loyalist troops.

On May 24, Cornwallis left Petersburg and marched north. For the next month and a half he would pursue a course of maneuvers northeast to Till's Ordinary, west to Point of Forks, and southeast back to Portsmouth. The offensive resembled the serpentine route of a blindman's buff (see map on overleaf). Neither side accomplished its objective. The British detachment under Simcoe was instructed to destroy stores at Point of Forks, while Lt. Col. Banastre Tarleton was assigned to disrupt the state legislature at Charlottesville. Tarleton ultimately reached Monticello and narrowly missed the capture of Jefferson. All detachments were to reunite at Richmond.

Meanwhile, the American forces gathered. Wayne joined Lafayette on June 10 at Brook's Bridge camp. Brig. Gen. William Campbell brought in 600 Virginia riflemen. Later, they were joined by another 450 under Maj. Gen. Friedrich von Steuben. These combined troops dogged the British move along a parallel course 20 miles north of their line of march first to Richmond and then to Williamsburg. On June 26 Lafayette sent out an expedi-

tion under Col. Richard Butler to intercept another raid by Simcoe on a supply depot on the Chickahominy River. A heated skirmish followed at Spencer's Tavern, six miles northwest of Williamsburg.

Cornwallis had remained in Richmond only four days and his security at Williamsburg was also short. He crossed the James River on July 6 en route to Portsmouth and prepared a trap for his pursuers. Suspecting an advance against his rear guard at the river crossing, Cornwallis hid some of his men. The Americans under Wayne attacked at Green Spring and prevented their own destruction only by their commander's bold counterattack. This action was the only significant encounter between the two forces. Wayne lost 28 killed, 99 wounded, and 12 missing. British casualties totaled 75.

Cornwallis withdrew to Suffolk and then to Portsmouth, where he began a correspondence with Clinton over the most suitable location for a naval base. Clinton continued to grow increasingly dispirited and frustrated as he watched last year's laurels at Charleston wither away in Virginia's summer sun.

The map of Cornwallis's march is probably the work of Edward Fage, Royal Artillery, who was with Cornwallis in Virginia. It excludes the skirmish at Spencer's Tavern and the attack at Green Spring. The map below shows the defenses at Portsmouth.

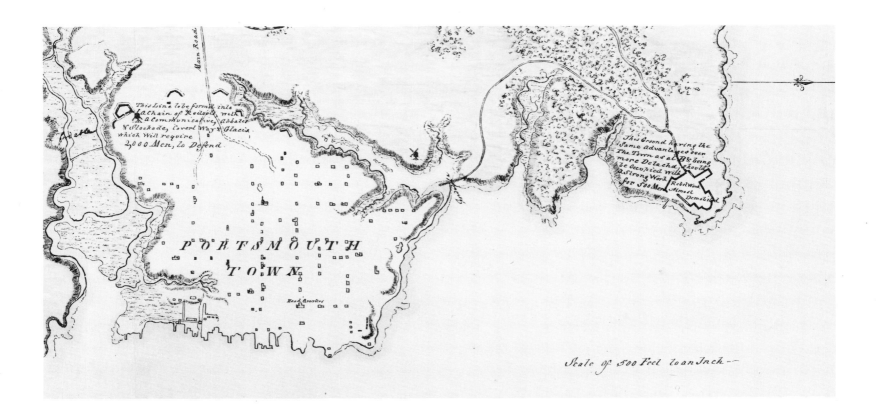

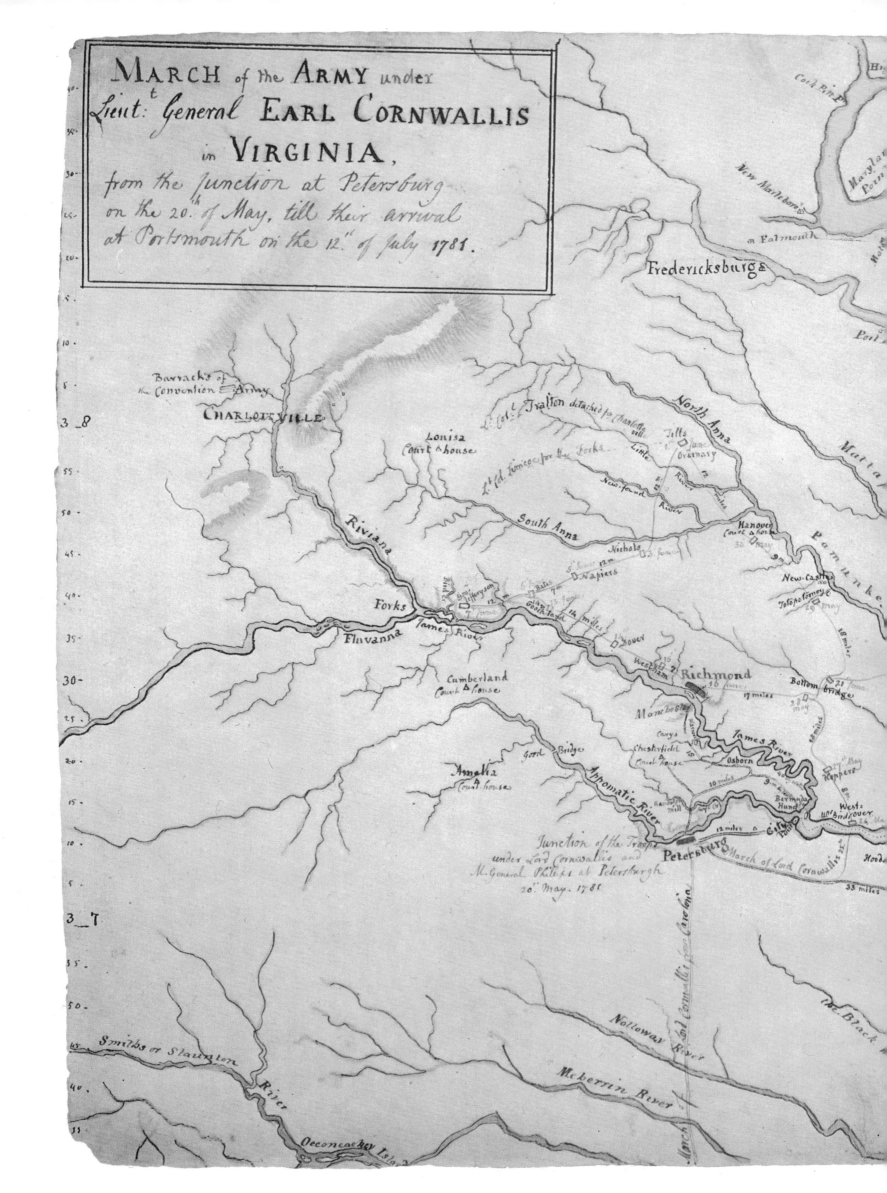

MARCH of the ARMY under Lieut.t General EARL CORNWALLIS in VIRGINIA, from the Junction at Petersburg on the 20.th of May, till their arrival at Portsmouth on the 12.th of July 1781.

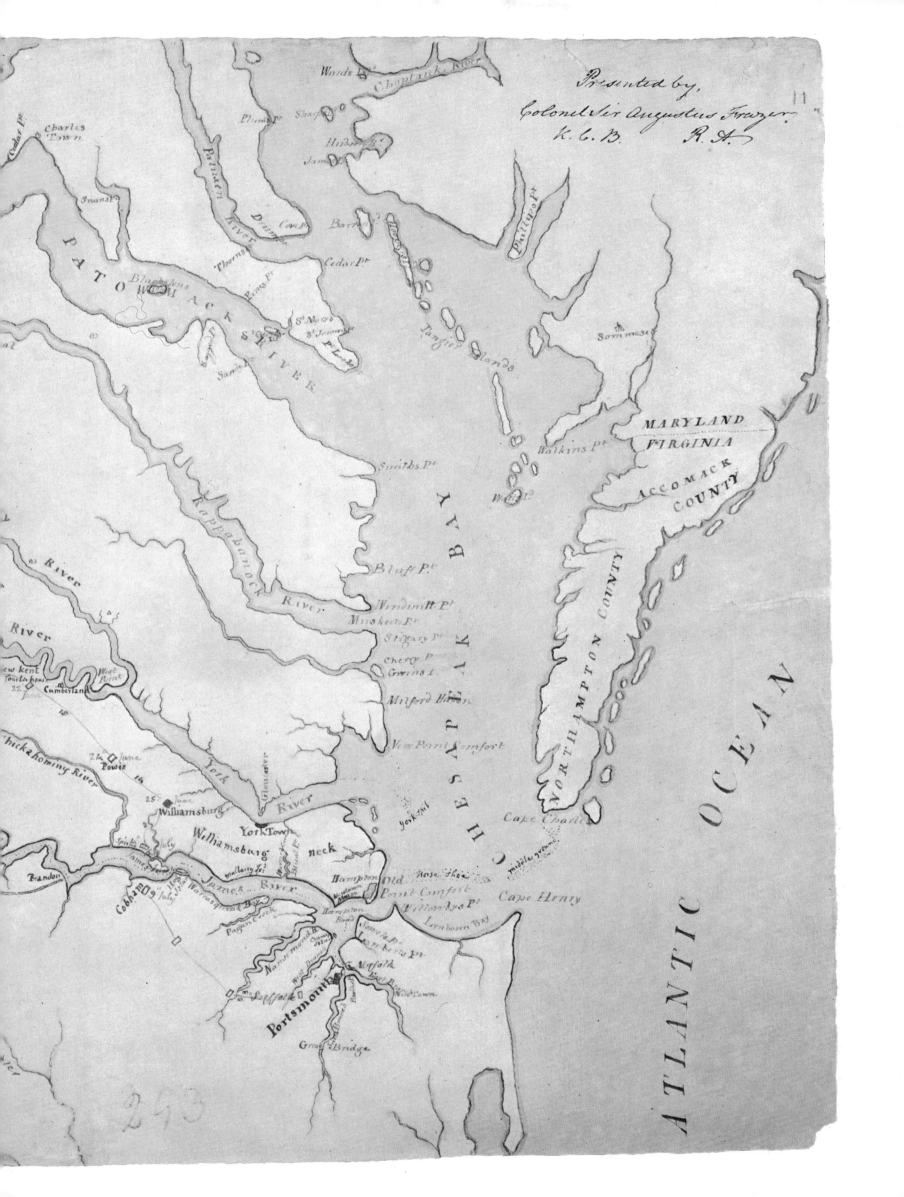

Yorktown

In late spring of 1781 New York City, not Yorktown, was Washington's objective for a joint attack with the French. A conference in Connecticut between Washington and the Comte de Rochambeau, commander of the French troops at Newport, resulted in a diversionary move. The plan was designed to force Sir Henry Clinton in New York to recall men from Virginia, thus relieving pressure on the American commanders in the South—Maj. Gen. Nathanael Greene and the Marquis de Lafayette. Washington had received the promising report that a large French force under Adm. de Grasse was headed for the West Indies and might later move north; but de Grasse's timing was too indefinite to enlarge allied strategy.

Washington's letter to Lafayette outlining this plan was captured by the British. Nonetheless, Clinton wrote to Lord Cornwallis in Virginia requesting him to send part of his troops to New York. In addition, he was expecting reinforcements from England and also more naval support. Even with his limited troop size, Clinton considered raids on Philadelphia and Rhode Island, while attempting to protect New York from the approaching allied force.

Rochambeau's 4,000 troops joined Washington's 3,500 Continentals at Dobbs Ferry on July 6. They reconnoitered the northern defenses of Manhattan and concluded that an attack would require siege operations which could not be accomplished. They resorted to jabs and threats, and waited for word of de Grasse's movements.

"In this quarter," commented loyalist William Smith in New York, "we continue. . .peaceable as lambs. The fashionable language is *there is no object*." It was true that Clinton's disagreeable relations with his naval commander had dampened his Rhode Island scheme. Clinton also lacked political favor in London, and Lord George Germain had plainly pinned his expectations for victory on Cornwallis in the South.

The tension between Clinton and his second in command had been exacerbated by Cornwallis's independent shift of his army to Virginia. Cornwallis reached Williamsburg on June 25. Clinton tried to make the best of his subordinate's brashness and ordered Cornwallis to take up a defensive post at Portsmouth, Old Point Comfort, Yorktown, or Williamsburg. He was to fortify his position, hold it with 4,000 troops, and send 3,000 men to New York. Clinton's next letter changed the latter's destination to Philadelphia; a third letter directed the men to New York again and urged Cornwallis to choose a Virginia base readily accessible to the navy. Meanwhile, Cornwallis had not sent a single soldier to New York. He misinterpreted Clinton's confusing directions and did not recognize that Clinton was allowing him discretion in the number of troops to send North. Finally, on July 20, a letter informed Cornwallis to keep all his troops if he needed them.

Cornwallis decided Yorktown was the best base for operations, with a secondary position across the York River at Gloucester. He occupied the two posts in August with 6,000 regulars and 1,500 to 2,000 marines, sailors, and armed loyalists.

On August 14 Washington received electrifying news from Adm. de Barras at Newport. De Grasse was indeed on his way to the Chesapeake with 29 warships and 3,100 marines under the Marquis de St. Simon. However, he could stay only until the middle of October. Washington immediately revised his strategy to encircle Cornwallis.

Maj. Gen. William Heath was left in the Highlands with 2,000 men. The combined force of 6,500 French and Americans crossed the Hudson at Stony Point in late August. They started marching southward down the west bank. Some of them carried pontoons as a ruse for the watchful British. When Clinton heard of this movement, he believed that the long-delayed attempt on the city was coming, presumably from Staten Island. He was heartened by the timely arrival of Rear Adm. Samuel Hood with 14 ships from the West Indies to augment the squadron under Adm. Samuel Graves. The newcomer had seen nothing of any French fleet, but Graves learned that de Barras had left Newport. The two admirals joined their squadrons and set off southward on August 31 in search of the French. Clinton remained unaware that the allied troops had suddenly turned southward, dropped their deceptive pontoons, and were hurrying across New Jersey. Not until September 2, when the American advance was tramping through the streets of Philadelphia, did Clinton realize their real objective and write to Cornwallis.

Cornwallis needed no warning from Clinton of impending trouble. De Grasse had sailed into Chesapeake Bay on August 31. He landed St. Simon's marines at Jamestown on September 2 in order to join Lafayette. This accretion meant that the allies in Virginia already outnumbered Cornwallis's force. As the French ships anchored between the capes, Cornwallis's only hope rested on access to the sea and the British navy.

Graves and Hood arrived off Chesapeake Bay on September 4 with 19 ships and were astonished to find de Grasse not only in the bay but with 29 vessels. For a week the two fleets circled and fought and finished in a draw. But it was a strategic defeat for the British; with damaged ships they limped back northward for repairs. De Grasse returned to the Chesapeake and found that de Barras had arrived with 7 ships carrying heavy siege guns and 1,500 barrels of meat rations. Strangely, Cornwallis did not learn until September 17 of the failure of the British navy, of the increase in the French navy, or of Washington's approach. Still, he might have taken one last chance to break out of the ring and fight his way southward. But he was deterred by another letter from Clinton promising relief. By September 22 Washington's troops were pouring into Williamsburg to join Lafayette's larger force, and six days later the combined armies marched to within sight of Yorktown. Cornwallis had no option.

British soldiers along with slaves had worked desperately on trenches and redoubts in a semicircle around Yorktown. Following a creek running from south to northwest, Cornwallis established outer works and continued them for two miles around to the southeast. Washington's chief engineer Maj. Gen. Louis Duportail began siege operations in the standard tradition of the eighteenth century. With the Americans taking their positions on the right and the French on the left (as agreed in their formal alliance), they formed an arc opposite the British line. The allies outnumbered their enemy three to one.

Even before Washington's reconnaissance could produce a map for directing the siege, Cornwallis made a mistake. On the evening of September 29, he received a message from Clinton that the navy was starting southward on October 5 with reinforcements of 5,000 men. That night Cornwallis abandoned his outer works and withdrew to his earthworks closer to the village to wait out the ten days. Clinton later insisted that the positions at *F* should have been retained and supported at *H* (see his emendations on the back endpaper map).

As the Americans and French dug trenches, built infantry redoubts, and prepared batteries for their siege guns, they were constantly cannonaded. At night, raiding parties were sent out to harass them. Cornwallis had dispatched Lt. Col. Banastre Tarleton's cavalry, which was of no use in the enclosed town, to Gloucester to strengthen that post. Virginia militia, with a French reinforcement under the Marquis de Choisy, followed; and after an unsuccessful charge by Tarleton, Choisy surrounded the village.

By October 9 the borrowed French cannon were mounted in the Americans' first parallel and opened up on Yorktown. The destruction was terrifying to civilians and soldiers alike. Cornwallis's headquarters was blasted. More than 80 persons were killed, and many wounded. French artillerymen were in a position to fire on Cornwallis's transports and small boats. A new messenger from Clinton slipped in with the bleak news that the expected ships could not leave New York until October 12.

The allies opened a second parallel closer to the town and found that redoubts nine and ten blocked their path to the river. On the night of October 14 the redoubts were overtaken in bayonet assaults led by Lt. Col. Alexander Hamilton and Lt. Col. de Deux-Ponts. The two actions cost Cornwallis 26 killed and 73 taken prisoner. The allies lost 24 killed and 102 wounded.

Caught in this critical situation, Cornwallis tried to buy time with another sortie. On October 16 a predawn raid to spike cannon brought only temporary success. The guns were soon back in working order; perhaps a hundred were now pounding the town to pieces. In a last gamble, Cornwallis attempted to ferry his army across to Gloucester that night. One-third of them were landed; then a squall blew up. When the weather calmed, it was too late to make other trips, so the first detachment was ordered to return. Late in the morning of October 17 Cornwallis sent out an officer waving a white handkerchief. An American ran out to blindfold him, and he was brought to Washington with a letter from Cornwallis proposing a cessation of hostilities while terms of surrender were settled.

The garrisons of Yorktown and Gloucester surrendered as prisoners of war to the Americans; the navy personnel to the French. Cornwallis tried to protect the loyalists from all punishment, but Washington insisted that this was a matter for Congress to judge. The ceremony was set for the next afternoon. On October 19 the redcoats and Germans marched out and stacked their arms while a band played "The World Turned Upside Down." Behind the two lines of Americans and French, civilians from the countryside crowded to see the sight. Cornwallis pleaded illness and sent Lt. Col. Charles O'Hara to offer his sword. The latter preferred to surrender to the French and approached the Comte de Rochambeau. With exquisite politeness, Rochambeau waved him over to Washington who, in turn, pointed to his second, Maj. Gen. Benjamin Lincoln. That same day in New York a British task force started south on a futile rescue mission.

The sketch below was drawn by Alexander Sutherland, Cornwallis's chief engineer, who had, according to Clinton, "very honestly confessed that he had never surveyed the ground the siege stood on." As in the French map on the overleaf, Yorktown is depicted in the final stages of the attack with the outer works captured and linked to the closest trenches of the allies. Sutherland's finished map on the back endpaper represents the siege at its inception with all British positions intact.

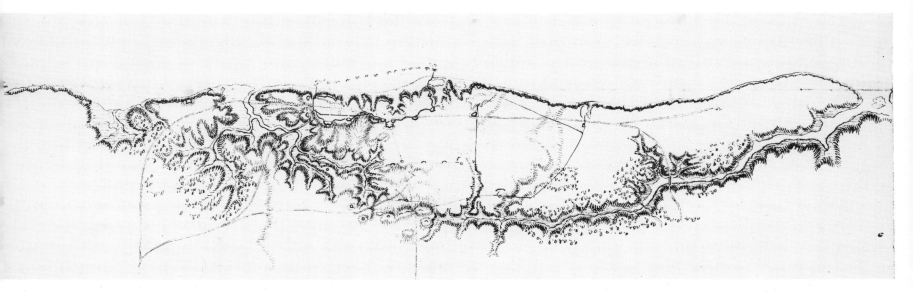

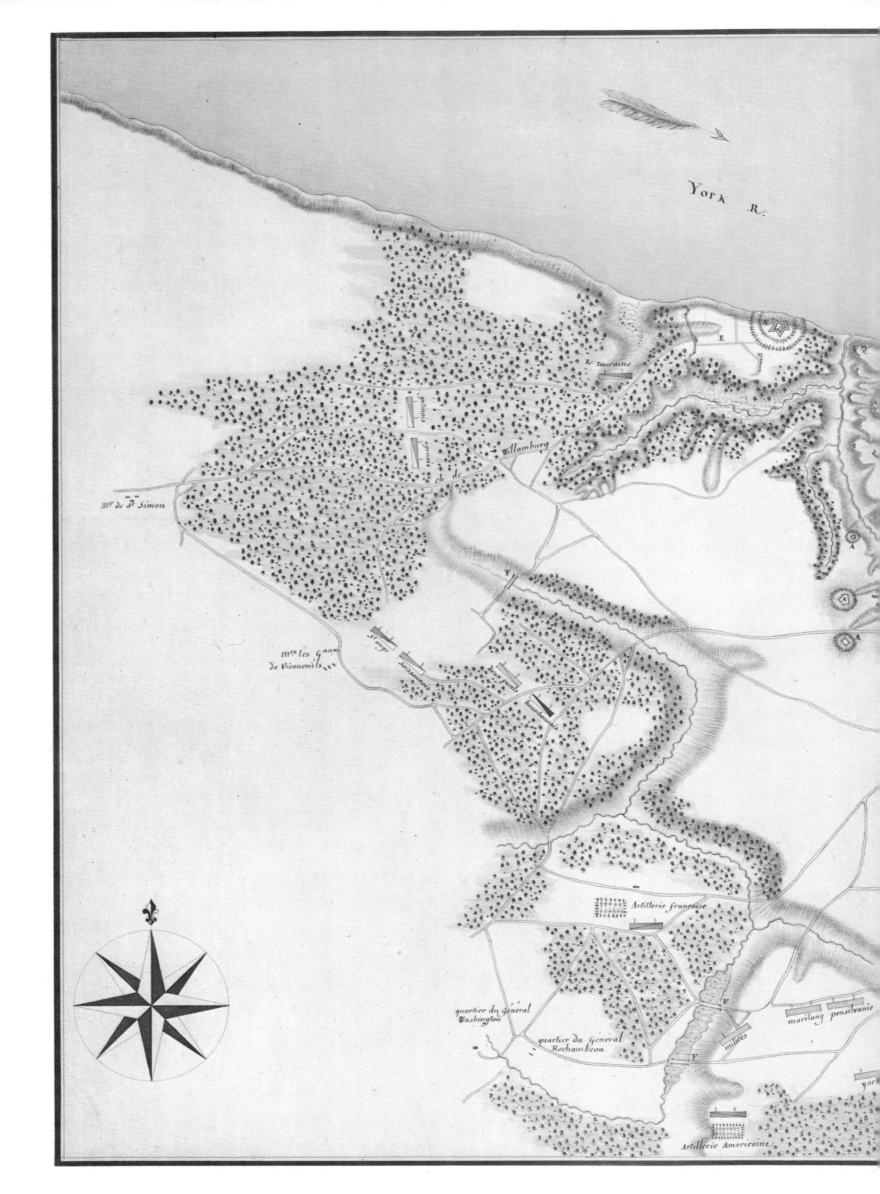

New London

Sir Henry Clinton authorized the September 6, 1781, attack on New London as a small-scale diversion to Washington's movements against Virginia. Clinton saw the raid as an opportunity to rid himself of the presence of Brig. Benedict Arnold while fulfilling an earlier promise made to Lord Cornwallis about relieving pressure in the South. Arnold was an appropriate choice for the mission. He was born in nearby Norwich, Connecticut, and knew the area well. In addition, Arnold had besieged Clinton and London politicians with complaints of inactivity and requests for an independent command. Although the residents of New London were to view the tragic raid as an act of revenge, to Arnold it was an opportunity to demonstrate his military talents.

New London was a prime target for a major raid. It was the chief seaport of Connecticut and a principal naval station near New York. During the Revolution the port was a center for privateering activity. Sanctioned by Congress and financed by wealthy families the privateers were far more damaging to British shipping than the diminutive Continental navy. Throughout the war nearly 500 British merchantmen were seized and brought into Connecticut harbors, most to New London. In the words of British Commodore George Collier, "The place was a famous receptacle for privateers, and was thought on that account to injure British trade as much as any harbor in America." Its commerce served to mark the town for British reprisals.

New London was poorly defended. Its main fortifications, Forts Trumbull and Griswold, were authorized in 1775 by the local Committee of Safety. Their guns had come from Commodore Esek Hopkin's 1776 raid on the Bahamas. The fort on Town Hill was built in 1779. The value of all three defenses was lessened by a constant shortage of powder and trained troops.

Arnold left New York on September 4 with over 1,700 men, nearly one-half of whom were loyalists. His planned night attack was delayed by adverse winds. The British flotilla was spotted and the customary warning signal fired. The British, however, were aware that the sound of two guns was the signal to summon the militia, and by the careful firing of a third cannon succeeded in confusing the warning. On the morning of September 6 Arnold landed with one division at the west bank of the Thames River. Across the river Lt. Col. Edmund Eyre went ashore and marched toward Fort Griswold. Using loyalists as guides, Arnold dispatched men to take Fort Trumbull and moved toward New London with the main body of troops. The small group of Americans at Fort Trumbull fired a single volley and fled across the river to Fort Griswold. The handful of defenders at the Town Hill fort were quickly dislodged. In the retreat one frustrated American shouted to Arnold, "Welcome Goddamn you to Fort Nonsense." On the map opposite the cartographer identified the fort as "Fort Folly."

Reaching New London, Arnold sent out torch parties guided by local loyalists to burn military stores. He issued strict orders prohibiting looting and indiscriminate burning. Although most looting was actually the work of local vagrants, the Americans blamed Arnold's soldiers. Arnold attempted to maintain personal supervision over the fire and managed to save the house of one old friend. For his trouble, he was nearly shot by the man's wife. At the river nearly a dozen vessels were burnt at their moorings. The burning, whether accidental or intentional, was widespread. Even the homes of reputed loyalists were fired to protect them against reprisals. The total damage included the destruction of 143 buildings with 97 families left homeless.

Lt. Col. William Ledyard commanded the defense of New London from within Fort Griswold. He had spent the morning hastily trying to recruit additional forces. Ledyard sought to impress sailors from privateers in the harbor but their captains had fled up the river to save the ships. He could not agree with his officers over the procedure to follow. Ledyard rejected a suggestion to fight a delaying action and chose to remain in the fort, despite the small number of men available to defend it. Many of the local militia feared being trapped and refused to enter the fort. Fort Griswold had only 158 defenders when the British troops under Eyre assembled before it. Eyre acted under earlier orders from Arnold to quickly seize the fort and snare the American privateers upstream. Later, the attack was countermanded, but the orders reached Eyre too late to stop the fighting.

The Americans fiercely contested the attack and British casualties were high. During a brief lull in the fighting a random shot severed the American flag. Even though it was quickly replaced, many British troops thought the fort had struck her colors and rushed forward. But upon fire from the fort, the British troops felt deceived. Enraged, they broke through the defenses as Ledyard signaled a surrender. Many of his men were unaware of the capitulation and continued firing from behind cover. Discipline gave way as the British troops fiercely bayoneted Americans who had laid down their arms. Ledyard was one of the first to fall. Seeing this, other Americans resumed fighting. Before British officers gained control of their men over 85 Americans lay dead and 35 wounded. All but three had fallen after the surrender. The British themselves lost 47 dead and 133 wounded, including Eyre. Capt. Stephen Broomfield assumed command, set a fuse to the magazine that was later extinguished, and hurriedly joined Arnold at the waiting British ships. The American wounded were released and the remaining prisoners taken aboard ship.

The events at Yorktown the following month obscured the New London action. The net result of the raid was to assist American propaganda. Embellished accounts of atrocities within Fort Griswold filled the local press. Arnold and his loyalists were castigated as word of the killing quickly spread throughout the states.

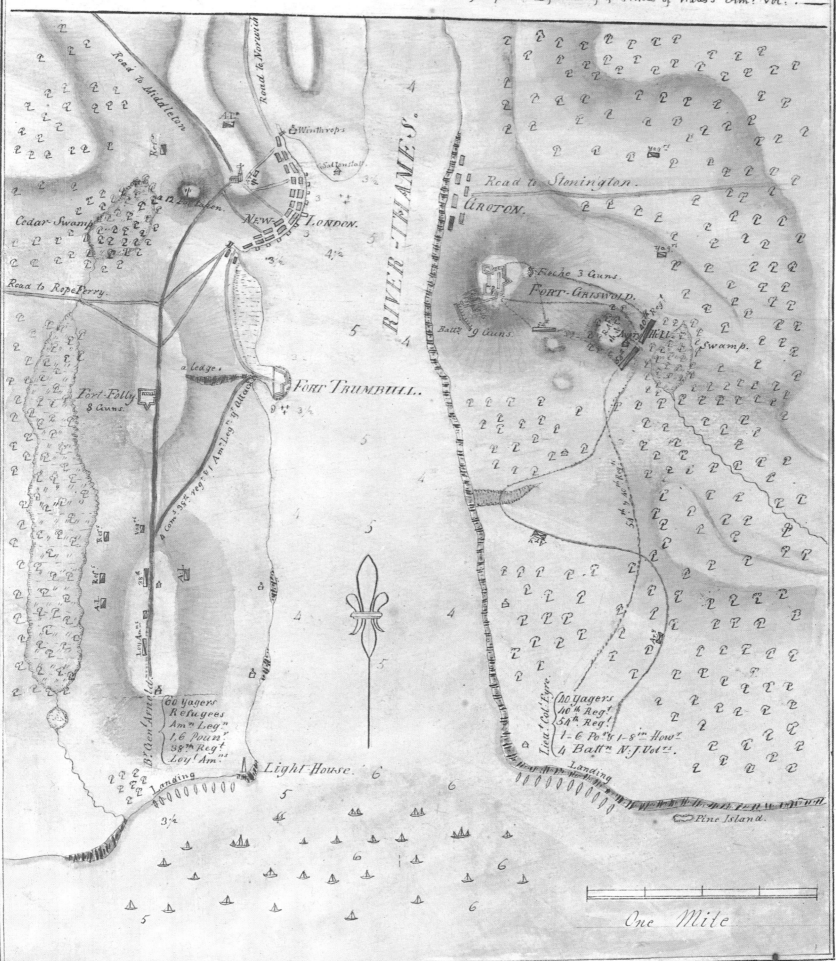

FORTS TRUMBULL & GRISWOLD,
by the BRITISH TROOPS
Under the Command of Brigr. GENERAL ARNOLD Sepr. 6th 1781.

By Captain Lyman of ye Prince of Wales's Amn. Volrs.

Road to Middleton

Road to Norwich

Winthrops

Saltonstall

A 12 Por taken

NEW- LONDON.

Cedar Swamp

Road to Rope Ferry

a ledge.

Fort Folly 8 Guns.

FORT TRUMBULL.

RIVER THAMES.

Road to Stonington.

GROTON.

Fleche 3 Guns.

FORT-GRISWOLD.

Batty. 9 Guns.

Swamp.

Br. Gen. Arnold.

60 Yagers
Refugees
Amn. Legn.
1 6 Poun.
38th Regt.
Loyl. Ams.

Light House.

40 Yagers
40th Regt.
54th Regt.
1 - 6 Por & 1 - 8in How.
4 Battn. N. J. Volrs.

Lieut. Col. Eyre.

Landing

Pine Island.

One Mile

Pensacola

After Field Marshal Don Bernardo de Gálvez, the Spanish governor of Louisiana, had taken Mobile in March, 1780, he began operations against Pensacola—the main British base in West Florida.

Pensacola had been ceded from Spain in 1763 as part of the settlement of the French and Indian War. It was a larger town than Mobile, and its living conditions were better. In 1767 Pensacola had profited from the efforts of Brig. Frederick Haldimand on the advice of surgeon John Lorimer. Streets were widened, providing improved air circulation, and the troops stayed healthier. Also in contrast to Mobile, a strong new fort, Fort George, was constructed in December, 1779, 1,000 yards from Pensacola on a 60-foot hill overlooking the town. Sir Henry Clinton reported in 1778 that the older fortifications "were fallen into ruin as soon as finished." A second fort called Red Cliffs guarded the entrance to the harbor.

Pensacola had an important function in keeping the southern Indian tribes loyal to Great Britain. During the later years of the Revolution, between two and four ships per year unloaded their cargo of Indian presents at Pensacola. In the summer of 1780, the transport *Content,* provisioned from Britain via the West Indies, carried £6,665 of goods destined for the Indians. Besides the usual trinkets, the gifts included 96 cases of guns, 6 casks of flints, 40 barrels of bullets, and 400 quarters of gunpowder. But after the declaration of war with Spain in June, 1779, the passage of storeships became a problem. Frequently, British ships were forced to travel in convoy or request naval escort to ensure protection against the Spanish.

Pensacola was garrisoned by 1,300 British troops of which 40 percent were Pennsylvania and Maryland loyalists and 25 percent were in the Waldeck Regiment from Germany. In addition, Maj. Gen. John Campbell, the commander, could assemble 300 sailors, 600 civilians, 300 armed blacks, plus numerous Indian allies when needed. Gálvez had been thwarted in his attempt of May, 1780, to seize the remainder of West Florida. That August, he appealed for aid to Spanish military authorities in Havana. A fleet of 63 ships and transports carrying 4,000 men were provisioned from Cuba to attack Pensacola in October. They were scattered by a five-day hurricane, and the British were spared again.

In January, 1781, Campbell dispatched a force of 400 troops and 300 Indians to overtake a small village and Spanish outpost on the east shore of Mobile Bay. The British were repulsed with the loss of several officers and men; this encounter encouraged Gálvez to continue his campaign for an attack on Pensacola. Eventually, the Cuban war council agreed to supply 1,315 troops from Havana. The transports sailed in February, accompanied by a 74-gun warship and four smaller frigates. They were to be joined by 1,348 men from New Orleans and 905 from Mobile. Gálvez was given command over all army and navy operations, yet he had to force the naval captain to risk taking the ships into the harbor under the guns of Red Cliffs on March 18.

Spanish troops established a camp near Pensacola on March 26. Most of April passed without progress on siege operations. Indian raids caused a few casualties, but Gálvez seemed preoccupied with reconnoitering the British fortifications. Toward the end of the month, a force of 3,675 soldiers and sailors (one-third of them French) unexpectedly arrived from Havana. Sir Peter Parker, who commanded the Royal Navy in the West Indies, had been preoccupied with the French. His force of only four warships was powerless to prevent the Spanish fleet from leaving Havana in April. Gálvez now commanded a total of 7,000 men.

Fort George was too strong to be taken by direct assault, and siege batteries could not be constructed in the open. A second Spanish position, therefore, was assumed as shown on the map. Troops were detailed for a trenching operation which took three nights to complete. A battery was installed on May 1, and a second trench and redoubt were begun on the adjacent hill. The British advanced and forced the Spanish back to their initial trench. Four guns were spiked in the assault, two officers were captured, and 34 suffered casualties.

The Spanish regained the position and repaired the damage. They continued artillery fire and on May 8 a shell rolled in the open door of a bombproof powder magazine at Fort George. The explosion killed at least 85 British soldiers and opened a breach. The Spaniards pushed up light artillery and fired on the center redoubt, wounding 31 more. Campbell could no longer work his guns and finally ran up a white flag at 3:00 P.M. Terms were reached on the night of May 9-10, and the entire province of West Florida was surrendered to the Spanish.

Spanish reports indicated that 1,113 prisoners were taken, in addition to 65 deserters who had been captured previously. Another 300 loyalists and British soldiers fled to Georgia while negotiations were in progress. A considerable amount of armament and supplies also fell into Spanish hands. The king of Spain was particularly gratified by the action of Gálvez, and increased his governorship to include the conquered territories. Gálvez was promoted to the rank of lieutenant general.

The British prisoners were treated with consideration. On June 1 they sailed for Havana and continued on to New York where they arrived on July 12.

The map was drawn by Capt. Lt. Henry Heldring of the Waldeck Regiment. He was an acting engineer at Pensacola and participated in its defense.

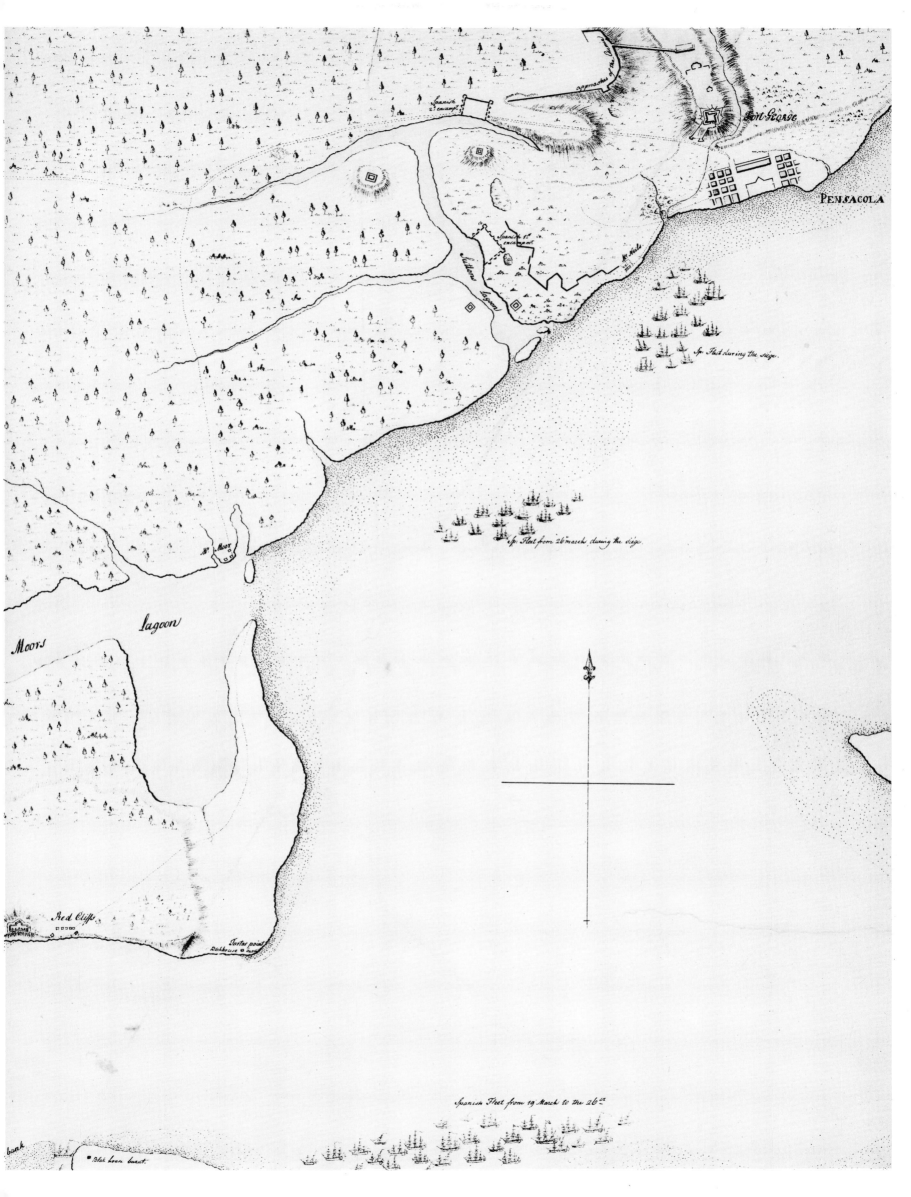

Spanish 2d encamp

Spanish 1st encampmt

Fort George

PENSACOLA

Indian Lagoon

Mr Moor

Sp: Fleet during the siege.

Sp: Fleet from 26 march during the siege.

Moors   Lagoon

Red Cliffs

Tartar point
Storehouse & work

Spanish Fleet from 19 March to the 26th

bank

Blck house burnt.

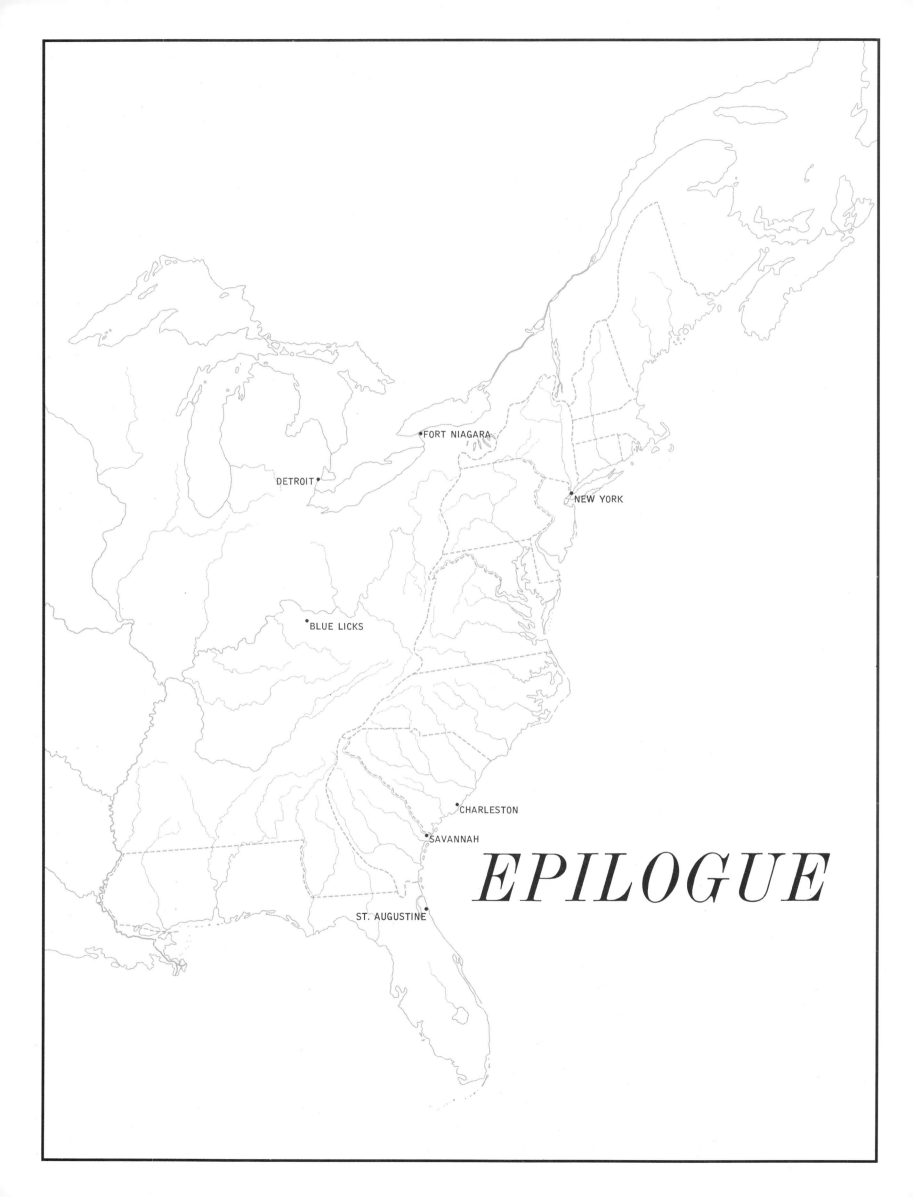

FORT NIAGARA

DETROIT

NEW YORK

BLUE LICKS

CHARLESTON

SAVANNAH

EPILOGUE

ST. AUGUSTINE

The masts which had filled New York harbor since early summer were suddenly gone. A brisk wind from the northwest billowed a final sail out past Governor's Island on the bright morning of November 25, 1783, and it receded hull down over the horizon. Aboard the H.M.S. *Ceres*, Lt. Gen. Guy Carleton reported that the last 2,000 British troops had been evacuated smoothly. The war in America was over.

British initiative had disintegrated in the 25 months since the surrender at Yorktown. Carleton arrived in New York on May 5, 1782, to relieve Sir Henry Clinton of command. Military activity declined from 196 reported engagements in 1781 to 53 in 1782 to 5 in 1783. Canada was retained but the four enclaves within the rest of North America were abandoned: Savannah and Charleston before the end of 1782; St. Augustine and New York in the fall of 1783.

Upon their return to England, the defeated officers refought the war in books and pamphlets, and in Whitehall and the houses of Parliament. They blamed each other, the ministry, the navy, and the guile of the Americans. Some generals went on to redeem their reputations —Carleton in Canada, Sir William Howe in the Ordnance, and Lord Cornwallis in India. Others were finished— Thomas Gage, John Burgoyne, and Clinton. Any balanced assessment for what had happened was lost amidst a welter of recrimination and nostalgic battle narratives.

The task of sorting out the reasons for British failure has been left to historians. Most agree that British conquest was possible, at least before the entry of France. Recent interpretations have focused on problems of strategy and tactics, command structure, ministerial direction, generalship, transport, and logistics. This study has examined the army in relation to its ability to obtain and disseminate geographic information. That geography, and its empirical expression in cartography, influenced the outcome of the war has never been debated—but the questions have remained: when, where, and how much?

British maps of the Revolution were influenced by several elements—military control of territory, technical capacity, the numerical strength, training, professional objectives of the cartographers, and the priorities of the local commander. The war began with scarcely any maps useful for military operations in the 13 colonies. To the extent that reliable knowledge of roads, fords, settlements, and terrain features were required for maneuver, the British army started from a disadvantage. Unless authority over a hostile countryside could be reasserted, surveyors would be limited in what they could accomplish.

A further complication for the British at the inception of war was the absence of a body of skilled professional cartographers. Only one member of the Corps of Engineers was at Boston, the Ordnance draftsman had died (not to be replaced), and Samuel Holland's colonial survey team was soon dispersed. But by 1776 the problem had been alleviated. In that year, mapmaking talent was available among 24 officers of the Corps of Engineers—two-thirds of the total complement to serve in America during the war. In addition, three skilled draftsmen had been identified and hired into the engineer staff outside the normal control of the Board of Ordnance, four of Holland's gifted surveyors had received army commissions, and other officers (at least three with known cartographic training) were serving as assistant engineers.

As the British army acquired bridgeheads in New York, Rhode Island, Pennsylvania, and eventually in South Carolina and Virginia, the demand for large-scale maps increased. Reliable reconnaissance was needed in the small war to choke off rebel commerce and to raid supply bases, as well as in the constant routine of foraging and the requisition of livestock and fuel. Maps were equally important in the larger effort to seize a vital land mass and thus break the Revolution into containable segments —through New York in 1777; across the South in 1780–81.

The evidence indicates that the army did not possess the maps it needed for war in America. In part, organization itself can be blamed. As the engineers were confronted with more pressing duties of field fortification and siege-craft, cartography became a tertiary consideration. In fact, only one-half of the members of the Corps of Engineers can be proven to have possessed surveying or drawing skill. And that skill was exercised for advancement within the professional army rather than toward describing the unfamiliar landscape. This accounts for the predominant number of commemorative battle plans—attractive, simple to construct, and made after the event itself. The emphasis was on skillful brushwork and the effect was designed to flatter the commander whose victory was depicted; maps of defeat are proportionately less evident. However gratifying the ornamental quality of these maps, they diverted the supply of talented manpower from more important projects. Yet those colorful battle plans may have influenced promotion prospects. Of eight engineers who obtained a position on the army staff all but one were appointed from among those who possessed mapmaking ability. Another organization, the Corps of Guides and Pioneers, was created to answer the demand for topographic reconnaissance and, by the end of the war, it had produced some impressive surveys—such as the following map of New York harbor. However, no attempt was made to map contested territory, and surveyors were not usually assigned to scouting expeditions. Even South Carolina, temporarily pacified in 1780, went unmapped.

Although it was the larger issues of ends and means which defeated the British army, inadequate maps contributed to the problem. It is not possible to determine every time military decision making was affected by topographic ignorance, but at a basic level this uncertainty worked against consistent planning and execution. What emerges was the need for a systematic reconnaissance network which the British command never clearly recognized nor resolved.

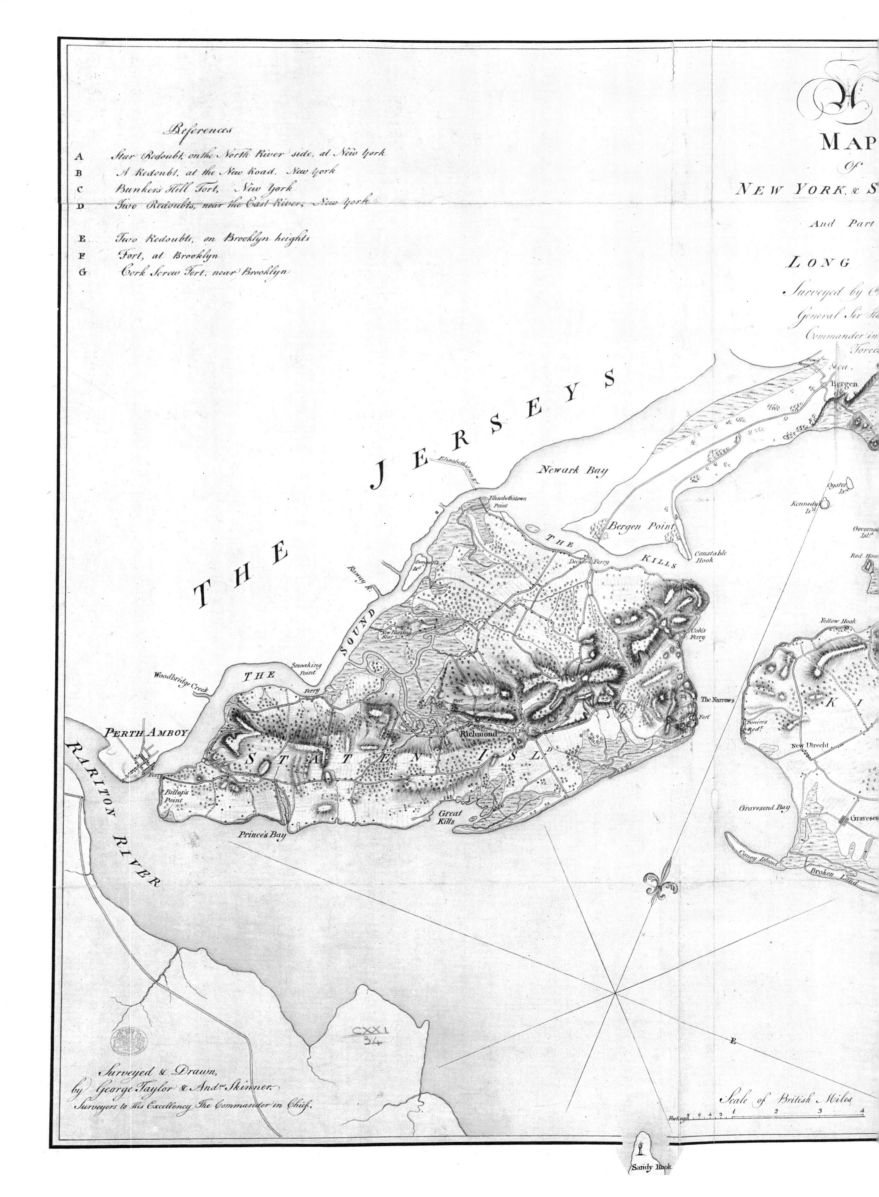

References

A   Star Redoubt, on the North River side, at New York
B   A Redoubt, at the New Road, New York
C   Bunker's Hill Fort, New York
D   Two Redoubts, near the East River, New York

E   Two Redoubts, on Brooklyn heights
F   Fort, at Brooklyn
G   Cork Screw Fort, near Brooklyn

MAP
OF
NEW YORK, & S
And Part
LONG
Surveyed by
General Sir
Commander in
Sea.

THE JERSEYS

Elisabethtown Rd.
Newark Bay
Elisabethtown Point
Bergen Point
THE KILLS
Constable Hook
Decker's Ferry
Donoho's Rd.
New Blazing Star
Cole's Ferry
Raway R.
SOUND
Smoaking Point
Ferry
THE
Woodbridge Creek
Fort
Richmond
The Narrows
Fort
PERTH AMBOY
STATEN ISLd
Ferry
Billop's Point

Kennedy Isld.
Oyster Is.
Governor's Isld.
Red Hou
Yellow Hook
KI
Bonica Reef
New Utrecht
Gravesend Bay
Gravese
RARITON RIVER
Prince's Bay
Great Kills
Coney Island
Broken Island

CXXI
34

Surveyed & Drawn,
by George Taylor & Andr. Skinner.
Surveyors to His Excellency The Commander in Chief.

Scale of British Miles

Sandy Hook

Sources

This is a partial list of references which were found useful in the preparation of the preceding narratives. It is not intended as a general bibliography of the Revolution. Works pertinent to particular engagements have been cited below under the individual map headings.

Fruitful research was conducted among the papers of Thomas Gage, Sir Henry Clinton, and Frederick Mackenzie in the Clements Library; the Conolly manuscripts on British military engineers, Royal Engineer Corps Library, Chatham; War Office papers, especially class 46 and 55, Public Record Office, London; and the Montresor family archive, in the possession of Lt. Col. John Montresor, RE. Also useful were the calendared papers of Sir Guy Carleton and the published diaries of Archibald Robertson, Stephen Kemble, John Montresor, John André, Henry de Berniere, and Frederick Mackenzie. Sir Henry Clinton's *The American Rebellion* (ed. by William B. Willcox and first pub. by Yale U. Pr., 1954), is the only narrative of the entire war written by a general officer of either side.

The reliable histories of the Revolution which follow will not be repeated under specific map headings: John R. Alden, *A History of the American Revolution* (Knopf, 1969); Mark M. Boatner, *Encyclopedia of the American Revolution* (McKay, 1966); Don Higginbotham, *The War of American Independence* (Macmillan, 1971); Piers Mackesy, *The War for America 1775–1783* (Harvard U. Pr., 1964); Howard H. Peckham, *The War for Independence* (U. Chicago Pr., 1958); Hugh F. Rankin, *The American Revolution* (Putnam, 1964); Christopher Ward, *The War of the Revolution,* 2 v. (Macmillan, 1952).

Excellent military biographies have supplemented this material: Douglas S. Freeman, *George Washington,* especially v. 3–5 (Scribner, 1951–52); Ira D. Gruber, *The Howe Brothers and the American Revolution* (Atheneum, 1972); Franklin and Mary Wickwire, *Cornwallis: The American Adventure* (Houghton Mifflin, 1970); William B. Willcox, *Portrait of a General: Sir Henry Clinton in the War of Independence* (Knopf, 1964).

Our awareness of logistical, cartographic, and statistical considerations has been aided by scholars whose work acknowledges research in the Clements Library collections: R. Arthur Bowler, *Logistics and the Failure of the British Army in America, 1775–1783* (Princeton U. Pr., 1975); Christian Brun, *Guide to the Manuscript Maps in the William L. Clements Library* (Clements Library, 1959); William P. Cumming, *British Maps of Colonial America* (U. Chicago Pr., 1974); Peter J. Guthorn, *American Maps and Mapmakers of the Revolution* (Freneau, 1966) and *British Maps of the American Revolution* (Freneau, 1972); J. B. Harley, *Mapping the American Revolutionary War* (scheduled pub. 1976); Charles H. Lesser, ed., *The Sinews of Independence: Monthly Strength Reports of the Continental Army* (U. Chicago Pr., 1975); Howard H. Peckham, ed., *The Toll of Independence: Engagements and Battle Casualties of the American Revolution* (U. Chicago Pr., 1974); David Syrett, *Shipping and the American War, 1775–1783: A Study of British Transport Organization* (Athlone, 1970).

Modern rules for capitalization have been applied to the source quotations.

FRONT ENDPAPER

[Untitled map of roads between Philadelphia and New York with adjacent counties]

SIZE 42.5 x 61.6 cm. *SCALE* 1:210,988/1 in. to 3.33 mi. *REDUCTION* 1:.75

The cartographer of this map can be determined from the lettering style. It is the work of Capt. John Montresor, Corps of Engineers, whose career is described below (see sources for "The Siege of Boston"). It was probably drawn in the winter of 1777–78.

The vectors have been overlaid to indicate the position of 34 towns on the map in relation to their actual positions of longitude and latitude. The plot was taken from a computer program designed by Waldo R. Tobler, Geography Department, University of Michigan, and modified in collaboration with Douglas W. Marshall. Using this method, geographic accuracy of any early map under 200 miles in area can be analyzed. The standard deviation for the towns on the map represents an average inaccuracy of 3.7 miles. Each of the positions in relation to their nearest neighbors indicates an average dislocation of 3.25 miles and a staggering distortion of 52 degrees. Thus, travel between towns would be difficult if not impossible using only this map and a compass.

Map from the Clements Library; Clinton map 247; Brun, *Guide,* no. 522.

LEXINGTON AND CONCORD

[Untitled map of roads from Cambridge to Medford]

SIZE 38.1 x 60.3 cm. *SCALE* 1:76,032/1 in. to ca. 1.2 mi. *REDUCTION* 1:.4

Sketch by a British participant unskilled in cartography or drawing. The calligraphy does not resemble that of Lt. Frederick Mackenzie, who accompanied Earl Percy's relief column and took sketches.

Map from the library of the Duke of Northumberland, Earl Percy Collection.

A plan of the town and harbour of Boston . . . 19th April 1775

SIZE 19.5 x 30.5 cm. *SCALE* 1:126,720/1 in. to 2 mi. *REDUCTION* 1:.8

It appears that this map came into Percy's possession from an officer at Boston. Yet a letter of August 8, 1775, in the Dartmouth calendar notes, "Carver and Dacosta have finished a new plan of Boston at the request of Whitworth." This refers to the engraved map with a larger ground plan and figures of troops, dedicated to Richard Whitworth, M. P. A reproduction can be found in Emerson D. Fite and Archibald Freeman, *A Book of Old Maps* (Harvard U. Pr., 1926; reprint, Dover, 1970), p. 40. "Carver" is Capt. Jonathan Carver, who had been in England since 1769. As a native of Massachusetts, perhaps he contributed to the topography and added military details from London newspaper accounts. However, it is implausible to attribute the manuscript in Percy's possession to Carver.

Map from the library of the Duke of Northumberland, Earl Percy Collection. Specific sources for the text include Allen French, *The First Year of the American Revolution* (Houghton Mifflin, 1934) and Arlene Phillips Kleeb, *Lexington and Concord* (Clements Library, 1975). For the machinations of Jonathan Carver, see William P. Cumming and Douglas W. Marshall, *North America at the Time of the Revolution,* pt. 3 (Margary, 1975).

THE SIEGE OF BOSTON

View from the blockhouse Dorchester Neck

SIZE 15.2 x 48.9 cm. *SCALE* variable *REDUCTION* 1:.5
Map from the Clements Library; Clinton map 49; Brun, *Guide,* no. 260.

A draught of the towns of Boston and Charlestown . . . 1775

SIZE 42.5 x 43.8 cm. *SCALE* 1:26,280/1 in. to 730 yd. *REDUCTION* 1:.75
Capt. John Montresor (1736–99) was one of the most ambitious and enterprising British officers to serve during the Revolution. He spent 23 years on duty in this hemisphere and became chief engineer in America in 1775—a post previously occupied by his father James from 1758 to 1760. Forced to relinquish control of the corps because of insufficient seniority, John Montresor obtained an appointment to the headquarters staff of the army commander Sir William Howe. The engineer returned to England on October 19, 1778, five months after his commander had gone home. Montresor's cartographic skill was acquired between 1750 and 1754 at Gibraltar, where his father served as chief engineer.

A study for this map of Boston and a rough draft are in the Library of Congress and the Clements Library, respectively. Finished copies survive in the Earl Percy collection, Alnick Castle; the Duke of Cumberland archives, Windsor Castle; the R. U. S. I. Collection, British Library; and the Library of Congress copy reproduced here. Only the Clements and the Alnick copies are signed. A map with the same ground plan and orientation, but with a different drawing and lettering style, is in the New York Public Library. Dated July 25, 1775, it is titled "Plan of the town of Boston and the circumjacent country. . . ." Its calligraphy is that of Philip D'Auvergne, RN, who drew at least two other surviving maps of Boston Harbor. He died a midshipman in 1782.

Map from the Library of Congress, Geography and Map Division. Specific sources for the text include French, *The First Year* and John Shy, *Toward Lexington: The Role of the British Army in the Coming of the American Revolution* (Princeton U. Pr., 1965).

BREED'S HILL

[Untitled sketch of Charlestown peninsula and battle]

SIZE 44.4 x 28 cm. SCALE indeterminate REDUCTION 1:.8

This hasty sketch was drawn probably during Page's recovery from the amputation of his foot. At the battle, he served as aide-de-camp to Pigot, who commanded the attack of marines and regulars on the left. Like Montresor and other resourceful members of the Corps of Engineers, Page had been able to obtain a coveted appointment to the staff of a general officer.
Page served in America for only 11 days. Upon his return to London, a map of the battle was published by William Faden, for which this sketch is a study. Historian Allen French has noted that the printed map omitted important military and topographical details. Page probably acquired drawing skill while attending the Royal Military Academy at Woolwich—an institution which trained many engineer and artillery aspirants. While attending the school in 1765, he had been awarded the gold medal in fortification on its first presentation. He continued on active duty in England after 1776, published seven pamphlets on military engineering, and was knighted and elected to the Royal Society in 1783.
Map from the Library of Congress, Geography and Map Division. A particular reference used for the text was Richard M. Ketchum, *The Battle for Bunker Hill* (Doubleday, 1962).

GREAT BRIDGE

A view of the great bridge near Norfolk . . .

SIZE 26 x 18.7 cm. [overall] SCALE 1:12,000/1 in. to ca. 1,000 ft. ENLARGEMENT 1:1.1

This map was thought to be the work of Francis Hastings, Lord Rawdon, but it is more likely attributable to Capt. Samuel Leslie of the 14th Regiment. The handwriting on the map resembles that of Leslie, who conducted the operation at Great Bridge. He had been on duty in Boston since the time of the 1770 massacre and later served in Florida. His company of 60 soldiers, 6 sergeants, and 2 lieutenants arrived off Norfolk on July 31, 1775. After the battle Leslie stayed aboard the transports along the Virginia coast until at least May, 1776. He was promoted to major in 1777 and disappeared from the *Army List* after 1779. The map demonstrates a drawing style which surpasses the usual crude efforts of line officers who had no training in surveying or perspective.
Map from the Clements Library; Clinton map 281; Brun, *Guide,* no. 588. Specific sources used for the text include Peter Force, ed., *American Archives,* ser. 4, v. 4 (1843) and E. M. Sanchez-Saavedra, "All fine fellows and well armed: The Culpeper Minute Battalion, 1775–1776," *Virginia Cavalcade,* v. 24, no. 1 (1974).

INTO CANADA

Sketch of different passes into Canada . . .

SIZE 33.6 x 16.8 cm. [overall] SCALE 1:2,534,400/1 in. to 40 mi. REDUCTION 1:.9

Outline map from an unidentified cartographer submitted to Lord George Germain, Secretary of State for America during the Revolution.
Map from the Clements Library; Brun, *Guide,* no. 142. Specific sources for the text include Justin H. Smith, *Our Struggle for the Fourteenth Colony,* 2 v. (Putnam, 1907); and Kenneth Roberts, ed., *March to Quebec: Journals of the Members of Arnold's Expedition* (Doubleday, 1938).

CHARLESTON HARBOR

Sullivan's Island [title from verso]

SIZE 20.3 x 32.4 cm. SCALE indeterminate REDUCTION 1:.7

This map was drawn by Capt. Lt. Abraham d'Aubant who accompanied the expedition. He learned mapmaking techniques while working in the Drawing Room at the Tower of London for five years before being commissioned into the Corps of Engineers in 1759. D'Aubant, who served in America throughout the war, held appointment as commanding engineer at Rhode Island, 1776–79, and again at New York in 1782. By the process of longevity and seniority he came to head the Royal Corps of Engineers in England for three years before his death in 1805.
Map from the Clements Library; Clinton map 304; Brun, *Guide,* no. 633.

Charleston Harbor and the British attack of June 1776

SIZE 62.2 x 98.4 cm. SCALE 1:36,000/1 in. to 3,000 ft. REDUCTION 1:.55

This carefully drawn map is similar to another version in the Clinton collection signed "John Campbell." The calligraphy and content, however, are not identical. Both are probably derived from a survey made by Capt. Lt. John Camble, Corps of Engineers. Camble spent only eight months as a gentleman cadet at the Royal Military Academy before obtaining his engineer commission in 1762. Perhaps his cartographic skill was acquired earlier in Scotland. This memorial map could have been drawn at any time during the war. Sir Henry Clinton was so obsessed with his failure in the 1776 operation that he asked to have the Sullivan's Island-Long Island part of the harbor recharted when the British army returned in 1780.
Map from the Clements Library; Clinton map 302; Brun, *Guide,* no. 607. Specific sources for the text include Frances Reece Kepner, "A British View of the Siege of Charleston, 1776," *Journal of Southern History* XI (Feb., 1945) and Edward McCrady, *The History of South Carolina in the Revolution, 1775–1780* (Russell and Russell, 1969; reprinted from 1901 edition).

LONG ISLAND

Plan of Long island . . .

SIZE 16.5 x 49.5 cm. SCALE 1:380,160/1 in. to 6 mi. REDUCTION 1:.5

The cartographer's penciled grid is still visible on this anonymous sketch of Long Island. His rudimentary English suggests this sketch was done by one of the Hessian officers stationed in the New York area.
Map from the Clements Library; Clinton map 120; Brun, *Guide,* no. 411.

A plan of the environs of Brooklyn . . .

SIZE 46.6 x 58.4 cm. SCALE 1:12,000/1 in. to 1,000 ft. REDUCTION 1:.8 [lower margin excluded]

George Sproule was born on Long Island in 1741, and was commissioned an ensign in the British army in 1762. He began work on the surveys under Samuel Holland in 1767 and received considerable training in surveying and drawing. Sproule was commissioned a lieutenant in the 16th Regiment in August, 1775. At least from July, 1777, his name appears on army returns as "Assistant Engineer." This survey was made by him in September, 1776, but the fair copy was not drawn until March, 1781. By 1784, he had disappeared from the *Army List,* but was later appointed the first surveyor general of New Brunswick.
Map from the Clements Library; Clinton map 132; Brun, *Guide,* no. 420. An additional source for the text was H. P. Johnston, *The Campaigns of 1776* (Long Island Hist. Soc., 1878).

WHITE PLAINS

White Plains

SIZE 35.5 x 32 cm. SCALE indeterminate REPRODUCTION 1:1 [margins deleted]

Lt. Col. John Graves Simcoe, age 24, probably sketched this map at the start of battle on October 28. He may have acquired some knowledge of drawing during the previous four years that he served as adjutant of the 35th Regiment. After 1777, Simcoe gained fame as commander of a loyalist regiment, and published *A Journal of the Queen's Rangers* in 1787.
Map from the Clements Library; Simcoe Papers; Brun, *Guide,* no. 462.

FORTS WASHINGTON AND LEE

A plan of the operations of the King's army . . .

SIZE 72.4 x 48.5 cm. SCALE 1:82,368/1 in. to 1.3 mi. REDUCTION 1:.6

Claude Joseph Sauthier received formal training in surveying and architecture in his native Strasbourg. He came to America at the age of 31 in 1767 as colonial surveyor for North Carolina. Four years later, he was reassigned to New York with Gov. Tryon. Sauthier completed a large-scale survey of Staten Island for Maj. Gen. Howe in 1776 and later served under Maj. Gen. Percy in the New York and Rhode Island campaigns. He returned with Percy to England in 1777 as personal secretary and estate surveyor.
This manuscript map was used by William Faden to engrave the copper plates for his printed map of Feb. 25, 1777. Two modern carto-bibliographers have acclaimed the map "most accurate," but Clinton termed it a "bad map."

Map from the Library of Congress, Geography and Map Division, Faden Collection. Transparency furnished by the Library of Congress. A reliable biography of Sauthier appears in Cumming, *British Maps*.

NEWPORT

New Port

SIZE 38.7 x 43.2 cm. *SCALE* 1:6,336/1 in. to 528 ft. *REDUCTION* 1:.75 [left margin deleted]

Charles Blaskowitz was appointed a cadet draftsman in the Tower of London in 1753 at the age of twelve. He later joined Samuel Holland's North American survey team on March 24, 1764. Blaskowitz was commissioned captain in the provincial regiment of Guides and Pioneers on May 3, 1777. He was prohibited from enlisting men to complete his own company in order to continue making surveys of roads. After 1783 he was on the half-pay list, and is presumed to have died in 1835. The map is taken from rough sketches with the grid still intact. The original survey was completed in 1774, and this copy was probably carried by Clinton on the British attack in 1776. Finished copies with slight variations in roads and topographic features were published by J. F. W. Des Barres in 1776 and William Faden in 1777.

Map from the Clements Library; Clinton map 67; Brun, *Guide,* no. 276.

LAKE CHAMPLAIN

The order of battle in crossing Lake Champlane

SIZE 36.8 x 24.8 cm. *SCALE* indeterminate *REDUCTION* 1:.85

This anonymous sketch of the proposed order for crossing Lake Champlain was made ten days before the battle of October 11, 1776. The escort vessels are indentified by name and number of guns. William Twiss, Corps of Engineers and aide-de-camp to Maj. Gen. William Phillips, directed the construction of the British fleet at St. Johns. The sketch demonstrates too little drawing ability to have been his, and more likely was the work of another officer.

Map from the Clements Library; Brun, *Guide,* no. 386.

NEW JERSEY INVASION

[The road from New Bridge to Burlington]

SIZE 34.9 x 44.9 cm. *SCALE* 1:380,160/1 in. to ca. 6 mi. *REDUCTION* 1:.65

The note in Clinton's hand reads: "Capt. Montresor after the misfortune of Trenttown this gentleman has forgot the Assompink Creek which is however here put in." This is one of seven maps in the Clinton papers to show troop dispersal. It was drawn by John Montresor about December 12, 1776, to indicate projected winter quarters for the army.

A computer analysis of the geographic accuracy of towns of this map indicates a standard deviation of 2.5 miles. However, the inaccuracy of each town in relation to its nearest neighbor is out of position by only 1.6 miles and 22 degrees, or less than one-half the inaccuracy in comparison with the larger map of New Jersey roads on the front endpaper. It suggests that maps of areas through which the army had passed were comparatively more accurate.

Map from the Clements Library; Clinton map 212; Brun, *Guide,* no. 507. An additional source for the narrative was William S. Stryker, *The Battles of Trenton and Princeton* (Houghton Mifflin, 1898).

PRINCETON

[Princeton]

SIZE 40 x 24.7 cm. *SCALE* indeterminate *REDUCTION* 1:.75

This crude manuscript map is John Cadwalader's only known attempt at cartography. Lacking any training in surveying or military affairs, Cadwalader had earlier left the College and Academy of Philadelphia to enter business with his brother. He became a brigadier general of the Pennsylvania militia by 1777, and twice declined Washington's offer of transfer in rank to the Continental army. The map was drawn on the basis of information furnished by a spy and sent to Washington on December 31, 1776.

Map from the Library of Congress, Geography and Map Division. A specific source for the text was Samuel S. Smith, *The Battle of Princeton* (Freneau, 1967).

DANBURY

Gov. Tryon's expedition to Danbury 1777

SIZE 46.3 x 36.8 cm. *SCALE* 1:95,040/1 in. to ca. 1½ mi. *REDUCTION* 1:.65

"Montresor" stamped on the verso of the map indentifies John Montresor as the cartographer.

Map from the Library of Congress, Geography and Map Division. An additional source for the text was the "Journals of Henry Duncan: Captain, Royal Navy, 1776–1782," in John Knox Laughton, ed., *The Navy Miscellany* v. 1 (Navy Records Society, 1902).

FORT SCHUYLER AND ORISKANY

Sketch of Fort Skuyler . . .

SIZE 40.6 x 26.7 cm. *SCALE* 1:5,976/1 in. to 166 yds. *REDUCTION* 1:.75

François Louis Teisseidre de Fleury had had nine years of service and training with the French army before joining Washington in May, 1777, as captain of engineers. He served in many of the major battles over the next two years. At Stony Point Fleury was recognized by promotion to lt. col. of engineers and a special medal awarded by Congress. Fleury left America for France in September, 1779, and later returned with the French army under Rochambeau.

This map is signed on the verso, "Col. Gansewoord I begg indulgence for so rough a sketch as it has been done without rule nor circle." Fleury was without drafting instruments for a time because his map of Fort Mifflin where he served as engineer during the attack is endorsed with a similar note. Two other 19th-century manuscript variations survive, one of which was published in 1831 and also in 1838.

Map from the New York Public Library, Emmet Collection.

BENNINGTON

Position of the detachment under Lieut. Col. Baum . . .

SIZE 29.8 x 37.8 cm. *SCALE* 1:7,200/1 in. to 200 paces *REDUCTION* 1:.65

Because of the initial "E," the manuscript has been incorrectly attributed to Elias Durnford. Actually, it was drawn by Lt. Desmaretz Durnford, Corps of Engineers, who was present at the battle of Bennington and taken prisoner. There is no direct evidence that he was related to the brothers Elias and Andrew Durnford, also with the Corps of Engineers in America and members of a remarkable family which sired six generations of British officers— mostly engineers. Desmaretz Durnford was probably named after John Peter Desmaretz, who served in the Drawing Room of the Tower until 1762. Durnford was commissioned in 1770, and assigned to the engineers in Canada in February, 1776. After capture at Bennington, he was exchanged and returned to England in July, 1778. He died in 1782. Nothing is known of his training in cartography. This copy of the map was used by William Faden as a model for the engraved map published in John Burgoyne's *A State of the Expedition* . . . (London, 1780).

Map from the Library of Congress, Georgraphy and Map Division, Faden Collection. An additional source for the text was Frank W. Coburn, *A History of the Battle of Bennington* (Livingston Pr., 1912).

SARATOGA

[Hudson River from West Point to Dobbs Ferry]

SIZE 40.3 x 32.4 cm. *SCALE* 1:ca. 126,720/1 in. to ca. 2 mi. *REDUCTION* 1:.95 [section]

Although this map was not used in Clinton's 1777 Hudson River raid, it represents the type of reconnaissance information being received at British headquarters. It was submitted to loyalist Gov. William Tryon on May 14, 1779, to induce an attack on Verdritige Hook, 40 miles north of New York City and just below Stony Point on the map. Its cartographer was the influential loyalist attorney, William Smith of New York. Smith's manuscript diary has now been published in several volumes and offers an important example of the political position of the Whig-loyalists. His map indicates geographic familiarity, proportion, and knowledge of transposition without demonstrating particular skill in cartography. Smith is not known to have been trained in either surveying or drafting.

Map from the Clements Library; Clinton map 170; Brun, *Guide,* no. 356.

Plan of the position of the army . . .

SIZE 48.3 x 71.1 cm. *SCALE* 1:7,200/1 in. to 200 yds. *REDUCTION* 1:.65

The cartographer of this map, Lt. William Cumberland Wilkinson of the 62nd Regiment, accompanied Burgoyne's expedition as assistant engineer. Apparently, he served as draftsman to Lt. William Twiss, Corps of Engineers, who was appointed commanding engineer of the expedition and conducted siege operations against Ft. Ticonderoga. The map shows evidence of formal cartographic training and may have been done in collaboration with Twiss who spent two years of study in the Drawing Room of the Tower of London. Wilkinson's training is unknown. William Faden published the map on February 1, 1780, and added the American positions and their attack of October 7, 1777. The printed map is titled, *Plan of the encampment and position of the army under his excelly. Lt. General Burgoyne at Braemus Heights . . .*

Map from the British Library, R. U. S. I. Collection. Specific sources for the text include John R. Cuneo, *The Battles of Saratoga: The Turning of the Tide* (Macmillan, 1967); Hoffman Nickerson, *The Turning Point of the Revolution* (Houghton Mifflin, 1928); and Rupert Furneaux, *The Battle of Saratoga* (Stein and Day, 1971).

BRANDYWINE

Plan de l'affaire de Brandewein . . .

SIZE 47.9 x 72.4 cm. *SCALE* 1:28,164/1 in. to 2,347 ft. *REDUCTION* 1:.8

Reinhard Jacob Martin was a captain in the Hessian Engineers and deputy quartermaster general for the German troops in America in 1778 and 1779. He was actively engaged in cartographic assignments before his death in New York City on May 27, 1780. This commemorative map was finished over a year after the battle.

Map from the Clements Library; Brun, *Guide,* no. 541.

PAOLI AND PHILADELPHIA

Progress of the British army . . .

SIZE 25.7 x 27.3 cm. *SCALE* 1:380,360/1 in. to ca. 6 mi. *REDUCTION* 1:.85

John André was one of the most remarkable officers in the British army. His administrative talent was recognized with successive appointments to the staffs of general officers and promotion to adjutant general in October, 1779. Before his capture and execution in October, 1780, for his role in the treachery of Benedict Arnold, André drew over fifty maps, including the illustrations for his military journal. The source of his cartographic training is unknown.

Map from the Huntington Library; HM 3086. An additional source for the text was Glenn Tucker, *Mad Anthony Wayne and the New Nation* (Stackpole, 1973).

GERMANTOWN

A sketch of the battle of German. Tn. . . .

SIZE 34.3 x 28 cm. *SCALE* 1:16,200/1 in. to 450 yds. *REDUCTION* 1:.8

A commemorative battle map by John Montresor who was not present at the battle. The positions of the 17th and 44th regiments have been penciled on this map but were neglected in coloring. Another copy of the map exists with an oval cartouche and with the missing units fully colored.

Map from the Library of Congress, Geography and Map Division.

FORTS MERCER AND MIFFLIN

[*Roads between Camden and Red Bank*]

SIZE 28 x 43.1 cm. *SCALE* 1:126,720/1 in. to ca. 2 mi. *REDUCTION* 1:.7

This road map should be compared with the same section of map on the front endpaper. It indicates the diversity of reconnaissance being received at British headquarters about a particular area. No cartographer can be attributed.

Map from the Library of Congress, Geography and Map Division.

Plan of the general attack . . .

SIZE 28.6 x 30.8 cm. *SCALE* 1:10,560/1 in. to ca. 880 ft. *REPRODUCTION* 1:1

This anonymous manuscript map has been attributed to Simon Fraser, a loyalist, but a positive identification cannot be made. Its style resembles a line officer's work without specialized training in shading. The map image and calligraphy are not identical to John André's map of this battle.

Map from the Clements Library; Brun, *Guide,* no. 544.

VALLEY FORGE

Plan of Washingtons position

SIZE 20.3 x 32.2 cm. *SCALE* 1:21,000/1 in. to ca. 1,750 ft. *REDUCTION* 1:.95

The identity of "Mr. Parker" remains uncertain. Perhaps, as a merchant, he was involved as a commissary in supplying the army. One loyalist, Capt. James Parker, a Virginia merchant who served under Lord Dunmore as an engineer was probably in Philadelphia that winter. As an engineer Parker may have had the interest and background to draw such a plan. The lettering on the map is in a different handwriting from that found on two letters from James Parker to Clinton in 1778 and 1780. But as an officer, Parker may have used a secretary to draft his formal correspondence. The accuracy of the map has been questioned by John F. Reed.

Map from the Clements Library; Clinton map 256; Brun, *Guide,* no. 546. Additional sources for the text were John F. Reed, *Valley Forge: Crucible of Victory* (Freneau, 1969), and John Joseph Stoudt, *Ordeal at Valley Forge* (U. Pennsylvania Pr., 1963).

MONMOUTH

Sketch of part of the road from Freehold to Middletown shewing the skirmish between the rear of the British army under command of His Excellency Genl Sir Henry Clinton and the advanced corps of the rebel army June 28th 1778.

SIZE 41.9 x 52 cm. *SCALE* 1:24,000/1 in. to ca. 800 paces *REDUCTION* 1:.95 [section]

From 1778 Lt. John Hills served as an "extra draughtsman" and an assistant engineer with the 38th and 23rd regiments, respectively. His drafting skill was put to frequent use by the army; he drew many maps from the basic work of other officers and colonial surveyors. Several of his maps were eventually printed by William Faden. Hills's formal cartographic training is unknown. After the Revolution he settled in Philadelphia and worked as a surveyor. There are four known copies of the Monmouth map, three in the Library of Congress—including one in the manuscript road atlas of New Jersey which was assembled by Hills for Sir Henry Clinton—and one in the Clements Library. Each is slightly different in detail. The map is part of a series which depicts the encampments of the British army's 1778 withdrawal across New Jersey. These maps and another series of the same march drawn by John André represent the only known British examples of route maps done in the French tradition by their corps of topographic engineers. John W. Shy has stated that none of the printed maps of the battle are accurate. This manuscript map is also misleading, and representative of the total British confusion.

Map from the Library of Congress, Geography and Map Division, Force Collection. Additional sources used for the text were Samuel S. Smith, *The Battle of Monmouth* (Freneau, 1964) and John W. Shy, "Charles Lee: The Soldier as Radical" in George Athan Billias, ed., *George Washington's Generals* (Morrow, 1964).

HESSIAN FORAGING

[*Position of the troops at Valentine's Hill*]

SIZE 24.7 x 39.4 cm. *SCALE* 1:10,080/1 in. to ca. 840 ft. *REDUCTION* 1:.95

The map shows the position of Hessian troop detachments just east of the Hudson River in September, 1778. The cartographer is unknown but the content and spelling suggest German origin.

Map from the Clements Library; Clinton map 156; Brun, *Guide,* no. 425.

RHODE ISLAND

[Newport]

SIZE 47.6 x 59.7 cm. SCALE 1:24,000/1 in. to 2,000 ft. REPRODUCTION 1:1 [section]

This is a section of a map by Edward Fage showing the British defenses around Newport and the French attack of August, 1778. Fage received formal cartographic training at Woolwich and was commissioned in the Royal Artillery in 1768. He was assigned to Rhode Island from 1777 to 1779 and drew several plans of the area. After the war Fage remained in the army reaching the rank of major general in 1808.

Map from the Clements Library; Clinton map 66; Brun, *Guide*, no. 277.

Plan of Rhode Island ...

SIZE 94.3 x 66.7 cm. SCALE 1:24,000/1 in. to 2,000 ft. REDUCTION 1:.5

Fage also drew this large topographic survey with soundings. It indicates considerable skill in triangulation and drawing and may have involved other surveyors. Rhode Island was one of the few areas in which the British had enough time and control to complete a formal survey.

Map from the Clements Library; Clinton map 62; Brun, *Guide*, no. 299.

KASKASKIA AND VINCENNES

A plan of Cascasqias ...

SIZE 28.9 x 39.8 cm. SCALE 1:4,800/1 in. to 400 ft. REDUCTION 1:.75

Philip Pittman acquired surveying training in England before coming to America with the army in 1758 at about the age of 20. He participated in the 1760–61 survey of Canada and was later sent to West Florida. Pittman's plan of Kaskaskia was drawn in 1766 and was published upon his return to England in *The Present State of the European Settlements on the Mississippi* (London, 1770). The stockade around the town was never constructed, and is not indicated on the printed map.

Map from the Clements Library; Gage Papers; Brun, *Guide*, no. 737. A supplemental source for the text is John D. Barnhart, ed., *Henry Hamilton and George Rogers Clark in the American Revolution* (Banta, 1951). A biographical note on the life of Pittman appears in Robert R. Rea's introduction to the facsimile edition of *The Present State* ...(U. of Florida Pr., 1973).

SAVANNAH

[Proposed fortification of Savannah]

SIZE 20.5 x 32.7 cm. SCALE 1:18,000/1 in. to 1,500 ft. REDUCTION 1:.7

Maj. Patrick Ferguson submitted this unfinished sketch of proposed fortifications while serving in the 71st Regiment in the year following the French and American attack. In addition to earlier sketches of fortifications and river passages, Ferguson made experiments with breech loading rifle design. He was killed at Kings Mountain in October, 1780.

Map from the Clements Library; Clinton map 328; Brun, *Guide*, no. 638.

Plan of the decent ...

SIZE 47 x 70.5 cm. SCALE 1:7,920/1 in. to 660 ft. REDUCTION 1.7:1

John Wilson joined the British army at the age of 13 in May, 1778, as a volunteer and assistant engineer in the 71st Regiment. He was commissioned a lieutenant in September, 1779. For a few months in 1781 Wilson held another commission as 2nd lieutenant in the Corps of Engineers. Wilson served during the war at Savannah, Charleston, and St. Augustine at the request of Maj. James Moncrief, Corps of Engineers. He was ordered to the Bahamas in the summer of 1783 and drew plans of the fort and harbor. His regiment was disbanded the next year and he retired at half pay in 1785. His obvious skill at drawing was acquired while serving in the Drawing Room of the Tower of London for six months in 1777.

Map from the Clements Library; Clinton map 324; Brun, *Guide*, no. 636. An additional source for the text was Benjamin Kennedy, ed. and trans., *Muskets, Cannonballs and Bombs: The Revolution in Georgia* (Beehive Press, 1974).

PREVOST IN SOUTH CAROLINA

Plan of the post ...

SIZE 18.7 x 21.6 cm. SCALE 1:5,040/1 in. to ca. 140 yds. REDUCTION 1:.85

Inset taken from beneath title on map below.

Draught of part of the Province of South Carolina ...

SIZE 51.4 x 72.4 cm. SCALE 1:179,498/1 in. to 2 5/6 mi. REDUCTION 1:.85 [south and west section deleted, scale repositioned]

An unsigned commemorative battle map probably the work of Lt. Alexander Sutherland, Corps of Engineers, assigned to Prevost's forces in 1779.

Map from the Clements Library; Clinton map 307; Brun, *Guide*, no. 611. An additional source for the text was Edward McCrady, *The History of South Carolina in the Revolution*.

CHESAPEAKE BAY

[Delaware and Chesapeake Bays]

SIZE 37.8 x 24.1 cm. [overall] SCALE 1:1,140,480/1 in. to 18 mi. REDUCTION 1:.8

Marginal notes in Clinton's hand relate to his criticism of Cornwallis in Virginia in 1781. The careful map is anonymous.

Map from the Clements Library; Clinton map 259; Brun, *Guide*, no. 555.

STONY POINT

[Stony Point and Verplancks Point]

SIZE 33.6 x 41.9 cm. SCALE 1:ca. 9,600/1 in. to ca. 800 ft. REDUCTION 1:.65

A note on the verso in Washington's hand indicates that this sketch was included in Maj. Gen. William Heath's letter of July 3, 1779. The letter has been lost, but Heath's journal entry for July 2 indicates that Putnam had reconnoitered the area positions. Putnam served as colonel of engineers for three months in 1776 before accepting command of the 5th Massachusetts Regiment. The map's disclosure of the unfinished works was a factor in the American decision to attack. After the British regained possession of Stony Point on July 19, they did not want the surprise repeated. A note on the refortification plan, Clinton map, no. 165, reads, "The exposing of this plan of the proposed work on Stony Point or allowing it to be copyd before it is in a thorough state of defence might possibly enable the Rebels to act against it with advantage."

Map from the Cornell University Library, Department of Rare Books, Sparks Collection. A particular reference used for the text was H. P. Johnston, *The Storming of Stony Point* (J. T. White, 1900).

PENOBSCOT BAY

A plan, profile and front view of Fort George Majabigwaduce

SIZE 46.7 x 63.5 cm. SCALE 1:240/1 in. to 20 ft. [view]; 1:1,200/1 in. to 100 ft. [plan] REDUCTION 1:.4

George William Dyail Jones produced several plans of Fort George while an assistant engineer with Rear Adm. George Collier's 1779 expedition to Castine, Maine. Jones was commissioned as a lieutenant in the 7th Regiment in 1778 and remained on the *Army List* until 1792. The source of his cartographic training is unknown.

This skillful drawing was completed in 1780 and probably submitted to show the finished state of the fort's defenses. Another virtually identical plan by Jones exists among the Clinton papers (Clinton map 34).

Map from the Clements Library; Clinton map 33; Brun, *Guide*, no. 158.

Sketch of the neck and harbour of Majabigwaduce ...

SIZE 31.4 x 48.2 cm. SCALE 1:9,792/1 in. to ca. 272 yds. REDUCTION 1:.9

This commemorative map was drawn by Jones shortly after the battle. It is identical to Clinton map 35, except for the deletion of the naval maneuvers and a shortened list of references. Jones may have submitted two copies of everything to ensure the safe arrival of at least one set.

Map from the Clements Library; Clinton map 36; Brun, *Guide,* no. 159. An additional source for the text was John Calef, *The Siege of Penobscot by the Rebels* (London, 1781).

PAULUS HOOK

Plan of the post at Paulus's Hook . . .

SIZE 36.8 x 41.9 cm.   SCALE 1:3,300/1 in. to ca. 275 ft.   REDUCTION 1:.5

The Library of Congress has two similar unsigned manuscript plans of Paulus Hook. They differ slightly; one fails to show "Howe's Bridge."

Map from the Clements Library; Clinton map 215; Brun, *Guide,* no. 502.

SULLIVAN'S EXPEDITION

[*Map of the expedition of the army under general John Sullivan against the Indians of West New York in the Seneca & Cayuga Lake regions, June 18th to September 15, 1779*]

SIZE 71.8 x 70.5 cm.   SCALE 1:316,800/1 in. to ca. 5 mi.   REDUCTION 1:.65 [section]

On September 17, 1779, Washington wrote that he possessed "no regular maps of the Western country" except for large-scale printed maps unreliable for military operations. Lt. Benjamin Lodge, assistant surveyor, was assigned to map Sullivan's route, and by May 7, 1780, Washington had received a copy of the survey. It was drawn originally on several sheets at a scale of one inch to two miles and a finished draft survives in the Erskine Collection of the New York Historical Society. This composite map at a smaller scale may have been drawn by the American army draftsman at headquarters in Morristown during the winter of 1780. Its style resembles British military topographic maps. A larger portion of this map is reproduced on a smaller scale in Guthorn, *American Maps.*

Map from the Library of Congress, Geography and Map Division. A particular source used in the text was *Journals of the Military Expedition of Major General John Sullivan* (New York Secretary of State, 1887).

MOBILE

Plan of Mobile

SIZE 28 x 45.7 cm.   SCALE 1:4,800/1 in. to 400 ft.   REDUCTION 1:.8

For a note on the cartographer see "Kaskaskia and Vincennes" in the sources section. Pittman's map of Mobile in 1768 was copied by William Brasier, the Ordnance draftsman assigned to the Corps of Engineers headquarters at New York from 1758 until his death in April, 1775. It was common practice for the draftsman to make several copies of maps and forward them to field commanders or influential politicians in England.

Map from the British Library, Map Room, Crown Collection; series 1, v. 2, no. 3. A particular source used for the text was John W. Caughey, *Bernardo de Gálvez in Louisiana, 1776–1783* (U. California Pr., 1934).

CHARLESTON

Plan of the seige of Charlestown in South Carolina

SIZE 26.3 x 29.5 cm.   SCALE 1:39,600/1 in. to 5 furlongs   REDUCTION 1:.8

This map may have been drawn in 1789 as indicated by a penciled note below the title. An anonymous printed version, however, was reproduced in Tarleton's 1787 history of the southern campaigns. Clinton acquired maps until his death in 1795, and manuscript maps taken from printed copies were not unknown.

Map from the Clements Library; Clinton map 308; Brun, *Guide,* no. 628. Additional sources for the text were Bernard A. Uhlendorf, ed. and trans., *The Siege of Charleston . . . Diaries and Letters of Hessian Officers* (U. Michigan Pr., 1938); and William T. Bulger, Jr., "The British Expedition to Charleston 1779–1780" (Ph.D. diss., U. Michigan, 1957).

CAMDEN

Plan of the battle of Gum Swamp . . .

SIZE 19.7 x 24.1 cm.   SCALE 1:147,629/1 in. to ca. 2 1/3 mi.   ENLARGEMENT 1:1.1

Lt. Thomas George Leonard Barretté had been in the army 12 years before Camden and had served in America since 1779. He came from a landed family in Kent with important political connections. Barretté was with Brig. Gen. Montfort Browne in the Bahamas in 1779 as aide-de-camp before rejoining the 23rd Regiment at Charleston. At some point before Camden, Barretté received extra duty pay as an assistant engineer, and may have learned drafting skills at that time. He wrote Sir Henry Clinton on August 26, 1780, and detailed his military services, as was the custom, and expressed his disappointment at slow promotion. This map drawn four days earlier was enclosed. Barretté apologized for its appearance, "having no sort of instrument with me, I was obliged to make use of a common pen and bad ink." Nevertheless, the map was intended to serve as an inducement to his own advancement. It represents at once a memorial of the victory and an indication of the cartographer's value to the army.

Map from the Clements Library; Clinton map 319; Brun, *Guide,* no. 625. An additional source used for the text was Hugh F. Rankin, *The North Carolina Continentals* (U. North Carolina Pr., 1971).

GUILFORD COURT HOUSE

Battle of Guildford fought on the 15 of March 1781

SIZE 20.9 x 18.4 cm.   SCALE 1:18,000/1 in. to ca. 1,500 ft.   ENLARGEMENT 1:1.2

This anonymous manuscript map was reproduced in Banastre Tarleton's *History of the Campaigns of 1780 and 1781, in the Southern Provinces . . .* (London, 1787), and in Stedman's 1794 history of the Revolution.

Map from the Clements Library; Clinton map 291; Brun, *Guide,* no. 592. An additional source for the text was Burke Davis, *The Cowpens-Guildford Courthouse Campaign* (Lippincott, 1962).

HOBKIRK'S HILL

Sketch of the battle of Hobkirk's Hill near Camden. on the 25th. April, 1781. Drawn by C. Vallancey. . . .

SIZE 43 x 29 cm.   SCALE indeterminate   REPRODUCTION 1:1 [title and margins deleted]

In an age of nonstandard spelling, it is possible that the cartographer of this map is the son and namesake of Charles Vallancey, who sired fifteen children and became director of engineers in Ireland in 1776 with responsibility for the military survey there. Certainly this would explain why Capt. Charles Vallancy of the 16th Regiment was assigned to assist the Corps of Engineers in America, as John Montresor's diary recorded in 1777. He served in the loyalist Volunteers of Ireland as lieutenant, and then as captain on the southern campaigns. He resigned his commission when his regiment was disbanded in 1783.

This is the only printed map included in the atlas. It was published by William Faden in 1783 after Vallancy had returned to England. Direct transactions between officers and publishers were not uncommon. With minor variations the map reappeared in Stedman's 1794 history of the Revolution.

Map from the Clements Library. Additional sources used in the text were Rankin, *The North Carolina Continentals;* and Henry Lee, *Memoirs of War in the Southern Department* (Force, 1827).

NEW HAVEN

A rough draught of New haven . . .

SIZE 22 x 30.2 cm.   SCALE indeterminate   REPRODUCTION 1:1

Capt. Nathan Hubbel's map resembles a graphic American primitive, without skill in surveying or drawing. It accompanied his letter of April 21, 1781, to loyalist Governor William Franklin of New Jersey, then serving as president of the Board of Directors of the Associated Loyalists. The map and an extract of the letter were later sent to Sir Henry Clinton.

Map from the Clements Library; Clinton map 112; Brun, *Guide,* no. 321. A specific source used for the narrative was Lloyd A. Brown, *Loyalist Operations at New Haven* (Clements Library, 1938).

VIRGINIA STRATEGY

Plan of Portsmouth on Elizabeth River from an exact survey made ye 21st January 1781. By James Straton. 2d lt. of engineers.

SIZE 48.9 x 61 cm. *SCALE* 1:6,000/1 in. to 500 ft. *REDUCTION* 1:.5 [title and margins deleted]

James Straton finished training at the Royal Military Academy, Woolwich, in 1769. He was commissioned in the Corps of Engineers in 1775 and arrived at Boston early the next year. Straton served in Rhode Island and New York before participating in the Virginia campaign of 1781. He returned to England in 1782 and attained the rank of major in 1797.

The map was enclosed in a letter from Benedict Arnold to Sir Henry Clinton, January 23, 1781. It was designed to show preparations for the British defense of Portsmouth. Straton apologized for the drawing with the statement, "this plan was done in a great hurry and partly by candle light."

Map from the Clements Library; Clinton map 277; Brun, *Guide,* no. 575.

March of the army under Lieut: General Earl Cornwallis . . .

SIZE 38.4 x 54.6 cm. *SCALE* 1:950,400/1 in. to ca. 15 mi. *REDUCTION* 1:.8

This map depicts Cornwallis's Virginia strategy up to his encampment at Portsmouth on July 12, 1781. It was probably drawn shortly after that date and before the British move toward Yorktown in August. Although the map is unsigned, the lettering style closely resembles that of Edward Fage (see sources for "Rhode Island"). Fage was assigned to an artillery unit that joined Cornwallis at Petersburg on May 20 and later participated at Yorktown. Fage was present at the surrender.

The signature of Sir Augustus Frazer refers to his presentation of the map to the Royal United Services Institution in the early nineteenth century. Frazer was a colonel in the Royal Artillery and the only son of Lt. Col. Andrew Frazer, Corps of Engineers. Wilkinson's map of Saratoga is also marked in this way.

Map from the British Library, Royal United Services Institution Collection. Additional sources used for the text were B. F. Stevens, *Campaign in Virginia, 1781,* 2 v. (London, 1888), and Banastre Tarleton, *A History of the Campaigns of 1780 and 1781.*

YORKTOWN

[British works at Yorktown]

SIZE 26.7 x 40 cm. *SCALE* 1:24,000/1 in. to ca. 2,000 ft. *REDUCTION* 1:.6 [Gloucester portion deleted]

Alexander Sutherland had been a messenger to the artillery field train at Woolwich in 1759 before entering the Royal Military Academy as a gentleman cadet in 1767. He was commissioned in the Corps of Engineers in 1770 and served in America from September, 1776, until Yorktown. Lieutenant Sutherland accompanied Cornwallis throughout Virginia in 1781.

A note on the verso in Clinton's hand reads, "The only plan of York I could obtain from Southerland L[ord] C[ornwallis's] Chief Engineer and the person he said that had made an Exact survey and Examination of it."

Map from the Clements Library; Clinton map 272; Brun, *Guide,* no. 567.

Carte des environs de York . . .

SIZE 47.6 x 67.9 cm. *SCALE* 1:4,788/1 in. to ca. 190 toises *REDUCTION* 1:.65

Edouard Charles Victurnier Colbert, Comte de Maulevrier (1758–1820), drafted several manuscript battle maps during two years of service with the French fleet in America. Maulevrier first came to the United States in 1780 as part of Adm. Ternay's squadron, and was later assigned to Adm. de Grasse's squadron in June, 1781. That fall he was with de Grasse at Yorktown. He spent another three years in America after 1796 an as émigré from revolutionary France. Maulevrier eventually returned home and attained the rank of rear admiral.

French maps of the Yorktown siege derived from a basic engineer plan. The progression of letters on the map image exceeds the number of explanations in the references beneath the title. Thus, Maulevrier used the source map common to all the French engineers for his own drawing.

Map from the Clements Library; Brun, *Guide,* no. 569. An additional source for the text was Henry P. Johnston, *The Yorktown Campaign* (Harper, 1881). For a biographical sketch of Maulevrier and a study of French mapping during the Revolutionary War in America, see Rice and Brown, *Rochambeau's Army.*

NEW LONDON

A sketch of New-London & Groton with the attacks made on Forts Trumbull & Griswold . . .

SIZE 33 x 28 cm. *SCALE* 1:21,120/1 in. to 1,760 ft. *REDUCTION* 1:.8

Maj. Daniel Lyman (1757–1809) was among several Connecticut loyalists to accompany Arnold on his raid. Lyman received an appointment as captain in a loyalist regiment in October, 1776. He saw action in many of the major battles of the war; being twice wounded. In 1783, Lyman emigrated with other loyalists to Canada. Although Lyman was educated at Yale, there is no indication of the source of his cartographic training. His map was later copied by John Hills and both maps were submitted to Clinton.

Map from the Clements Library; Clinton map 109; Brun, *Guide,* no. 322. A specific source used for the text was Walter L. Powell, "The New London Raid" (M.A. thesis, Kent State U., 1975).

PENSACOLA

Plan of the Harbour of Pensacola . . .

SIZE 47.6 x 68.6 cm. *SCALE* 1:31,680/1 in. to ½ mi. *REPRODUCTION* 1:1 [section]

Lt. Capt. Henry Heldring went to Pensacola with the 3rd Waldeck regiment of Germans at the end of 1778. Heldring served as acting engineer and finished several plans of Pensacola while strengthening the inadequate defenses of the fort. In correspondence between Sir Henry Clinton and Maj. Gen. John Campbell, Heldring's services as an engineer were praised and he was recommended for a British army commission in the 60th Regiment. But Pensacola was overrun before the appointment could be made.

Map from the Clements Library; Clinton map 337; Brun, *Guide,* no. 653. An additional source for the text was Robert B. Rea, "Pensacola Under the British (1763–1781)" in James R. McGovern, ed., *Colonial Pensacola,* v. 1 (Pensacola Series, 1972).

EPILOGUE

Map of New York . . .

SIZE 72.4 x 101.6 cm. *SCALE* 1:63,360/1 in. to 1 mi. *REDUCTION* 1:.4

George Taylor and Andrew Skinner were a Scottish surveying team who had published a series of maps and road books of England, Scotland, and Ireland between 1776 and 1778. In 1780 the two men left Ireland for New York where they became official surveyors for Sir Henry Clinton. Taylor and Skinner produced numerous plans during their short stay in America, working both individually and as a team. This map was drafted by Taylor. Taylor served as a captain in the loyalist regiment of Guides and Pioneers, and a later reference in a 1785 road book of Scotland lists him as a captain in the "Duke of Cumberland's late regiment of foot." Skinner is not known to have held a commission in a specific army unit. After the war, Taylor returned to Scotland and later Ireland, while Skinner is known to have completed surveys in the Bahamas in 1788.

Map from the British Library, King's Topographical Collection; CXXI34.

BACK ENDPAPER

Sketch of the posts of York Town . . .

SIZE 45.7 x 64.8 cm. *SCALE* 1:10,800/1 in. to 300 yds. *REDUCTION* 1:.7

This memorial map of Yorktown is by Lt. Alexander Sutherland. The orientation of the map, with such a prominent view of the York River, gives a feeling of dependence on water as a sanctuary. The positions of the French and the Americans were never colored in, although the references indicate that intention. The British outer works at Yorktown appear to take advantage of high ground between marsh areas. The added note is not in the hand of Sir Henry Clinton and may be an afterthought by an officer at British headquarters in New York. It suggests how Yorktown might have been successfully defended.

Map from the Clements Library; Clinton map 270; Brun, *Guide,* no. 585.

SKETCH OF THE POSTS OF
YORK TOWN and GLOUCESTER POINT
shewing the *french* and *rebel* attacks upon the former in
October. 1781.

References

A. Redout, held 'till the post was surrender'd.

B. Redouts which the enemy carried by assault on the 14th.

C. Line of communication from one Flank to the other.

D. Magazines. bomb-proof

E. Line of stockade enclosing the Town.

F. Redouts made to strengthen the right flank of the British Troops, in their advanced position, previous to the 30th Septr.

G. Flèches, to defend the dams on the left flank of the troops.

N.B. The lines, and batteries, tinged yellow are *french*; the blue, are *rebel*.

H. The redoubt which would have rendered his exterior position respectable and within 300 yds of marshes I.

Scale 300 Yards to an Inch.

Lieut. Sutherland Engineer

Y